BONA OPERA

BIBLIOTHECA

HUMANISTICA & REFORMATORICA

VOLUME XXXI

CARL E. MAXCEY

BONA OPERA

A Study in the Development
of the Doctrine
in Philip Melanchthon

NIEUWKOOP
B. DE GRAAF
1980

IN MEMORIAM

MY FATHER

Ira Honley Maxcey

ACKNOWLEDGMENT

Appreciation, above all, is due to B. de Graaf for publishing a revision of my 1979 doctoral dissertation from Marquette University, "Bona Opera: A Study of the Development of the Doctrine in Philip Melanchthon." I wish to thank Professor Kenneth Hagen of Marquette who directed the original dissertation and as mentor provided me with much sagacious counsel. Persons to whom I also am deeply grateful for their assistance in the preparation of this work include: Professors Joseph Lienhard, S.J., Robert Wild, S.J., John Sheehan, S.J., Thomas Caldwell, S.J., William Kelly, S.J., and Mr. Guy Carter, all at Marquette University. I owe much to the encouragement and continued support of Professor John Bigane of Xavier University in Cincinnati.

Without Professor Earl A. Weis, S.J., the Chairperson of the Theology Department at Loyola University of Chicago, I would not have had the opportunity to prepare this work. My thanks to Mr. Daniel J. Eberle, a graduate student at Loyola of Chicago, for his valuable help in the preparation of the index. In addition, I am grateful to Mr. Thomas Bennett and the Research Services Office at Loyola of Chicago for procuring the necessary typing help on the revised copy. I am deeply grateful to Professors Robert Kolb and

vii

Ralph W. Quere for reading the manuscript and providing me with invaluable suggestions.

Finally, I wish to thank my wife. She has assisted me with all facets of the preparation of this work. Her love has sustained and guided me, I am lucky to call myself her husband.

I wish to dedicate this work to my father. "May light perpetual shine upon him." Amen.

TABLE OF CONTENTS

ACKNOWLEDGMENT vii

INTRODUCTION 1

Chapter

I   THE DOCTRINE OF GOOD WORKS IN THE CATHOLIC
CONFUTATIO AND MELANCHTHON'S APOLOGY 13

      Introduction 13
      The Apology and the Role of the Mediator . . . 35
      Righteousness by Reason in the Apology 40
      Merit and Reward in the Apology 44
      The Apology and the Terrified Conscience . . . 47
      The Terrified Conscience, the Sinful Human
         Condition, and the Apology 53
      The Meaning of Faith in the Apology 55
      Faith with Works in the Apology 58
      Faith, the Fallen Human Condition,
         and the Apology 61
      Conclusion 65

II   THE DOCTRINE OF GOOD WORKS IN THE COMMENTARY
ON ROMANS OF 1532 AND THE LOCI OF 1533 67

      Introduction 67
      Commentary on Romans of 1532 74
      The Doctrine of Good Works in the Loci
         of 1533 84
      Reward and Punishment in the Loci
         of 1533 87
      The Meaning of Faith in the Loci
         of 1533 92
      Person and Work in the Loci of 1533 93
      The Loci of 1533 and the
         Sinful Human Condition 96
      The Christian as Pronounced Just
         in the Loci of 1533 99
      The Loci of 1533 and the Function
         of the Law 101
      Syllogistic Arguments with the Loci
         of 1533 103
      Conclusion 111

ix

Chapter
III   THE DOCTRINE OF GOOD WORKS IN THE
LOCI OF 1535 115

Not without Works 115
Introduction to the Loci of 1535 118
The Loci of 1535 on Works as Necessary 126
The Worth of Works in the Loci of 1535 130
Causes for Doing Good Works
in the Loci of 1535 133
Natural Law as a Cause for Doing
Good Works in the Loci of 1535 136
The Loci of 1535 and the Moral
Law as Necessary 141
Corrupt Works as Pleasing to God
in the Loci of 1535 146
The Meaning of Faith in the Loci in 1535 . . . 151
Rewards for Works in the Loci of 1535 158
Syllogistic Arguments in the Loci of 1535 . . . 164
Conclusion 170

IV   THE DOCTRINE OF GOOD WORKS IN THE INTERIMS
AND THE LOCI OF 1559 176

Introduction 176
The Interims 181
Introduction to the Loci of 1559 192
The Necessity of Good Works in the
Loci of 1559 195
Three Causes for Doing Good Works in the
Loci of 1559 202
Melanchthon's Refutation of Merit in
the Loci of 1559 208
The Loci of 1559 and the Sinful
Human Condition 215
The Distinction between Human and
Divine Righteousness in the Loci of 1559 . . 221
The Loci of 1559 and the Pleasing
Works of the Reborn 224
The Loci of 1559 and the Possibility of
Meriting Rewards 228
The Meaning of Faith in the Loci of 1559 . . . 231
The Role of Natural Knowledge in the
Loci of 1559 240
Natural or Moral Law and the Loci of 1559 . . . 243
Syllogistic Arguments in the Loci of 1559 . . . 254
Conclusion 278

CONCLUSION 287

ABBREVIATIONS 298

BIBLIOGRAPHY 300

INDEX 320

INTRODUCTION

The Counter Reformation author Thomas Stapleton
said that the sixteenth century doctrine of justification
was the "principium proprium et propinquum controversarium."
Martin Luther would have agreed with him because he was of
the opinion that the article of justification is the
article on which the Church stands or falls.

Luther incorporated an existential religious
experience of God's righteousness into a doctrine which
ruled out man's cooperating in his justification. God's
gracious mercy or favor is given to men through faith alone.
Justification is not achieved by works or merit, but God
accomplishes justification and places mankind into a new
relationship with himself. Man is passive and receives
God's righteousness through faith. Man will do good works,
says Luther, but not so that justification may be achieved
through works. Rather, those who are righteous will do good
works, just as the healthy tree will bear good fruit. Good
fruit will not bring forth a tree, but it is the healthy
tree which bears the fruit.

The essence of Luther's doctrine was the attempt to
rid the Christian teaching of a perverted emphasis on the
merits of good works and an autonomous Christian life-style

which seemed to do quite well without Christ. Luther
wanted to turn our attention from ourselves to the Incarnate
God. To look to Christ alone is to understand that we are
justified by faith alone through grace alone. As a
consequence, Luther was not particularly concerned with a
doctrine of good works, because he felt works had been
preached enough and that Christianity had ignored Christ
as the only mediator.

Philip Melanchthon was to take over the leadership
of the German Evangelical party after Luther's death in 1545.
Melanchthon was considerably different in background and
temperament than Luther. Melanchthon was more philosophical
and was interested in the ethical effect of philosophical
and theological teachings. Melanchthon was also more
interested in the unity of Evangelical principles and
attempted to systematize them into a whole. Luther said
that he was more interested in chopping down and that Philip
was more interested in building up. The doctrine of good
works (rather than justification by faith alone) was pushed
to the forefront of controversy as a result of the following
conditions: Melanchthon's ethical concerns, Catholic attacks
stating that the Evangelicals preached against works, and a
growing antinomianism. It was assumed by both Catholics and
Anabaptists of the early Sixteenth century that the Evangelicals
praised faith and avoided works. The second generation
Lutherans attended to problems which were derived from

original theological tenets proposed by Luther himself.

The issue of good works, as dealt with by Melanchthon and his followers, continued to be a problem even up to the Formula of Concord in 1580. Even though the Formula decided against a certain position of Melanchthon's on good works, seventeenth century Lutheranism continued to be divided between supporters of Melanchthon and those who felt that Melanchthon had wavered from the original teaching of Luther. This divergence in Lutheran teaching continued in the eighteenth century (Pietism, Rationalism), the nineteenth century (Liberalism, Pietism), and up to the present day. Witness the failure to come to an agreement on justification by delegates at the Fourth Assembly of the Lutheran World Federation at Helsinki in the summer of 1963.[1]

Since Melanchthon is recognized as the first systematizer of Evangelical doctrine, it is not surprising that Lutheranism itself has taken its form from Melanchthon rather than Luther. There are even some who claim that

---

[1]Another indication of the divergent views within Lutheranism is the result of a survey conducted by M. P. Strommen, M. L. Brekke, R. C. Underwager, and A. L. Johnson published by the Augsburg Publishing House in 1972. It was found that only 40% of the Lutherans surveyed believed in salvation through faith alone. In addition, when asked to respond to the statement: God is satisfied if a person lives the best life he can; 50% said yes, 43% said no, 5% did not know, and 2% did not respond. For details see Merton P. Strommen et al., A Study of Generations: Report of a Two-Year Study of 5,000 Lutherans Between the Ages of 15-65; Their Beliefs, Values, Attitudes, Behavior. (Minneapolis: Augsburg Publishing House, 1972), pp. 145-146, 277, 289, 369.

Lutheranism might readily be referred to as "Melanchthonianism."
At the same time much more research has been done on Luther
and post-Luther Lutheranism than on Melanchthon. Melanchthon's
teachings, while perhaps more influential than Luther's are
still less known today. In this study, I shall identify that
line of thought at its source and investigate the meaning of
good works in Melanchthon.

Philip Melanchthon was born Philip Schwartzerd on
February 16, 1497 at Bretten, Germany.[1] He was educated at

---

[1]Biographies of Melanchthon include: Karl Hartfelder,
Philipp Melanchthon als Praeceptor Germaniae (Berlin:
A. Hofmann and Co., 1889; reprint ed., Nieuwkoop: B.
DeGraaf, 1964). J. W. Richard, Philip Melanchthon: The
Protestant Preceptor of Germany, 1497-1560 (New York:
Putnam Press, 1898; reprint ed., New York: Lenox Hill, 1974).
Georg Ellinger, Philipp Melanchthon. Ein Lebensbild. Mit
einem Bildnis Melanchthons (Berlin: R. Gärtners, Heyfelder,
1902). Rudolf Schaefer, Philipp Melanchthons Leben, aus den
Quellen dargestellt (Gütersloh: C. Bertelsmann, 1894). Clyde
L. Manschreck, Melanchthon, The Quiet Reformer (New York:
Abingdon Press, 1958). Robert Stupperich, Melanchthon
(Berlin: W. De Gruyter and Co., 1960). Nikolaus Müller,
Philipp Melanchthons letzte lebenstage, heimgang und
bestattung nach den gleichzeitigen berichten der Wittenberger
professoren. Zum 350. todestage Melanchthons (Leipzig:
Verlag von M. Heinsius nachfolger, 1910). Peter Meinhold,
Philipp Melanchthon; der Lehrer der Kirche (Berlin:
Lutherisches Verlagshaus, 1960). Leo Stern, Philipp
Melanchthon: Humanist, Reformator, Praeceptor Germaniae.
Festgabe des Melanchthon-Komitees der Deutschen Demokratischen
Republik (Halle: 1960). Nello Caserta, Filippo Melantone
(dall'umanesimo alla Riforma) (Rome: Edizioni Ita, 1960).
DThC X, 502-513. RGG3 IV, 834-841. LThK[2]VII, 247-249.
EKL II, 1282-1286. NCE IX, 624-625. ODCC[2] 898-899.

Pforzheim, Heidelberg, and Tübingen for four years, and in
1518 he moved to Wittenberg, where he was called to teach
Greek. At Wittenberg, he met Martin Luther who turned
Melanchthon's attention to theological pursuits. As
Luther's Evangelical teachings became more widely known,
Melanchthon became increasingly embroiled in religious
controversy for he had become a devout supporter of Luther.

Even while a member of the philosophy faculty at
Wittenberg, Melanchthon's classical interests are revealed
in the fact that he offered courses in Cicero, Terence,
Virgil, and Livy. Melanchthon began his theological studies
before 1518, but they were certainly intensified by his
meeting with Luther at Wittenberg. Even though trained as
a humanist and classicist, Melanchthon soon rejected philosophy
and turned to Evangelical theology. His constant interest in
good works and his attempts to systematize Evangelical
principles prove that his conversion to Evangelical thought
was qualified with certain ethical and philosophical presuppositions.

Up to the time of his death in 1560, Melanchthon
wrote treatises dealing with rhetoric, philosophy, Scripture,
astronomy, medicine, physics, and ethics. Interpreters of
those writings have seen him as a humanist, philosopher,
systematic theologian, enemy of Lutheran orthodoxy, orthodox
forerunner of the Formula of Concord, synergist,

crypto-Calvinist, semi-Pelagian, and even

crypto-semi-Pelagian.[1] It is not my attempt in this study

to prove that Melanchthon was right or wrong, synergist or

not, or whether or not he is a "true" Lutheran. Rather, I

wish to ask topical questions and examine in detail his

writings in order to clearly discern the answers. My question

is this: what did Melanchthon say about good works?

It is acknowledged by many that Melanchthon conceded

far too much to the Catholics during the period of the

---

[1]Among those who have compared Luther and Melanchthon, with the greater emphasis on Luther are: Martin Greschat, Melanchthon neben Luther. Studien zur Gestalt der Rechtfertigungslehre zwischen 1528 und 1537 (Witten: Luther Verlag, 1965). Ragnar Bring, Das Verhältnis von Glauben und Werken in der Lutherischen Theologie (Munich: Kaiser Verlag, 1955). Rolf Schäfer, Christologie und Sittlichkeit in Melanchthons Frühen Loci (Tübingen: J. C. B. Mohr, 1961). The notes of Schäfer refer, above all, to Luther's works in the WA, and his references to Melanchthon's writings are most difficult to follow. Those who prefer to treat Melanchthon in comparison with Lutheran confessional literature include: F. Bente, "Historical Introductions to the Symbolical Books of the Evangelical Lutheran Church." In Concordia Triglotta (St. Louis: Concordia Publishing House, 1921), pp. 1-256. (Bente blames Melanchthon for all unorthodox tendencies found in Lutheranism). Ralph Quere, "Christ's Efficacious Presence in the Lord's Supper: Directions in the Development of Melanchthon's Theology after Augsburg." Lutheran Quarterly 29 (February 1977):21-41. Lowell C. Green, "Faith, Righteousness, and Justification: New Light on their Development under Luther and Melanchthon." The Sixteenth Century Journal 4 (April 1973):65-86. Lowell C. Green, "Influence of Erasmus upon Melanchthon, Luther, and the Formula of Concord in the Doctrine of Justification." Church History 43 (June 1974):183-200. Eugene F. Klug and Otto F. Stahlke, Getting Into the Formula of Concord. A History and Digest of the Formula (St. Louis: Concordia Publishing House, 1977).

Interims. In particular, it is felt that he conceded excessive significance and importance to the performance of good works. No one would say that Melanchthon taught the Catholic theory of merit, but precisely what did he say about good works?

The most important study dealing with the meaning of works in Melanchthon is that of Ragnar Bring.[1] The thrust of his study is a comparison of the psychological and spiritual aspects of faith and works in Melanchthon and Luther. His real contribution is his penetrating insight into the outward psychology of works as signs of the inner faith. Unfortunately, Bring does not contextualize the development of the meaning of works in Melanchthon. He systematizes works for Melanchthon and does not consider their significance as developmental and highly nuanced in Melanchthon's writings. It is unlikely that Melanchthon had such a clear cut and formal understanding of a very complicated issue, which surely took on many characteristics throughout his career.

An outgrowth of just such a developmental understanding of the doctrine of works in Melanchthon is the confusing issue surrounding the use of the phrase, "necessary

---

[1]Ragnar Bring, Das Verhältnis von Glauben und Werken in der Lutherischen Theologie (Munich: Chr. Kaiser Verlag, 1955).

for salvation." Robert Kolb tells us that Melanchthon taught that good works were necessary for salvation, but that he withdrew the use of that phrase "after a controversy over its use involving one of his disciples, Casper Cruciger."[1] Eugene Klug, on the other hand, is of the opinion that Melanchthon should never have stated that good works were necessary for salvation, and that he just began to maintain this position from 1535 onwards.[2] Martin Greschat, in agreement with Kolb, says that Melanchthon dropped the use of the phrase after 1535, due to the controversy surrounding Cordatus and Cruciger.[3]

Ragnar Bring holds that Melanchthon did maintain the proposition (necessary for salvation) before 1532, but he does not examine its meaning as it develops for Melanchthon, nor does he indicate whether or not Melanchthon dropped the

---

[1]Robert Kolb, "Georg Major as Controversialist: Polemics in the Late Reformation." Church History 45 (December 1976):459.

[2]Eugene F. Klug and Otto F. Stahlke, Getting Into the Formula of Concord. A History and Digest of the Formula (St. Louis: Concordia Publishing House, 1977), p. 39. There are far too many popular works which assume Melanchthon held this or that without any desire on the part of reputable scholars to do the critical work necessary to establish precisely what he did maintain.

[3]Martin Greschat, Melanchthon neben Luther, pp. 217-230. Greschat far too often quotes the WA as though everything contained there were written personally by Luther.

use of the phrase.[1] Finally, F. Bente is of the opinion
that Melanchthon did repudiate the use of the phrase, which
he himself had introduced.

> Nowhere, however, did he reject it or advise against
> its use because it was inherently erroneous and
> false as such, but always merely because it was
> subject to abuse and misapprehension, - a qualified
> rejection which self-evidently could not and did
> not satisfy his opponents.[2]

From the above it is clear that confusion exists not
only concerning Melanchthon's use of this phrase, but concerning the overall picture of what Melanchthon actually
said about good works. Did Melanchthon maintain the use of
the phrase "necessary for salvation" before 1535 and then
drop it? Did he only begin to hold this phrase in 1535?
How did he qualify its meaning? Did the meaning of the
phrase ever change for Melanchthon? The overall question
to be answered, then, is what did Melanchthon maintain
concerning good works? What ancillary categories did
Melanchthon use in order to establish a particular position
in regard to good works? Using a developmental manner, I
shall attempt to examine in detail selected writings of
Melanchthon in order to discern precisely what he meant by
works, their need and reasons for doing them. Treatises
have been written touching on Melanchthon's doctrine of
justification as he presented it in various periods of his

---

[1]Ragnar Bring, Das Verhältnis, pp. 92-106.

[2]F. Bente, "Historical Introductions to the
Symbolical Books ...", p. 115.

life (Greschat, Green, Maurer, Bring, Eichhorn,

Engelland, Mayer) but no one has examined, developmentally

and in detail, how he understood the role of good works.[1]

---

[1]In addition to the doctrine of justification in
Melanchthon, some have treated ethical theory as understood
by Melanchthon. Among both include the following works:
Albert Herrlinger, Die Theologie Melanchthons in ihrer
geschichtlichen Entwicklung und im Zusammenhange mit der
Lehrgeschichte und Culturbewegung der Reformation (Gotha:
Friedrich Andreas Perthes, 1879). Charles Leander Hill,
"An Exposition and Critical Estimate of the Philosophy
of Philip Melanchthon." (Ph.D. dissertation, Ohio State
University, 1938). C. Baur, "Melanchthons Naturrechtslehre."
ARG 42 (1951):64-98. According to Baur, natural law is
something that Melanchthon develops over his life time
and finally integrates into his theology in the Loci of
1559. The truth is that natural law operates as an ethical
presupposition in all of Melanchthon's writings after 1531.
Ottmar Dittrich, Geschichte der Ethik. Die Systems der
Moral vom Altertum bis zur Gegenwart. vol. 4. Von der
Kirchenreformation bis zum Ausgang des Mittelalters. I.
Die Reformatoren und der lutherischkirchliche Protestantismus
(Leipzig: Felix Meiner, 1932). Cornelius Meyer,
"Rechtfertigung durch Werke?" Theologische Quartalschrift
154 (1974):118-136. Karl Thieme, Der Geist der
lutherischen Ethik in Melanchthons Apologie (1531-1931)
(Giessen: Alfred Töpelmann, 1931). Adolf Sperl, Melanchthon
zwischen Humanismus und Reformation. Forschungen zur
Geschichte und lehre des Protestantismus vol. 15. (Munich:
Chr. Kaiser Verlag, 1959). Robert Stupperich, Der unbekannt
Melanchthon. Wirken und Denken des Praeceptor Germaniae in
neuer Sicht (Stuttgart: W. Kohlhammer Verlag, 1961).
Vilmos Vajta, ed. Luther und Melanchthon. Referate des
zweiten Internationalen Kongresses für Lutherforschung
(Göttingen: Vandenhoeck and Ruprecht, 1961).
Siegfried Wiedenhofer, Formalstrukturen humanistischer
und reformatorischer Theologie bei Philipp Melanchthon
(Frankfurt/M. and Munich: Peter Lang, 1976). Wilhelm
Maurer, Der junge Melanchton. Zwischen Humanismus und
Reformation. vol. 2. Der Theologe (Göttingen: Vandenhoeck
and Ruprecht, 1969). H. Engelland, Melanchthon: Glauben
und Handeln (Munich: C. Kaiser, 1931). Just a few of the
most recent works dealing with the Lord's Supper in
Melanchthon are: W. H. Neuser, "Melanchthons Abendmahlslehre

The texts examined in this study deal extensively
with the doctrine of good works. Other writings touched
on the subject as well, but the writings selected provide
a more thorough exposition of the doctrine in particular
periods of Melanchthon's life. The writings examined
include the Apology, the Commentary on Romans of 1532, the
Loci of 1533, the Loci of 1535, the Interims, and the Loci
of 1559. In addition, other writings examined include:
those which dealt with various colloquia, those pertaining
to disagreements with Eck, Agricola, Flacius, and Osiander;
the Regensburg book; and a number of Melanchthon's letters
which pertain to his teaching on good works.

The various texts and letters examined will
indicate the development of Melanchthon's teaching on good
works. This development does not mean that from year to
year Melanchthon adopted a new teaching. This study will
rather expound on his teaching, either old or new to his
thinking, within various periods of his life.

First of all, the method followed in this study was

---

und ihre Auswirkung im unteren Donauraum." ZKG 84 (1973):
49-59. Ralph Quere, Melanchthon's Christum Cognoscere:
Christ's Efficacious Presence in the Eucharistic Theology of
Melanchthon. Bibliotheca Humanistica and Reformatorica,
XXII. (Nieuwkoop: B. DeGraff, 1977). Ralph Quere,
"Melanchthonian Motifs in the Formula's Eucharistic
Christology." Discord, Dialogue, and Concord. Studies
in the Lutheran Reformation's Formula of Concord. Ed.
by L. W. Spitz and W. Lohff. (Philadelphia: Fortress
Press, 1977), pp. 58-73.

to provide pertinent historical data surrounding a given text in order to reveal the current situation, the questions, and problems Melanchthon was dealing with. This historical contextualizing will show particular influences on Melanchthon as he developed a teaching on good works. Secondly, the individual texts will be thoroughly examined so as to reveal the specifics regarding Melanchthon's teaching on good works. Finally, there will be a conclusion incorporating the categories Melanchthon employs, the answers to questions initially proposed, and any development within Melanchthon's writings.

CHAPTER I

THE DOCTRINE OF GOOD WORKS
IN THE CATHOLIC CONFUTATIO AND MELANCHTHON'S APOLOGY

Introduction

With the presentation of the Augsburg Confession,
work was soon underway by the Catholics to prepare an answer,
or, as it came to be known, the Confutatio. The first
Confutatio was prepared primarily by the Catholic professor
of Theology at Ingolstadt, Johann Eck.[1] By July 8, 1530 Eck
had completed the text and had consulted other theologians
regarding the matter in Augsburg.[2] He first presented a
copy to the cardinal legate at Augsburg, Campeggio, on the
twelfth of July. Campeggio approved this copy and sent it
on to the emperor who received the response on the thirteenth.[3]
The emperor was so displeased with the invective and the

---

[1]For a discussion and presentation of this first
edition see Johannes Ficker, Die Konfutation des Augsburgischen
Bekenntnisses. Ihre erste Gestalt und ihre Geschichte.
(Leipzig: Verlag von Johann Amrosius Barth, 1891).

[2]Judith Law Williams, "Philip Melanchthon as an
Ecclesiatical Conciliator, 1530 through 1541" (Ph.D.
dissertation, The University of North Carolina at Chapel
Hill, 1973), pp. 76, 88.

[3]CR 2:193-196; WAB 5:475-478; StA 7/2:215-217;
James William Richard, Philip Melanchthon, the Protestant
Preceptor of Germany, 1497-1560. (New York: Putnam, 1898;
reprint ed., New York: Lenox Hill, 1974), p. 211; MBW
I, p. 405, #970; MBW I, p. 406, #973.

13

polemical tone that he sent it back in order to have it
reworked.

During this period Melanchthon was writing to
Luther and other friends expressing his anxiety as he
awaited a look at the rebuttal.[1] Finally, the Confutatio
was formally read in the Diet of Augsburg on the third of
August, 1530.[2] It was chiefly (as presented) the work of
Eck, Faber, Cochlaeus, and Wimpina. The following day
Melanchthon wrote to the legate's secretary Bonfio stressing
the importance for his party that the marriage of priests
and the reception of the cup during communion be maintained.
For the sake of unity he did offer to recognize the juris-
diction of bishops.[3] Bonfio agreed to meet with Melanchthon,
but rather than discuss the matter Bonfio offered Melanchthon
a lump sum of money and a yearly pension if he would accept
the Confutatio and convince the princes to accept it also.[4]

The Confutatio itself did not seem to frighten
Melanchthon concerning its content and effectiveness for he
wrote to Veit Dietrich, Luther's friend at Coburg, saying

---

[1]CR 2:217, 218, 229, 240, 241.

[2]CR 2:249-252. WAB 5:479-481, CR 2:252-253,
259-260; MBW I, p. 421, #1014; I, p. 422, #1017; I,
p. 422, #1018.

[3]CR 2:248-249. See also MBW I, p. 420, #1010.

[4]Williams, Conciliator, p. 87.

that he was calmer and more secure in his position now because among the adversaries "there is no knowledge of religion."[1] Likewise, in a letter to Luther dated the sixth of August he refers to the Confutatio as being "puerile."[2]

The emperor agreed to abide by the Confutatio and ordered the minority party to accept it. This request they felt to be inordinate. Melanchthon was soon after asked to write an apology to the Confession explaining why they could not accept the Confutatio. This task he immediately undertook using notes that had been written by Camerarius at the time of the reading of the Confutatio.

The teaching concerning the doctrine of good works is located primarily in Articles 4, 6, and 20 of the Confutatio.[3] The authors specifically call attention to Article 4 of the Confession where Pelagian thinking in regard to works is condemned. In doing so, the Catholic authors agree that persons are not "able to merit eternal life outside the grace

---

[1]CR 2:253: "Intelligunt enim nullam apud adversarios religionis scientiam esse." See also MBW I, p. 421, #1013.

[2]CR 2:254.

[3]The Latin text of the Confutatio is found in CR 27:81-184. Bretschneider's introduction to the Confutatio in its various editions covers pp. 1-80. All subsequent references to CR 27, unless otherwise indicated, will refer to the Confutatio.

of God."[1] The first Confutatio written by Eck had maintained
that "no Catholic believes"[2] one is able to merit "without
the grace of God."[3]

Evidence from Scripture is brought to bear on the
defense of merit in Article 4 and Article 6 of the Confutatio.
Paul's reference in 1 Timothy 4 to fighting the good fight
and running the race in order to be rewarded the crown of
righteousness is used. The reference in 2 Corinthians 5
to the appearance before the judgment seat of Christ, so
that each may receive good or evil according to deeds performed in the body is also applied to merit.[4]

Old Testament references include: The promise of
Yahweh to reward Abraham, in Genesis 15; the reference to
reward and recompense, in Isaiah 40; and the statement of
God to Cain, in Genesis 4: "If you do well, will you not
be accepted?"[5]

Not only, according to Article 6, does James 2

---

[1]CR 27:92-93.

[2]Ficker, Die Konfutation, pp. 10-13, 66.

[3]Ibid. In a 1534 treatise of Cochlaeus concerning
the Confession he states: "Etenim a meritoriis operibus
nostris nusquam secludimus fidem, nusquam gratiam Dei,
Scimus enim ex Paulo Heb. XI quod impossibile est sine fide
placere Deo, Scimus nos gratia Dei id esse quod sumus."
CR 27:95-96.

[4]CR 27:93-94.

[5]CR 27:94.

state that faith without works is dead, "but the entire
Scriptures summon us to works."[1] Allusion to the use of
the hands in Ecclesiastes 9 and Genesis 4, as well as God's
rewarding "acts" in Genesis 18 and 22 are given as examples
of a meritorious relationship between God and humankind.
Paul also states that we should "do good to all, especially
to those within the household of faith {Galatians 4:10}."[2]
In 1 Corinthians 13 all faith without love is considered to
provide one with nothing. Finally, the import of act is
evinced in John 15 where Jesus states that you "are my friends
if you do what I prescribe."[3]

A supposition of the Catholic party, expounded in
Article 6 and later attacked by both Luther and Melanchthon,
was that the Augsburg Confession excluded good works. The
Catholic party maintained that sola fide, "unlike the truth
of the Gospel,"[4] excludes good works. This is supported,
the framers of the Confutatio say, by Paul's statement in
Romans 2 that the Lord rewards each according to his works
and by the passage in Matthew 7 where Jesus warns that not
all who say "Lord, Lord" will enter into the kingdom of heaven,

---

[1]CR 27:98.

[2]CR 27:99.

[3]CR 27:100.

[4]CR 27:99-100.

"but those who do the will of my Father."[1] St. Paul's saying that we are not justified by works of the law means "in the end that works are not excluded."[2] For the Catholics, it is not works without grace or sola opera, but it is that "our works from themselves can merit nothing, but the grace of God makes them worthy of eternal life.[3]

---

[1]Ibid.

[2]CR 27:101-102.

[3]CR 27:95. Cochlaeus maintained as well: "Haec et id genus innumera alia scripturae testimonia contestantur nos per bona opera mereri, et laboribus nostris promissam reddi mercedem, nosque bonis operibus nostris per gratiam Dei dignos effici vita aeterna, iuxta illud Iohannis. Ambulabunt mecum in albis quia digni sunt, Apoc. 3." CR 27:96. He further endorses the position of the Confutatio: "Gratia Dei praevenit voluntatem, movet voluntatem, perficit voluntatem, ita ut opera, quae alioqui nulla essent assistente Dei gratia, aliquid sint et meritoria fiant. Non sane ex virtute propria, sed per gratiam et misericordiam Dei promittentis, et per meritum passionis Christi, mediatoris et advocati nostri." CR 27:96. It would be most beneficial for future study to investigate the specificity of theological positions taken within the polemics of Cochlaeus. His concept of the immutability of church teaching for instance as depicted in his Confutatio: "Unde fit, ut Christus dicat, (Matth. 16) Ecclesiam suam fundatam esse super firmam petram, et Paulus (I Tim. 3) nominet eam columnam et basim veritatis. Ideo a veritate et recta fide (custode ac ductore spiritu sancto) aberrare nunquam poterit." CR 27:87. The role of church authority and that of Scripture is brought out in the same treatise: "Nusquam item in sacris literis scriptum legitur, Symbolum istud, quod Apostolorum dicimus, ab Apostolis vel compositum vel conscriptum fuisse, Et tamen recte pie ac vere ita credimus, non quod in scripturis habeatur expressum, sed quia sic per spiritum sanctum edocta tenet pia mater Ecclesia." CR 27:91. The following treat Cochlaeus: Adolf Herte, Die Lutherbiographi des Johannes Cochläus. Eine quellenkritische Untersuchung. (Münster in Westfalen: Aschendorff, 1915); idem, Die Lutherkommentare des Johannes Cochläus, kritische studie zur Geschichtschreibung im Zeitalter der Glaubensspaltung.

The Catholic party in their Article 6 ended with an attack on the sola fide position. St. Paul and the entire Church, they say, testifies to the fact that "faith alone does not justify."[1] It is true that our works offer nothing useful to God, nor do they compare in any way to the divine reward. Rather, "faith and good works are gifts of God, to which is given eternal life by the mercy of God."[2]

Article 20 as well treats the argument by numerous citations from Scripture, some being repeated. The argument, however, Melanchthon begins in the interrogative. For example, if works are not meritorius, "why did Wisdom say God rewards the labors of holy men {Wisdom 10}?"[3] Why did the author exhort us to works, saying in 2 Peter 1: "Be zealous, brothers, in making certain your call and election by your good works?"[4] Why did Paul say in Hebrews 6 that God "is not so unjust as to overlook your work and love which you

---

(Münster in Westfalen: Aschendorff, 1935; idem, Das katholische Lutherbild im Bann der Lutherkommentare des Cochlaus. (Münster in Westfalen: Aschendorff, 1943); Hubert Jedin, Des Johannes Cochlaeus Streitschrift De libero arbitrio hominis (1525), ein Beitrag zur Geschichte der vortridentinischen katholischen Theologie. (Breslau: Müller und Seiffert, 1927).

[1]CR 27:100-101.
[2]CR 27:101.
[3]CR 27:122.
[4]CR 27:122.

showed in his name?"[1] It is not, the authors assert, that
we reject the merit of Christ, but that "our works are
nothing, are able to merit nothing, without the virtue of
the merit of the passion of Christ."[2]

Article 20 continues by pointing to the scriptural
references pertaining to the "bearing" of the cross of
Christ, as Matthew 10 and 16, and this means of discipleship.
One is to _ambulare_ if one is to _in Christo manere_. [One is
to walk in Christ if one is to remain in Christ.][3]

This article concludes tersely that these opinions,
those being impugned, "were a condemned and reproved 1100
years before, at the time of Augustine."[4]

According to a report composed on August 4, 1530 by
the Nuremberg delegates at Augsburg, the Catholic _Confutatio_
was publicly read on August 3 at 2 P.M.; it comprised more
that fifty pages.[5] During the reading John Cammermeister
(Camerarius) recorded the substance of the Articles "in
shorthand on his tablet, as far as he was able, and more

---

[1]CR 27:122.

[2]Ibid.

[3]CR 27:123.

[4]CR 27:123.

[5]CR 2:249-252.

than we could all understand and remember ..."[1] In a
letter to Luther dated August 6 Melanchthon indicates that
he was not present at the reading.[2]

The minority party was not able to accept the
Confutatio, nor to procure a copy in order to prepare a
reply. The notes taken by Camerarius during the reading
provided the only source. The Confutatio was not to be had
in print.[3] Melanchthon concluded his apology of the Augsburg
Confession by stating that had the Confutatio been given "to
us for inspection, we may have been more properly able to
answer these and further points."[4]

It was with those notes of Camerarius that Melanchthon
began to prepare what would be called the "Apology" to the
Augsburg Confession. He continued to work on the reply until
September 20, at which time he writes Camerarius telling him
that he has finished.[5] "I am remaining at home now and have

---

[1]CR 2:250. Also haben wir, so viel wir diess Mal
dess behalten mögen, den Effect davon Joachim Cammermeister,
so wir auch zu uns hinein genommen, verzeichnen lassen, der
es also mit Fleiss auf alle Artikel mit kurz in sein Täfelein
aufgezeichnet so viel ihm möglich, und mehr denn wir alle
verstehen und behalten können, wie S.W. aus beiliegender copey
vernehmen."

[2]CR 2:254.

[3]CR 9:929; CR 27:420.

[4]CR 27:378.

[5]CR 2:383. See also CR 2:438, 440. The work
probably was not begun until early September for the Nuremberg
delegates gave their opinion to Melanchthon on August 19.
CR 2:289. The text is found in CR 27:275-316.

written in these days the apology of our confession, which
if necessary, will also be delivered; for it will be opposed
to the confutation of the adversaries which you heard read.
I have written it sharply and quite vehemently."[1]

This work was offered to the emperor by Chancellor
Brück on September 22, but it was rejected. The Catholic
party later published a statement boasting that they had
refuted the Augsburg Confession by the Scriptures.[2]

On September 23, Melanchthon left Augsburg and
proceeded to Wittenberg, going to Coburg where Luther was
waiting. From there both men proceeded to their homes in
Wittenberg. Almost immediately after the Apology was refused
in Augsburg, Melanchthon set out to amend and expand upon its
text. Having come across a copy of the Confutatio, Melanchthon
diligently worked on the new copy of the Apology even while
they traveled back to Wittenberg. It is reported that while
they were staying at Spalatin's home in Altenburg, Melanchthon
was writing constantly. He was said to be writing during a
Sunday meal when Luther snatched the pen from his hand saying,
"God can be honored not alone by work, but also by rest and
recreation; for that reason He has given the third commandment

[1]CR 2:383

[2]Bente, Concordia Triglotta, p. 41; Richard, Philip
Melanchthon, p. 216.

and commanded the Sabbath."[1]

In February, 1531 Melanchthon writes to John Brenz commenting on his revision: "I am redoing the Apology and it will be much larger and more fortified. Presently, the part where we speak of faith and not love as that which justifies men is treated fully."[2] We must know that we are justified by faith. The justification "by love is justification by the law, not the Gospel."[3]

In the end, Melanchthon's revisions were to take from November 1530 to April 1531. In a November 12 letter to Dietrich he states that he is endeavoring to polish the Apology.[4] On November 13 he writes to Camerarius saying that he hopes his work in revising will be of some usefulness and bring results.[5] He mentions, in a letter to Camerarius dated January 1, 1531, that his labor concerns primarily the article on justification.

Again, in February, 1531 he writes Brenz saying that he exhaustively treated the article on justification by faith.[6]

---

[1]This story from Mathesius' Seventeen Sermons on the Life of Luther is found in Bente, Ibid., pp. 41-42 and Richard, Ibid., p. 217.

[2]CR 2:484.

[3]Ibid. See also CR 27:420.

[4]CR 2:438.

[5]CR 2:440.

[6]CR 2:484.

On March 17 he writes to Camerarius lamenting the "tardy progress" he is making.[1] He mentions illness as a partial cause for delay in a March letter to Baumgartner.[2] In an April 7 letter to Jonas he says that he has completed the section on marriage and the following day he writes to Brenz saying: "We have almost finished the Apology."[3] In a tone of seeming despair he tells Camerarius (April 11) that his Apology "will appear one of these days."[4]

At last in mid-April Melanchthon writes to Bucer: "My Apology has been published in which I have treated articles on justification, repentance and others in a way that our adversaries will find themselves quite troubled."[5]

The Apology was first intended to be what its name implied, an apology for the Augsburg Confession in light of the critique provided by the Catholic Confutatio. Melanchthon wrote the Apology as a refutation of the various charges made by the Catholics. The structure, as a consequence, is much akin to that of the Confutatio and the Apology consists of articles which were specifically in dispute.

---

[1]CR 2:488.

[2]CR 2:485.

[3]CR 2:493-494.

[4]CR 2:495.

[5]CR 2:498.

Even though accepted later as confessional by
Lutheran churches, the Apology is the first major treatise
of Melanchthon's which extensively examines and provides a
systematic, well thought out, theology of good works.
Melanchthon has not simply defended but actively systematized
a new theology of good works.

As an answer to the Catholic party's charge that the
Evangelicals omit works, Melanchthon states quite directly
that "we require good works."[1] It is important, however,
that we understand the impossibility of loving God apart
from faith, even if this love is demanded. For, states
Melanchthon, it is because "of Christ" that we are able to
worship, "to fear and to love God, as John teaches in his
first epistle."[2] Melanchthon says that "we praise and require
good works" and present many reasons why they "ought to be
done."[3] Abraham, for instance, accepted circumcision as a
sign, just as Abel offered sacrifice, not to be justified
by a work.[4] Their acts were meant to be "exercises" of faith
or putting that which was received into action.[5]

Works are not to be excluded, nor separated from

---

[1]CR 27:449.

[2]Ibid.

[3]CR 27:479-480.

[4]CR 27:480.

[5]Ibid.

faith. "Love and works ought to follow faith," but a trust
in love or a work as a merit for "justification is excluded."[1]
We maintain that "love ought to follow faith," for Paul says
in Galatians 5:6 that in Christ Jesus "circumcision is not
valid at all, nor uncircumcision, but faith working through
love."[2]

The consequential dimension of love or works is most
important for Melanchthon. Indeed, he considered it to be
the ethical mandate inherent in the Christian calling.
Melanchthon points to the example used by the Catholic party
which avails itself of 2 Peter 1 in which the author exhorts
the readers to make firm their calling. From this passage
the adversaries, says Melanchthon, have "artificially judged
whatever is pleasing from Scripture. Namely, make firm your
calling by good works. Therefore, good works merit the
remission of sins."[3] The argument makes sense, according
to Melanchthon, if the example of the magistrate who remits
the punishment of one guilty of a serious offense is used.
The magistrate actually withholds punishment, so it comes
from another, thus, punishment comes from outside ourselves.
"Therefore merit is relief from punishment, which is withheld
by another. Therefore, the argument is not from a cause,

[1]CR 27:440.

[2]CR 27:446.

[3]CR 27:586.

but provides a cause."[1] Peter, on the other hand, speaks
of works <u>following</u> the remission of sins and teaches that
the people make firm their calling. A person does not
exercise his calling by a life of sin.[2] One does good works
as one perseveres in one's calling. The gift of the calling
is not lost by the works that follow "but it is retained by
faith and faith does not remain in those who lose the Holy
Spirit, and who throw away penance," simply because "faith
comes forth in penance."[3]

The operation of the Holy Spirit is most important
in order that works have any significance. In a variant
reading from an early edition (1531) Melanchthon remarks
that the love of God is a tendency "which the Holy Spirit
awakens in man, and we teach that love and good works ought
to follow faith."[4] Human nature without the Holy Spirit does
not know nor fear nor believe in God. The gift of the Holy
Spirit "begins in the believer eternal life which is revealed
through a new disposition and movement (<u>motus</u>)."[5]

---

[1]CR 27:586-587.

[2]CR 27:587.

[3]Ibid. Melanchthon uses the word <u>existere</u>.

[4]CR 27:474. This is from an early draft of 1531.
which Melanchthon removed. See CR 27:460-478.

[5]Ibid. There are four principal editions of the
Apology. They are: 1) 4º Editione principe a. 1531 quaternariae
formae, 2) 8º Editione anni 1531 octavae formae, 3) 4º Editione
a. 1535-1540 quaternariae formae, 4) 8º Editione a. 1541-1542
octavae formae. Any variants will be noted by the following:
Eds. 1, 2, 3, or 4.

An analysis of Melanchthon's use of language is
very important in understanding why he tells us we should do
good works. Particularly important in the Apology are three
verbs. These verbs are used in enunciating the doctrine of
good works. They include oportet (it is fitting), debeat,
(it ought to be), and now necesse est (it is necessary).
Melanchthon uses this last phrase in explaining the import of
works in the course of his investigation of the moral exhortation found in Isaiah 1:16-18. There, the prophet proclaims,
as a word of the Lord that the people are to wash themselves
and to remove evil from their sight, to cease doing evil and
to pursue good, to seek justice and correct oppression, and
to defend the fatherless and plead for the widow.[1] Melanchthon
examines the prophet's emphasis on works and concludes that
he does not say "by these works, works such as relieving the
oppressed and pleading for the widow, we are able to merit
the remission of sins ex opere operato, but he does propose
those works to be necessary in a new life."[2] He adds that
Christ himself preached penance when he said, "Forgive and
you will be forgiven."[3] Christ did not say, however, that
those forgiving works of ours "merit the remission of sins
ex opere operato, as they call it, but he requires as

---

[1]CR 27:492.

[2]CR 27:492-493.

[3]CR 27:493.

certainly necessary (<u>necesse est</u>) a new life. In the
meanwhile he desires that we receive the remission of sins
by faith."[1]

Melanchthon is very cautious in not proposing a
causal relation between the consequent good works and the
remission of sins. With faith a new life "necessarily
(<u>necessario</u>) creates new tendencies and works."[2] For when
the author of the epistle of James speaks of faith and works
he "rightly denies that we are justified by a faith which is
without works. He does not say that we are justified by
faith and works, for certainly we are not reborn by works."[3]
The causal principle is the key for Melanchthon. It is "not
that Christ is partly (<u>partim</u>) propitiator and our works are
partly our propitiator."[4] The example from James does not
indicate the manner or mode of justification (<u>modum
justificationis</u>), but it describes those who are just "after
they are justified and reborn."[5]

Following this consequential understanding of works
are examples from variant texts using different verbs to
highlight the "reasons" for works. Works, he says, are to

---

[1]Ibid.

[2]CR 27:491.

[3]Ibid.

[4]Ibid.

[5]Ibid.

be done "because God requires them and they are the effect
of regeneration as Paul teaches in Ephesians 2. For we
are created in Christ Jesus for good works, which God has
prepared, so that we should walk in them."[1] Thus, "good
works ought to follow faith," so that "our confession will
invite others to piety."[2]

Using one of Luther's typical images, that of the
good fruit, Melanchthon charges that we know works are
"necessary" even though they "do not merit the remission of
sins or justify us before God."[3] It is, rather, "fitting in
this life to project a confession of faith" because "a new
life ought to have new fruit ..."[4] This life "points out
hypocrisy and a sham of penance unless good fruit follows."[5]
Melanchthon pursues this image in the Apology, not to establish
works as a propitiation, but for two specific reasons. One
is that after reconciliation "good fruits necessarily ought
to follow" or hypocrisy toward faith is indicated. The other
cause is that "for us a work is to have outward signs" of
the promise in order to calm a frightened conscience.[6]

---

[1]CR 27:478. Eds. 2-4.

[2]Ibid.

[3]CR 27:477. The early 1531 edition.

[4]Ibid.

[5]CR 27:518. Eds. 2-4.

[6]CR 27:497.

The consequent significance of works for Melanchthon
is elucidated when, in the first part of the Apology, he
speaks of the possibility of love toward others. It is after
(postquam) we are justified and reborn by faith, he says,
that we begin to love, to fear, and to entreat God. The
same applies to our love of neighbor whom we begin to love
"because {reborn} hearts have spiritual and holy inclinations."[1] These are not possible until "after (postquam) we
are justified by faith and are reborn by receiving the Holy
Spirit."[2]

Even though it "is necessary to do good works" we
"are obliged to render all honors to Christ."[3] This is because
the importance of works for Melanchthon, is relational. It is
by "faith because of Christ that we are reputed just before
God, that we are not reputed just because of works, without
Christ as mediator ... our works are not able to oppose the
anger and judgment of God, nor are they able to vanquish the
terrors of sin."[4]

This justification, from which it is necessary to
do good works, is not just a reputed state for Melanchthon.[5]

---

[1]CR 27:447.

[2]CR 27:448.

[3]CR 27:482-483.

[4]Ibid.

[5]CR 27:509.

Indeed, we are justified "so that we will do good works and begin to obey the law of God. Therefore, we are renewed (regeneramur), we receive the Holy Spirit, so that this new life has new works, new dispositions, fear, love of God, {and} the hatred of lust, etc."[1]

The final cause for doing good works is "because of the command of God" in exercising or confessing the faith.[2] On account of this cause "good works necessarily ought to be done" and those who remain in the flesh and do not live the renewed (renovata) life retard "the movement (motus) of the Holy Spirit."[3]

This consequential ethical mandate will become even more pronounced in Melanchthon's later works. For now he states that faith which "receives the remission of sins in the terrified heart and flees sin does not remain in those who submit to lust, nor does it exist with mortal sin."[4]

Such an ethically responsible life, acting in accord

---

[1]Ibid. Other passages emphasizing necesse esse include: CR 27:446, 449, 451. The later emphasis on the importance of the law is inferred from CR 27: 451: "Profitemur igitur quod necesse sit inchoari in nobis, et subinde magis magisque fieri legem."

[2]CR 27:478.

[3]Ibid.

[4]CR 27:450. In the early 1531 edition he states: "Propterea necessario debent honesta opera facere, ne plus peccant, Et scire debent Deum non solum aeterna morte, sed etiam corporalibus poenis punire istos, qui violant iusticiam civilem." CR 27:464.

with God's command, does not go unrewarded. God praises civil acts or justice of reason, even if human nature cannot provide any great good.[1] He even "commends corporal rewards," yet not to the extent that it is a "praising with an affront to Christ."[2]

It is "because of faith" that works "are holy, divine, and sacrifices," which act as an announcement to the world.[3] By them Christ extends his reign in the world by sanctifying hearts, denouncing the Devil, pronouncing the good news, "and in our helplessness declaring his power."[4]

According to Melanchthon, these works are "heavenly," "divine" and "holy" (sancta) because they proclaim God's capability in and through our incapacity.[5] These works are recognized as important, but they do not make us sons of God or co-heirs with Christ. This is due to the fact that justification and eternal life are "not merited by our works."[6] Faith itself establishes works as pleasing before God.

---

[1]CR 27:432.

[2]Ibid. Good works are considered pleasing due to faith. See Eds. 2-4, CR 27:457: "Sola igitur fides iustificat, et bona opera propter fidem placent."

[3]CR 27:478. Here works are called "divine" (divina) by Melanchthon insofar as they are joined to the work of Christ.

[4]Ibid.

[5]Ibid.

[6]CR 27:479.

Melanchthon is quite cautious in relating works
and merit in any way. He does affirm that God proposes
works to be performed and rewards are promised.[1] "We teach
that good works are meritorious, not for the remission of
sins, grace, or justification."[2] They follow upon faith,
and as a consequence, will be granted corporal and spiritual
rewards "in and after this life because Paul states as much.
Each will receive a reward comparable to his labor. There
were different rewards, because of different labors."[3] The
labor affects the meriting and the reward; thus there exists
a "degree of rewards."[4] For "he who sows sparingly, sparingly
reaps and he who sows plentifully, plentifully reaps.
Clearly the kind of reward is connected to the kind of work."[5]

For Melanchthon, the commandment exhorting honor of
mother and father and the commensurate reward for such action
is just such an example. For the "law sets forth a certain
reward for a certain work. Therefore, the fulfillment of the
law merits the reward."[6] The fulfillment of the law is not
pleasing to God, unless we are justified and reborn. Once

---

[1]Ibid.

[2]Ibid.

[3]Ibid.

[4]CR 27:511.

[5]Ibid.

[6]Ibid.

we are received as sons of God by faith, "the beginning
fulfillment of the law is pleasing, and has reward in and
after this life."[1]

Being justified means that "those who in their
hearts believe in God, are pronounced just, and thereafter
they bear good fruit which is pleasing because of faith."[2]
It does not follow, according to Melanchthon, that "works
merit the remission of sins," or act as a propitiation or
do "not require Christ as the propitiator."[3] These works,
even if they are "far removed from perfection of the law,
nevertheless are pleasing because of faith," which is
"reputed to be just because we believe we are reconciled
to God because of Christ."[4] Thus, faith is that which
both produces works and make them acceptable.

The Apology and the Role of the Mediator

Any principle of causality applied to the Christian
mystery of salvation must refer to only one cause. According
to Melanchthon, works cannot merit salvation for this would

---

[1]Ibid.

[2]CR 27:491.

[3]Ibid.

[4]CR 27:500-501. Melanchthon remarks here that we
are, once reborn, able to obey the law. "Haec fides imputetur
pro iusticia coram Deo, Romans IV. Et cum hoc modo cor
erigitur et vivificatur fide, concipit spiritum sanctum,
qui renovat nos, ut legem facere possimus, ut possimus
diligere Deum, verbum Dei, obedire Deo in afflictionibus, ut
possimus esse casti, diligere proximum, etc."

provide yet another cause and detract from Christ's glory.
It is because of Christ, "not because of our works" that
"the remission of sins is given to us. For what was the
work of Christ who was given for our sins, if our merits are
able to make amends for our sins?"[1]

All human virtues are under sin and men are not able
to fulfill the demands of the law.[2] "We are not able to be
free from sin and to be justified by the law, but the
promise of the remission of sins and justification is given
because of Christ who was given for us. This was so that
he would make amends for the sins of the world and be established as mediator and propitiator. This promise does not
have our merits as a condition."[3]

Melanchthon discusses the importance of having a
mediator when he speaks of being justified by faith. Three
objects come together (concurrere) in this doctrine. These
are: promise, the gratuitousness of God, and the merits of
Christ as reward and propitiation.[4] "The promise is received

---

[1]CR 27:436.

[2]CR 27:434.

[3]Ibid. In an early edition of the Apology: "Primum
quia obscurat gloriam Christi, quia qui suis operibus conatur
mereri iustificationem, is non sentit sibi donari isuticiam
propter Christum, sed propter propria merita. Itaque omisso
mediatore Christo, propria merita opponit irae Dei, loco
mediatoris." CR 27:463.

[4]CR 27:436.

by faith, the gratuitousness excludes our merits and
signifies that only by mercy are we offered {God's} favor.
The merits of Christ are the reward because it is fitting
that another person be the propitiation for our sins."[1]

It is by faith alone that we receive the remission
of our sins and the Holy Spirit for the "reconciled are
reputed to be just and sons of God, not because of their
purity (mundiciem), but by mercy because of Christ if this
mercy is embraced by faith."[2] Therefore, Scripture testifies
"that we are reckoned as just by faith."[3]

In the letter to the Romans (3:28) Paul states that
man is justified by faith apart from the works of the law.
Melanchthon considers Paul to be speaking here "not only of
ceremonies, but of the entire law."[4] This Melanchthon takes
to be the Decalogue.[5] For if the fulfillment of the biddings
of the Decalogue or "if moral works merited the remission of
sins and justification, then the work of Christ was nothing"
and the promise to which Paul addresses himself is
meaningless.[6]

---

[1] Ibid.

[2] CR 27:442.

[3] Ibid.

[4] CR 27:443.

[5] Ibid. See also CR 27:429.

[6] CR 27:443.

This work of Christ is not simply one cause of salvation and our works another. Christ "does not cease being mediator after we are renewed. They err who maintain that Christ has merited only the first grace. Thereafter, we please God by the fulfillment of the law and we merit eternal life. Christ remains mediator ..."[1] Thus, only one cause is responsible for salvation, and that is Christ alone. If, says Melanchthon, we attribute anything to our works or consider them in any way to be a propitiation or to merit the remission of sins, then we deny that "we are reputed to be righteous before God" by faith and on account of Christ as propitiation.[2] This is to remove from Christ the honor of mediator (honorem mediatoris).[3]

If our works are worthy of eternal life then we "transfer the glory of Christ to our works. Further, we are pleasing because of our works and not because of Christ."[4] It would omit the mediatorial function of Christ "who is perpetually mediator not only in the beginning of justification."[5] Since he is mediator, the "merits of Christ are given to us, so that we are reputed to be righteous by trust

---

[1] CR 27:454.

[2] CR 27:482.

[3] Ibid.

[4] CR 27:504.

[5] Ibid. See also CR 27:487, 514.

in his merits."[1] When we "believe in him, we have then,
as it were, personal merits."[2]

For Melanchthon there is no sense in contrasting
any human work or act with the mediatorial death and sacrifice
of Jesus on the cross. If eternal life is not freely given
to us because of Christ what human work can be found that
"stands worthy of eternal life?"[3] If we need to fulfill
the demands of the law in order to merit the remission of
sins, then what achievement or accomplishment has the Gospel
provided us? Even more directly, what has "Christ accomplished,
if the remission of sins follows due to our work?"[4]

Finally, Melanchthon accuses the Catholics of
actually proposing a justice of law and not one from the
Gospel. Men cannot simply be saved by their works. The God
whom Melanchthon envisages is wrathful due to the sin in the
world. No amount of love nor "works are able to be a
propitiation for sin."[5] Christ alone as mediator saves and
the glory and the honor of Christ ought "not to be transferred
to our works."[6]

------

[1]CR 27: 590.
[2]Ibid.
[3]CR 27: 505.
[4]CR 27: 549.
[5]CR 27: 550.
[6]Ibid.

Righteousness by Reason in the Apology

    With the rejection of Christ as the only mediator
follows, says Melanchthon, the teaching of a "justice of
reason, namely, civil works" and the doctrine "that reason
without the Holy Spirit is able to love God above all things."[1]
Thus, arises the teaching that one is able to provide works
as a propitiation and merit the remission of sins.

    This justice of reason is much like a veil or as
Melanchthon says, an effort to be secure in hypocrisy.
Those who feel they can fulfill the law "arouse presumption,
an inane trust in works, and comtempt for the grace of
Christ."[2] According to John 8:36, Christ says if "the Son
frees you, you will truly be free."[3] For Melanchthon the
meaning is that "we are not able to be freed from sin and
merit the remission of sin by our reason."[4] As also stated
in John 3, if you are "not reborn by water and the spirit,
you will not be able to enter the kingdom of God."[5]

    No apostle, according to Melanchthon, believed that
"our love conquers sin and death, that love is the propitiation

---

    [1]CR 27:430. Again, I begin with the Apology
because it is Melanchthon's first synthesized presentation
of his theology of good works.

    [2]CR 27:432.

    [3]CR 27:433.

    [4]Ibid.

    [5]Ibid.

because of which God is reconciled (to the world) neglecting Christ as mediator, or that love is justice without the mediator, Christ."[1] This type of love is a "justice of the law, not of the Gospel. The latter promises us reconciliation and justice if we believe that God is reconciled because of Christ the mediator and that the merits of Christ are given to us."[2]

This justice or righteousness is more a justice or righteousness of philosophy rather than the Gospel. Melanchthon asks, "If this is Christian righteousness, what difference exists between philosophy and Christian doctrine?"[3] If we are able to merit the remission of sins by our works, what did Christ accomplish? "If we are able to be justified by reason and the works of reason to what end is the work of Christ or being born again?"[4] Those who would maintain such a position actually deny the Gospel and "expound the ethics of Aristotle."[5] Aristotle did write most learnedly, asserts Melanchthon, in regard to civil morality. Yet, if one proposes the remission of sins by works of reason, then "there exists no difference between the righteousness of

---

[1]CR 27:488-489.

[2]Ibid.

[3]CR 27:430-431.

[4]Ibid.

[5]Ibid.

philosophy, i.e. Pharisaism, and Christianity."[1]

Buttressing this same contention, Melanchthon maintains, in his early edition of the Apology (1531), that there is no "difference between philosophy and theology" when one proposes merit.[2] Many have "carried Aristotle into the church" to replace Christ.[3] The writings of Zeno and Socrates are compared with Christ and the consensus is that they all taught certain moral precepts, but not the promise of the remission of sins.[4]

If human worship is "deserving of justification, grace, and the remission of sins, then plainly the reign of the Anti-Christ is established."[5] For the reign of the "Anti-Christ is a new worship (cultus) of God, invented on

---

[1]Ibid.

[2]CR 27:463.

[3]Ibid.

[4]Ibid. In this early edition Melanchthon discusses this justice: "Initio autem hoc praefandum est, nos cum de iustificatione loquimur, non loqui de iusticia civili seu morali, sed de iusticia, qua coram Deo iusti sumus, seu iusti reputamur, quam Paulus vocat iusticiam Dei, id est, qua nos Deus iustificat. Nam de iusticia civili, seu ut vocant in scholis, de operibus moralibus, et hoc exteriori conversatione, subiecta rationi humanae, sic sentimus, quod Deus exigat illam civilem iusticiam ab omnibus, et quod sit aliquo modo in potestate humana efficere eam."

[5]CR 27:575. Here Melanchthon actually means human deeds (cultus). For the classical and medieval meanings of the word see respectively: Lewis and Short, A Latin Dictionary (Oxford: Oxford University Press, 1879), pp. 488-489; J. F. Niermeyer, Mediae Latinitatis Lexicon Minus (Leiden: E. J. Brill, 1976) p. 287.

human authority and repudiating Christ."[1] For the Muslim
has "worship and works by which he wishes to be justified
before God," not knowing that it is because of Christ and
by faith that one is justified.[2] The "papacy (Papatus)
will be equal to the reign of the Anti-Christ if it defends
human worship as justifying."[3]

Condemning the "naturalism" of justification by
works Melanchthon (Apology, ed. of 1531) equates this teaching
with "the dogma of the Epicureans and Muslims."[4] There is
little difference from Judaism if one were to hold to the
teaching of external works.[5] "What is that justification
without faith in Christ unless it is philosophy or indeed
Judaism?"[6]

---

[1]CR 27:575. See also Niermeyer, Ibid., p. 287.

[2]CR 27:575. See also Niermeyer, Ibid., pp. 624.
627. Hereafter, all references to Lexicon will be references
to Niermeyer.

[3]CR 27:575.

[4]CR 27:471.

[5]Ibid. Within the Apology Melanchthon criticizes
the "naturalism" of works: "Et haec opinio, quia naturaliter
blanditur hominibus peperit et auxit multos cultus in
Ecclesia, vota Monastica, abusus Missae, Et subinde alii
alios cultus atqueobservationes haec opinione excogitaverunt."
CR 27:430.

[6]CR 27:473.

Merit and Reward in the Apology

Lest there be any question on the Apology's treatment of works and/or merit Melanchthon provides clear assertions regarding the state of these doctrines. "It is false that we merit the remission of sins by our works. It is not true that men are reputed to be just before God because of the righteousness of reason."[1] "It is not true that reason {by its own strength} is able to love God above all things and abide by the law of God."[2]

In examining the meaning of the law, Melanchthon is assured that the teaching of the law does not remove the Gospel nor Christ as propitiator.[3] However, those who interpret the fulfillment of that law as meritorious bear the curse of the Pharisees whom Jesus chastized.[4] Merit becomes significant for humankind because the conscience anguishes and "is seeking by works the remission" of sins.[5]

The distinction was made, among those who defended the possibility of merit, between congruous and condign merit.

---

[1]CR 27: 432.

[2]Ibid. As Melanchthon says in the early 1531 Apology: "Non igitur justificamur nomine operum nostrorum, sed nomine Christi, quod fide apprehenditur." CR 27: 469.

[3]CR 27: 495.

[4]CR 27: 495-496.

[5]CR 27: 498-499. In variants Editions 2-4 Melanchthon remarks: "Quae tandem insania est, praeferre nostras satisfactiones, satisfactioni Christi?" CR 27: 564.

For Melanchthon, those "who make a distinction between
meritum congrui et meritum condigni are only playing a game
obviously not seeing this as Pelagian (πελαγιανιζειν)."[1]
If God "necessarily gives grace for meritum congrui, then it
is not meritum congrui but meritum condigni."[2]   The intention
of the act or "the doing does not distinguish kinds of merits,
but the hypocrite" wishes to be secure by the worth of
works.[3] On the other hand, the terrified or frightened
conscience doubts all works.[4]

When one doubts all works one is attempting,
according to Melanchthon, this meritum congrui. Because of
the doubt with regard to the works done one seeks to do even
more. "They seek other works in order {to attempt} congruo
mereri, but then they doubt and operate without faith until
despair occurs."[5] In other words, the meritum de congruo
cannot be a "means" for winning grace, for then it would be
meritum de condigno. Likewise, if this "means" is eradicated
as possible one must turn then to other means (i.e. that of
a mediator).

------

[1] CR 27:431.

[2] Ibid.

[3] CR 27:505.

[4] Ibid.

[5] Ibid.

For Melanchthon, the entire teaching of these two
kinds of merit escapes the impurity of the heart and the
inability of works to please God.[1] Such a "doctrine of
reason" cannot save us for "reason cannot see the impurity
of the heart."[2] The concept that would assert that works
are actually pleasing to God drives man to invent more and
more tasks to resolve the "terrors of the conscience."[3]

History teaches us that "Gentiles and Jews offered
human sacrifices and undertook many other extremely difficult
works to appease the wrath of God."[4]

These doctrines or teachings concerning merit must
be regarded, says Melanchthon, as false due to the fact that
we are reconciled by grace and not by law. If we are justified by "works, then it is not by grace."[5] The justice of
God "is now revealed without the law. That is, the remission
of sins is offered by grace."[6] It would be useless if the
remission of sins and reconciliation depended upon our merits,
for we are entirely unable to fulfill the law.[7]

---

[1]CR 27:499.

[2]Ibid.

[3]Ibid.

[4]Ibid.

[5]CR 27:434.

[6]CR 27:434-435.

[7]Ibid.

Melanchthon concludes his investigation and analysis
of merit by an examination of the meaning of reward (mercedes).
According to Melanchthon, the Catholic party held that
eternal life is called "reward". By this "it is then
necessary to merit (de condigno) by good works."[1]
Melanchthon's response is that Paul speaks of "eternal gift"
or "reward" because it is justice given "on account of
Christ, just as John says, we are made sons of God and
co-heirs with Christ. He who believes in the Son has
eternal life."[2]

If, states Melanchthon, our adversaries concede
"that we are reputed to be just by faith because of Christ
and that good works are pleasing to God because of faith,"
thereafter we will not vehemently disagree "concerning the
word 'reward' (merces)."[3] "We acknowledge eternal life to
be a reward because it is a thing owed (debita) because of
the promise" and not "because of our merits."[4]

The Apology and the Terrified Conscience

As inferred within the prior section, the condition
of the "terrified conscience" causes Melanchthon to attack

---

[1] CR 27:510.

[2] Ibid. See merces in Niermeyer, Lexicon, pp. 672-673.

[3] CR 27:510.

[4] Ibid.

any salvific causal significance given to good works. It
is only the hypocrite who feels secure in being able "to
merit de condigno, either having that habitus or not,
because naturally men trust in their own righteousness, but
those with a terrified conscience are undecided and doubt."[1]
Those desiring merits seek to accumulate many works so they
may finally rest one day. They never know themselves "to
merit de condigno and they sink into despair" unless they
come to know from the Gospel the remission of sins by grace
and the righteousness which comes from faith.[2]

The despair, for Melanchthon, comes from the failure
to live up to the law. This is a result of our carnal nature.
All who are born into this world "have concupiscence and are
not able to have true fear and trust in God."[3]

Trust in the blessings of God is received because
of mercy and "not because of our merits."[4] This is the
"most ample consolation for all afflictions. This kind of
consolation the adversaries abolish when they diminish
faith" and teach men "to walk with God by works and merits."[5]

The acceptance of grace is because of mercy and is

---

[1]CR 27:431-432.

[2]Ibid.

[3]CR 27:422.

[4]CR 27:438.

[5]Ibid.

necessarily by faith. "The law always accuses us and always reveals the wrath of God."[1] God is not loved, then, until after (postquam) we accept God's mercy by faith.[2] Further, this wrath of God "we are not able to oppose by our love and our works."[3]

One impact of the terrified conscience is the uncertainty innate in any system that depends on works. The question constantly arises: how many are needed? "If the remission of sins is received by faith due to love, the remission of sins will always be uncertain, because we never love as much as we should."[4] The truth is, we actually do not love, "unless hearts stand assured that the remission of sins is given to us."[5] Melanchthon understands that uncertainty regarding the remission of sins will remain if and when one trusts or has faith in acts. This trust, is before the eyes of God "an empty trust (fiducia vana). As a consequence of it the conscience falls into despair."[6]

If the remission of sins depends not on Christ but on our love, "no one will have the remission of sins unless

---

[1]CR 27:448.

[2]Ibid.

[3]CR 27:441.

[4]CR 27:446.

[5]Ibid.

[6]CR 27:453.

he fulfills the whole law."[1]

For Melanchthon, the image of the terrified conscience carried with it the search for that which can provide peace. Peace cannot be found in works for God's favor and peace is due to Christ and to God's promise. "No amount of works is able to render peace to the conscience, but only the promise {of God}."[2] If further love and works are sought elsewhere in order to procure justification and "peace of conscience, then love and works do not justify, even if there are virtues and the justice of the law" for to what extent could they all have "fulfilled the law."[3]

The obedience to the law "justifies righteousness of the law, but this imperfect justice of the law is not acceptable to God, unless because of faith."[4] Therefore, the law "does not justify. That is, it neither reconciles

---

[1]CR 27:453. In the early edition: "Nihil mihi conscius sum, sed in hoc non iustificatus sum. Quia igitur mediatore Christo." CR 27:476. There is an obvious difference in Melanchthon's earlier assertions regarding the reborn's ability to fulfill the law. The position maintained here will become the norm hereafter.

[2]CR 27:457-458.

[3]Ibid.

[4]Ibid.

nor renews nor by itself makes one acceptable before God."[1]

The attempt by the saints to fulfill the law bears a certain order and reason for those who witness their good works. This order and reason suggests to those observers that the possibility of earning a reward exists. They judge "the saints to have merited the remission of sins and grace by these works. For that reason they imitate them and they feel that by like works they merit the remission of sins and grace."[2] They believe that those works and deeds appease the wrath of God, and consequently, "because of those works they are reputed to be righteous."[3]

This "impious opinion regarding works" Melanchthon vehemently condemns.[4] Such a judgment obscures the glory of Christ when men place before God "these works as if valuable and a propitiation."[5] There is no limit to the number of works sought by a person to ease his terrified conscience,

---

[1]Ibid. A partial reason for works' inability is impurity: "Hae sententiae et similes in scripturis testantur opera nostra immunda esse, et indigere misericordia." Editions 2-4. CR 27:437. Further, the role of the law is explained: "Lex enim semper accusat, cum legi nunquam satisfaciamus. Id quod tota Ecclesia confitetur. Paulus enim ait, Non quod volo bonum hoc facio, sed quod nolo, malum." Editions 2-4. CR 27:458.

[2]CR 27:480.

[3]Ibid.

[4]Ibid.

[5]Ibid.

yet peace will never come from works.[1] Further, there is
no one work that will comfort despair.

"The people of Israel saw the prophets sacrifice
in the high places."[2] Likewise, the examples of the saints
greatly move many to perform like works. The difficulty
is, however, that such an imitation and such works are
thought "to merit the remission of sins, grace, and justice."[3]
The prophets, indeed, sacrificed on the high places, but not
so that they would "by those works merit the remission of
sins and grace."[4] For they sacrificed in those very places
in order to proclaim, to teach, and to declare "here is a
testimony of our faith."[5]

When this testimonial function of works done in faith
is ignored and the recognition that works do not render peace
to the conscience occurs, it results in the following: "the
establishment of a new worship, new vows, and new ways of
acting the monk (monachatus). The additional work becomes a
further command of God, so that another great work is sought"
in order to "oppose the wrath and the judgment of God."[6]

----

[1]Ibid.

[2]CR 27:481.

[3]Ibid.

[4]Ibid.

[5]Ibid.

[6]CR 27:482. On Monachatus see Niermeyer, Lexicon,
p. 701.

The Terrified Conscience,
the Sinful Human Condition, and the Apology

Melanchthon argues that the antecedent cause of
the terrified conscience rests upon the inherent inability
of the person to fulfill the law. If we are not able to
fulfill the law, then we cannot love God. If the flesh "is
hostile toward God, then the flesh sins even when we do
external civil works."[1] If we cannot obey the law of God,
then we certainly sin. Even if we do excellent deeds and
human judgment deems them honorable and distinguished, we
cannot help but sin.[2] The contempt of God "adheres to the
nature of man" who sins even when "honest works are done
without the Holy Spirit" because they are done from an
impious heart.[3] Whatever is not done "from faith is sin."[4]

No one is able to claim, says Melanchthon, that
they are free from sin. Proverbs 20:9 maintains: "Who is
able to say 'My heart is clean? I am pure of sin.'"[5]
1 John 1:19 states that we do not have the truth in us if
we say we have no sin. Further, the saints pray on Sundays

---

[1]CR 27:433.

[2]Ibid.

[3]CR 27:433-434.

[4]Ibid.

[5]CR 27:506.

for the remission of sins, "and so the saints have sins."[1]

Faith is that which distinguishes all those who remain sinners, even the so-called saints. Faith makes the difference between those who have salvation and those who do not. "Faith makes the difference between those who are worthy and those who are not" because eternal life is promised to the justified and "faith justifies."[2]

In fact, Melanchthon believed that the state of having faith and of being justified because of Christ enabled one to do good works. Although there is no causal relation between good works and salvation, there exists one between salvation and works. As Christ said, "Without me you are able to do nothing."[3] If eternal life is rendered for works, it is given to the justified, because "men are never able to do good works unless they are justified and governed by the spirit of Christ."[4] Good works are not pleasing "without Christ as mediator and faith, for without faith it is

---

[1] Ibid. In the early 1531 edition: "Omne quod non est ex fide peccatum est. Item, sine fide impossible est placere Deo. Est enim fides quae vere sentit Deum remittere peccata." CR 27:463.

[2] CR 27:509. Or as is found in Edition 1531 8°, Edition 1540, and Edition 1542 8°; "Ita neque in hoc opere, imo nostra condonatio non est bonum opus, nisi cum fit a reconciliatis. Ideo nostra condonatio, quae quidem placet Deo, sequitur condonationem divinam." CR 27:517-518.

[3] CR 27:512.

[4] Ibid.

impossible to please God."[1]

Thus, for Melanchthon, all are unable to fulfill the law because of the sin which inheres in all, yet faith in Christ is that which separates one sinner from another. In addition, this faith is needed (with the help of the spirit of Christ) in order to do good works and it makes the sinner pleasing to God.

The Meaning of Faith in the Apology

It is important to examine the kind of faith that Melanchthon speaks of when he states that we are justified by faith and not by works. This faith "does not justify or save because it is a work worthy in itself," but only "because it accepts the promised mercy."[2] The Scriptures testify, he argues, that we are justified by faith. That faith is itself justice by which we are to be justified before God, clearly "not because it is a work worthy within itself, but only because it accepts (accipit) the promise of God."[3]

The act of receiving and accepting is paramount for

---

[1]Ibid.

[2]CR 27:437.

[3]Ibid. In Editions 2-4 Melanchthon states: "Idque affert fides, non quia per se sit opus dignum, sed tantum quia accipit oblatam promissionem, nihil respiciens propriam dignitatem." CR 27:456.

Melanchthon if Christ is to be the only mediator.
Throughout the Apology the salvific actor is Christ. Faith,
then, can only be that by which we are reputed just because
of the mediatorial role of Christ. "To have faith" means
"to rely upon the merits of Christ"; by these we are surely
reconciled to God.[1] For Melanchthon, defending the promise
of God because of Christ, means one must defend the doctrine
that we are justified by faith.[2] The law is unable to
grant the remission of sins; only the promise of God through
the merits of Christ can remit sins. Therefore, faith
justifies, for a promise is something that is received and
accepted; it is not to be possessed.[3] We do not receive the
remission of sins because of charity "or our own love, but on
account of faith alone."[4]

Melanchthon describes the importance of promise
when he differentiates between that faith which is an
acquaintance or a knowledge of history (noticia historiae)
and that which accepts or assents to the promise of God
(assentiri promissioni Dei). The remission of sins and
justification is offered by grace because of Christ. One
does not receive that remission and justification only

---

[1]CR 27:439.

[2]Ibid.

[3]See CR 27:439. One has faith that God will
fulfill his promise. One does not "possess" justification,
but has faith in God's promise of justification.

[4]CR 27:450

through knowledge (<u>noticiam</u>). To know the existence of the promise is not to accept in faith the promise of the remission of sins and justification.[1] This acceptance by faith is not to be found in those who perform evil deeds, or, in the demons.[2]

If one were to assert, says Melanchthon, that faith is in the intellect (even though those in the schools assert that the will commands the intellect to assent), we would maintain that "faith is not only knowledge in the intellect, but also a trust in the will."[3] This means it is to wish and "to receive that which is offered in the promise, namely, reconciliation and the remission of sins."[4]

Thus, for Melanchthon, faith is that which accepts or receives the righteousness of God and that by which we are reckoned as just. In 2 Corinthians 5:21, Paul states that God made Jesus "who knew no sin, to be sin for us, that we might be made the justice of God in him."[5] Here Paul means that faith is the "imputative justice," i.e., "it is that by which we are made acceptable to God on account of

---

[1]CR 27:436

[2]CR 27:502

[3]CR 27:503

[4]Ibid.

[5]Ibid.

the imputation and ordinance of God."[1]

Another dimension of this receiving faith is its acceptance of the future now. Following Hebrews 11:1, Melanchthon defines faith as "the substance of things hoped for."[2] For Melanchthon, the object of present hope is actually "a future event, but faith is concerned with future and present things and receives in the present the remission of sins offered in the promise."[3] It is not that we possess that future justice now, but that the faith in the promise of the future is "justice in the heart."[4]

Faith with Works in the Apology

One current exegetical issue dealing with good works, both in the Confutatio and the Apology, was the passage from the letter of James 2:24. There the author of James states that man is justified by works and not by faith alone. The Catholic party maintained that this passage alone refuted the Lutherans. On this Melanchthon observed that whenever works of any kind are mentioned, the Catholics are wont to say that good works merit the remission of sins, "that good works are a propitiation" and a price or reward "through which God

---

[1]Ibid.

[2]CR 27:504.

[3]Ibid.

[4]CR 27:494.

is reconciled to us, that good works conquer the terrors
of sin and death," that they are accepted in God's sight
because of their own goodness, and "that they do not need
mercy and do not need Christ as mediator."[1] Melanchthon
advanced the argument that this passage actually refutes the
Catholics. First of all, James does not omit that faith "by
which we apprehend Christ as propitiator."[2] The Catholics
condemn this understanding of faith in "their writings and
by the sword and capital punishments, they endeavor to remove
it from the church."[3] According to Melanchthon, James does
not omit faith "or choose love over faith, but retains faith,
{which apprehends} and does not exclude Christ as propitiator
in justification."[4]

Secondly, Melanchthon claimed that the works spoken
of in James pertain to those works that follow upon faith and
prove that it "is efficacious and living in the heart."[5]
Therefore, James "did not believe that we merit the remission
of sins and grace by good works."[6] For James "speaks of the
works of those who have been justified," of those who are

---

[1]CR 27:489-490.

[2]CR 27:490.

[3]Ibid.

[4]Ibid.

[5]CR 27:490.

[6]Ibid.

already reconciled and who "have obtained the remission of sins."[1] Therefore, for Melanchthon, the Catholics err in inferring that James teaches "that we merit the remission of sins and grace by good works," and that we have access to God without Christ's being our propitiator.[2]

Thirdly, Melanchthon interprets James 1:18 as saying that we are a kind of first fruits of his creatures.[3] "When he says that we have by the Gospel been born again, he teaches," asserts Melanchthon, "that by faith we are reborn and justified."[4] Christ's promise is apprehended "only by faith, when we place against it the terrors of sin and death."[5] James, therefore, does not think that we are born anew "by our works."[6]

Melanchthon agrees with James in denying that we are justified by a faith that is without works.[7] He adds that James says that we are "justified by faith and works, he surely does not say that we are reborn by works."[8] Neither

---

[1] Ibid.

[2] Ibid.

[3] CR 27: 490.

[4] Ibid.

[5] Ibid.

[6] Ibid.

[7] CR 27: 491.

[8] Ibid.

does such a position propose Christ as partly propitiator
and works as partly propitiation.[1] According to Melanchthon,
James does not describe the mode of justification (modum
iustificationis), but the "nature of the just after they are
justified and reborn."[2] Those who act to fulfill the law are
justified: "they are pronounced just, who in their hearts
believe in God, and then bear good fruits, which are pleasing
because of faith."[3]

Faith, the Fallen Human Condition, and the Apology

The impossibility of works' possessing any inherent
value, and possibly merit, demands that faith itself cannot
be a habitus which inheres in the soul and confers value or
worth on human deeds. Faith is reckoned as justice or
righteousness because of Christ. Faith is righteousness
(iustitia) in us "imputatively, i.e. it is that by which we
are made acceptable to God because of the imputation and
ordinance of God."[4]

For Melanchthon faith may be called justice itself
insofar as it is obedience to another. It is obvious for
him that "obedience to the command of a superior is truly a

---

[1] Ibid.

[2] Ibid.

[3] Ibid.

[4] CR 27: 503. Romans 4:4-5.

kind of distributive justice (speciem distributivae
iusticiae)."[1] For us it is the obedience to the Gospel that
is reckoned as justice. Further, because of this obedience
"we apprehend Christ as propitiator, and obedience to the law
or good works is pleasing."[2] We are not able to satisfy the
law but are forgiven because of Christ. Therefore, faith
is not that which is honored, but that which honors (God).[3]

Since our fleshly existence is unable to fulfill
the law, the honor and glory of Christ are then imputed to
us. "We are reputed just, not because of the law," says
Melanchthon, "but on account of Christ because merits are
given to us if we believe in him."[4]

Melanchthon demonstrates this faith as being ad
alterum when he quotes Acts 13:38-39: "Let it be known to
you therefore, brothers, that through him is proclaimed to
you the remission of sins, and by him all that believe are
justified from all things from which you could not be justified
by the law."[5] Within this text, says Melanchthon, justification
by the law is omitted and the proper role of Christ is
emphasized. It is because of Christ that "we are reputed

---

[1] CR 27:503.

[2] Ibid.

[3] CR 27:503-504.

[4] CR 27:501.

[5] CR 27:444.

to be just, when we believe God to have been reconciled to us because of him."[1] Thus, if it is "through him," "by him," "on account of him," and "because of him" that we receive any righteousness, then the object of faith as <u>fiducia</u> cannot be self, but the other, namely, Christ.

The person "possessing" faith is not righteous or just <u>because</u> <u>of</u> that faith, but, as Paul says, (Romans 4:4-5) that faith is counted or reputed to be just.[2] Melanchthon maintains that here Paul clearly says that "faith itself is imputed for righteousness."[3] Faith is that thing (<u>res</u>) which God "pronounces to be just, and Paul adds that it {God's righteousness} is imputed freely."[4] The free act of imputation by God could not be accomplished "if it were due (<u>deberetur</u>) on account of works."[5] Hence, if works possessed any value or worth before God, faith could not freely be reckoned as righteous or just without the mediating quality of works.[6]

Obedience towards the law is always incomplete and

---

[1] Ibid.

[2] CR 27: 443.

[3] Ibid.

[4] Ibid.

[5] Ibid.

[6] Ibid. As Melanchthon states in an early 1531 edition: "Fides igitur est illa res, quam Deus imputat pro iusticia, quam Deus acceptat, et pronunciat esse iusticiam." CR 27: 465.

impure, for sin always remains.[1] Thus, obedience is not
"pleasing for its own sake, nor is it accepted for its own
sake."[2] Justification is not the beginning of the renewal,
but it is reconciliation. To begin that renewal, to begin
to fulfill the law, does not itself justify, "because
obedience is accepted only on account of faith."[3] Therefore,
this faith cannot be that which relies upon any amount of
works or any inherent worth of a deed, but only on Christ,
the other.[4]

---

[1]CR 27: 454.

[2]Ibid.

[3]Ibid. Along with the mention of an inchoate fulfillment of the law is that of a double justice tradition:
"Etsi necesse est renatos bene operari. Et virtutes legis,
quatenus obediunt legi, sunt iusticiae, et eatenus haec
obedientia legis, iustificat iusticia legis. Sed haec
imperfecta iusticia legis non est accepta nisi propter fidem,
nec potest conscientias reddere pacatas." CR 27:459.
Eds. 2-4.

[4]It must be noted that Werner Elert was quite
correct in saying that, in the Apology, Melanchthon "hammered
out and underpinned the essential characteristics of the
fourth article of the Augsburg Confession even more thoroughly,
if this was possible. Especially did he emphasize again
and again that justification and forgiveness of sins are
identical. As a result, no argument against the purely
receptive character of faith is left." Werner Elert, The
Structure of Lutheranism, trans. Walter A Hansen (St. Louis:
Concordia Publishing House, 1962), p. 97. Problematic with
this type of assertion, however, is the assumption that
"proper" Lutheran doctrine was in the womb with Luther and
waited for Melanchthon to be born to maturity. The imputation doctrine in Luther and Melanchthon has long been
overemphasized. Melanchthon did emphasize the glory of
Christ, consequently imputation, in order to deemphasize
any value in works. However, strong statements are made in
the Apology, and elsewhere, that stress the internal or

Conclusion

Even though Melanchthon repudiated philosophy and appeared adverse to it in general, he continued to employ its methods and schemata in his presentation and elucidation of theses. Therefore, the following systematized conclusion summarizes the meaning of good works given in the Apology.

In the Apology Melanchthon expounds his teaching on good works as follows: 1) good works are required of all Christians; 2) good works ought (debeat) to follow faith; 3) works follow the remission of sins, but are not therefore the cause of that remission; 4) works are fitting (oportet), they ought (debeat) to be performed, and they are necessary (necesse esse) for a morally Christian life; 5) we are renewed by justification and thereafter do good works; 6) we are commanded by God to do good works; 7) we are rewarded in and after this life for works performed; 8) works are not a propitiation and are not causally followed by salvation or the remission of sins.

Theses within the Apology which disavow the doctrine of merit are: 1) the doctrine of merit detracts from the glory of Christ; 2) works are not pure in and of themselves

---

renewal dimension of justification. As: "... quod sola fide iustificemur, hoc est, ex iniustos iusti efficiamur, seu regeneremur." CR 27: 446-447. In addition: "Et quia iustificari significat ex iniustis iustos effici, seu regenerari, significat et iustos pronunciari seu reputari." CR 27: 440.

and therefore the sacrifice of Christ is needed; 3) there
can be only one cause for the remission of sins and that
is Christ, for works cannot be a part of the cause which
grants the remission of sins; 4) we are reputed to be
righteous because of Christ and not on account of our works;
5) reason and the works provided thereby are not able to
provide the remission of sins; 6) the justice of the law is
not the justice of the Gospel; 7) merit posits no difference
between philosophy and the Gospel; 8) merit and external
works are the teachings of philosophy, of the Jews, and of
the Muslims; 9) the terrified conscience knows that no work
or amount of works can appease the angry God; 10) the
remission of sins is a reward for the deeds of another, not
for our own works; 11) works cannot fulfill the law because
all works are done from a contemptuous and impious heart;
12) works have no value in and of themselves, hence men
cannot merit anything; 13) whatever is not done from faith
is sin.

The effect that Melanchthon's understanding of
faith has on his doctrine of works becomes increasingly more
important in his later writings. Within the Apology faith is:
1) that which receives or accepts the promise of God; 2) not
a knowledge of history but an acceptance or assent to the
promise; 3) that which is reckoned as righteousness; 4) the
substance of things hoped for; 5) not that which possesses,
but that which relates to another, namely, Christ.

CHAPTER II

THE DOCTRINE OF GOOD WORKS IN
THE COMMENTARY ON ROMANS OF 1532 AND THE LOCI OF 1533

Introduction

Following the publication of the Apology Melanchthon was not only busy with lectures on Cicero,[1] Romans,[2] Homer,[3] and the fifth book of Aristotle's Ethics,[4] but was writing and publishing on astronomy,[5] a commentary on the epistle to the Romans,[6] a commentary on the first three books of Aristotle's Ethics,[7] a treatise on the Lord's Supper,[8] and a catechism for children.[9]

During this period Melanchthon was involved in a correspondence with John Brenz concerning the nature of justification and faith. The terms he uses shows that he was continually reflecting on the doctrine of works.

---

[1] See CR 16:1107, 1147, 1289.

[2] CR 28.42.

[3] CR 28:42.

[4] Ibid. See also CR 2:580.

[5] CR 28:40-42.

[6] CR 2: 611, CR 28:42.

[7] CR 2:585, CR 16:3.

[8] CR 23:729.

[9] CR 2:501-502.

Brenz was more of the opinion that we are justified by faith because we receive the Holy Spirit who renews us. This renewal enables us to fulfill the law because of the Holy Spirit. Melanchthon remarks, however, that it is because of Christ that we are accepted by God and discover peace of conscience and "not because of that renewal (novitas). For that renewal itself is not enough."[1] We are just because of faith "not because it is the root (radix)" . . . but because it apprehends Christ. Because we are received by him, of what effect is that "novitas, even if it necessarily ought to follow, since it does not pacify the conscience?"[2] Therefore, love does not justify but "faith alone, indeed, not because it is perfect in us, but only because it apprehends Christ."[3] It is not because of charity, not because of the fulfillment of the law, nor because of our "renewal (novitas), even if they are gifts of the Holy Spirit, but because of Christ," who is received only by faith.[4]

Melanchthon shows development here in his theological reflections on good works and justification for he exhorts Brenz to turn his mind from the law and the idea of the

[1] CR 2:501.
[2] Ibid.
[3] CR 2:501-502.
[4] CR 2:502.

fulfillment of that law in order properly to understand
this righteousness by faith, which Melanchthon calls "a
great and obscure controversy."[1] He tells Brenz that he
has attempted to explain this issue in the Apology, but
the calumny of his adversaries forces him to continue to
speak on the matter.[2] Melanchthon states, as he did in
the Apology, that to attribute justification to charity
or love is to have justification by works. Here he says,
"I understand work as accomplished by the Holy Spirit in
us."[3] The letter concludes with Melanchthon's hopes that
the Apology is of help, but he does say it is not understood unless one has a "certain consciousness."[4]

The principle of causality and the function of works
and faith becomes increasingly important for Melanchthon.
At this point Brenz evinces a concern for the meaning of
faith as a work. Within their correspondence of this
period Brenz tells Melanchthon that there are three types
of works: 1) that of satisfaction or merit, 2) that of

---

[1] Ibid.

[2] Ibid.

[3] Ibid.

[4] Ibid. Luther in an appendix to this letter attacks
the Catholic understanding of faith as a quality or habit:
"Sic dicit: ego sum via, veritas et vita. Non dicit: ego
do tibi viam, veritatem et vitam, quasi extra me positus
operetur in me." CR 2:503. Melanchthon's constant development and rethinking is evidenced by a June 7, 1531 letter
to Brenz. See CR 2:504-505.

instrument, 3) that of declaration. He says: The passion of Christ I call "[a work] of satisfaction and merit, faith I call an instrumental work, [and] works as the fruit of faith a declaratory work."[1] Therefore, justification does not depend on our love or faith, but only on Christ. The work of faith or its dignity does not merit justification. Nevertheless "as an instrument it affects justification, which is not affected by the fruit of faith or charity, thus _fides_ _sit_ _medium_ _inter_ _fidem_ _et_ _opera_."[2] Faith is the only means by which Christ can be accepted or received.[3]

Melanchthon answers Brenz by not concentrating on faith as _medium_, but rather on the distance between ourselves and Christ. It is, he says, not because of any purity of ours "that we are reputed just, that is, acceptable to God, but because of Christ, even if renewal necessarily follows the reception of the Holy Spirit."[4]

Here it becomes clear that Melanchthon discerns that whenever it brings one back to the self, a reflection on the nature of faith and works is problematic in character.

---

[1] CR 2:510-511.

[2] CR 2:511.

[3] Ibid.

[4] CR 2:517.

Brenz' concern with medium leads Melanchthon to emphasize a righteousness that is reputed. It is not by accident that he tries to evade what he considers to be too pedantic a position, or one that at this point would give his adversaries ammunition.[1]

On September 30 Melanchthon writes to Brenz stating that all the saints still have sin and this impedes the possibility of perfect works no matter how numerous the works. Christ, however, perfectly fulfills the law, doing that which no amount of works can.[2] He cautions Brenz not to be so open to the merits of the saints, and finds that Brenz is arguing in a subtle fashion from a doctrine of predestination. He himself says, "I, however, in all the Apology avoided that long and inexplicable disputation on predestination."[3] Melanchthon is quite concerned that people do not become immersed in what he calls "an inexplicable labyrinth."[4]

People are received as righteous because of faith in Christ, then they do works which have their rewards. Righteousness, he says, is acceptance by God and faith alone vivifies when it pacifies the heart.[5]

---

[1] This will become more clear with Osiander.
[2] CR 2:547.
[3] Ibid.
[4] Ibid.
[5] Ibid.

Melanchthon then curtly remarks that "these are clear and
easily understood" and should be satisfying.[1] Again, he
is concerned with pedantry, but here the reason is astral.
He concludes his letter by quickly asking for any
prognostica regarding the comet.[2]

On September 29 Melanchthon writes that a comet has
been seen in France and Italy.[3] On August 18 he writes to
Camerarius stating that he has seen it, the first he has
seen, and he wonders what it could possibly mean.[4] During
the same month Melanchthon writes a preface to a book by
Grynaeus dealing with the spheres of the heavens. There,
he agrees with Aristotle that the inferior world is governed by the superior, and the inferior causes by superior
causes.[5] This also applies to the inherent dispositions
and the given intellectual capacities of humans.[6] Further,
the signs provided by stellar movements within constella-
tions are seriously worthy of the Christian's consideration

---

[1]
 Ibid.

[2]
 Ibid. Melanchthon's interest in astrology and astronomy might appear to have little or no impact on the doctrine of justification and works, but this will also become more defined. Haley's comet was seen in 1532 and for
Melanchthon's reactions see CR 2:537-538, 545-546, 547, 551-
552, 598.

[3]
 CR 2:546. It is Haley's comet.

[4]
 CR 2:518-519.

[5]
 CR 2:533.

[6]
 CR 2:534.

for under Christ they bear direct significance on our lives.[1] As the Scripture says: "Do not fear the signs from heaven because the nations fear them [Jeremiah 10:2]."[2]

Shortly before and immediately after the appearance of the comet Melanchthon is found writing about an impending catastrophe.[3] His concern which is seemingly confirmed by the comet's appearance, is that it will occur very soon,[4] perhaps involve war,[5] and probably be due to the neglect of religion and proper doctrine.[6] What meaning, however, would this knowledge of astronomical signs and the conviction of an impending catastrophe have on Melanchthon's doctrine of justification and good works?

First, of all, it is not an indirect or purely analogical correlation among the astronomical signs, Melanchthon's emphasis on reputare, his concern for too "inexplicable disputations," and his conviction that there will be a catastrophe. Melanchthon had perceived that a social upheaval was about to occur, as indicated by the stars, and felt impatient with any attempt to debate the doctrine of justification and works beyond that which was

[1]
 CR 2:534-537.
[2]
 CR 2:535.
[3]
 CR 2:546, 551-552, 553, 554.
[4]
 CR 2:597, 598. On June 23, 1532 he states it will be this year and on June 24, 1532 he states that all the signs have appeared this year.
[5]
 CR 2:546.
[6]
 CR 2:551-552.

absolutely necessary. Further, Melanchthon feared any attempt to envision righteousness or glory as something _intra nos_ and was driven, by his own caution, to under-score the significance of reality _extra nos_. This meant that signs and portents from _without_ bear particular significance for us and it very well may have enlivened the "gravity" of an imputed righteousness.

The Commentary on Romans of 1532

Even though Melanchthon wrote to Corvinus in January 1532 stating that he intended fully to clarify the doctrine of justification in his commentary on Romans,[1] nevertheless, the tenor and substance of that work differed only slightly from those of the Apology.

As in the Apology the benefit for justification is transferred from merit to Christ. Melanchthon states that "the person is just, that is received (_accepta_), because

---

[1] CR 2:568: "Nunc expono ep. ad Rom., in quibus controversiam de iustificatione spero me sic illustraturum esse, ut nihil desiderari in ea causa dilucidius possit. Alia enim ratione utar, quam qua in Apologia usus sum." Contrary to Herrlinger's opinion Osiander wrote to Melanchthon on Feb. 15, 1534, but there appears to have been no problem regarding justification until much later. See MBW 2, no. 1407. Herrlinger maintained: " . . . mit dem Commentar zum Römerbrief von 1532, auf den Melanchthon selbst in jener Correspondenz den Brenz hingewiesen hat; es schliesst mit den interimischen Streitigkeiten. Von da an stehen alle Ausführungen des Dogma's bei Melanchthon nicht nur in be-wusstem Gegensatz zum Osianderismus, sondern auch unter sehr merklichen Einfluss desselben."

of Christ."[1] This "being accepted by," "received by,"
or "transferred" to Christ "does not depend on our
dignity but is imputed to the believer on account of
Christ" and is received by faith.[2] As a result, a "new
obedience is necessary (est necessaria), so that the
effect necessarily follows that imputation, because with
imputation there is renovatio which is the beginning of
a new and eternal life."[3] For truly the beginning of a
"new and eternal life is a new and spiritual obedience.
Therefore a new and spiritual obedience is necessary."[4]

One of the most important differences, if not
the most important one, between the commentary and the
Apology is the evidence of syllogistic arguments which
will become significant as a mode of disputation regarding justification and works.

First, Melanchthon refutes arguments pertaining
to the doctrine of sola fide. He gives three of them:
Demons are said to believe and yet are not righteous,
therefore to believe or have faith does not justify men.
Further, no nature is able to be righteous by knowledge

---

[1]CR 15:635. All references to CR 15, unless otherwise indicated, refer to the Commentary on Romans of 1532.

[2] Ibid.

[3] Ibid.

[4] Ibid.

(<u>noticia</u>) alone, faith is such a knowledge; therefore no one is righteous by faith. Finally, faith is itself a work, therefore we are just by works.[1]

In response to the first contention Melanchthon remarks that the demons indeed have faith and believe, but their belief is a knowledge or acquaintance of history (<u>noticia historiae</u>) and it is not an acquiescing trust in Christ as mediator.[2] Therefore, the proper definition of faith is to be used. Faith is the assent to all that which the Word of God transmits to us, it is the promise of grace, the "trust assenting to the promise," the promise of God on account of the mediator.[3]

Melanchthon further responds to his adversaries by denying the minor of their second syllogism: No nature is righteous by knowledge alone, faith is just such a knowledge, therefore we are not righteous by faith alone.[4] The denial of the minor proposition meant a redefining of faith. As in the first argument Melanchthon asserts that faith is an assent to the promise of God and not only <u>noticia historiae</u>.[5] Faith is this "trust (<u>fiducia</u>) in the

---

[1]CR 15:891.

[2]CR 15:891-892.

[3]CR 15:892.

[4]Ibid.

[5]Ibid.

will and heart assenting to the promise, that is, assenting to the God who promises on account of the mediator."[1]

The third argument Melanchthon presents syllogistically as follows: We are justified by faith; faith is a work; therefore we are justified by a work. Melanchthon's response to the major proposition is that we are not justified by any work in us, nor "because of the dignity of a human work do men have the remission [of sins] or are they justified."[2] The works found in us, such as love, charity, patience, or chastity, all come from God who moves the heart.[3] We do not have the remission of sins because of these works, and so "it is not on account of faith in so far as it is a quality or a work in us, but because of faith we acknowledge the mediator, and his benefits are applied to us" on account of faith. When one says *fide iustificamur* it must be a proposition that is correlatively understood.[4] It is *by* mercy *because* *of* a mediator that we are justified when his benefits are applied to us *because* *of* faith.[5] Therefore, the judgment in the major proposition is that we

---

1
Ibid.
2
Ibid.
3
CR 15:893.
4
Ibid.
5
Ibid. Editor's emphases.

have the remission of sins and we are just because of
Christ, that is, we are accepted or received.[1] "The
conclusion therefore does not follow that we are just
because of works."[2]

The doctrine of imputation, then, must be defended
for since no one in "this depraved nature is able to
fulfill the law," no one is just by the law and, in
addition, sins must be remitted or not imputed on account
of Christ. Melanchthon is careful to accentuate imputation
because persons like Osiander were positing the transfusing
of the divine life into the Christian and thereby inferring,
as Melanchthon viewed it, some consequent value to the
deeds of such a transformed person.[3] Even if it is true
that there is an inward renewal with the remission of
sins when the voice of the Gospel is "heard in the terrified
heart, the Son of God pronounces this consolation: Your
sins are forgiven (remittuntur)."[4] He does give the Holy
Spirit, but it is "one thing to speak of that renewal
(renovatione) and another to speak of the cause because of
which the person received the remission of sins and is

---

[1] Ibid.

[2] Ibid.

[3] CR 15:895. Melanchthon was cautiously aware
of Osiander's position, but major differences only came
about with the later development of Osiander's thought.

[4] Ibid.

accepted, or of the way we approach God."[1]

   To be just or righteous is to have the obedience
of the mediator imputed to us and sins remitted on account
of that obedience.[2] The faith, then, which accepts the
promise and the remission of sins is imputed to be just
(correlatively) in light of Christ the mediator.[3]

   Melanchthon provides a fourth argument in defense
of imputation and against the doctrine of good works as
follows: In the case of Abraham righteousness was imputed
before circumcision, therefore circumcision is not the
cause of Abraham's justification. This is clear for the
effect does not precede the temporal cause.[4] Abraham was
circumcised when he was ninety years old and he was called
from Haran when he was seventy-five, therefore there are
fifteen years from his call to this circumcision.[5] Using
Abraham as an example Melanchthon intended to show that
works do not justify. Circumcision has been regarded as a
sacrament or a sign of the justice of faith. All sacraments
or signs have two principal ends: first, they are

---

[1]Ibid.

[2]Ibid.

[3]Ibid.

[4]CR 15:896.

[5]Ibid.

part of the public ministry because God desires a united visible congregation that is ministered to; second, they pertain to the private individual as signs before men and even before God of the pledge of the promise of grace.[1] These signs truly call to mind the gracious promise of God and the fact that they pertain to each individual. The circumcision of Abraham was physical evidence which called to mind the promise of God which applied to Abraham personally.[2] Abraham's faith was that which looked to the promise he had received and our faith looks to the promise by which we are accepted by God and our sins truly are remitted "because of the mediator."[3] Because "faith is required in the use of the sacraments" it is clear that any position which asserts that works merit the remission of sins ex opere operato is impious."[4]

The fifth and final presentation proceeds as follows: "No promise depends on the conditions of the law for it to be established for us and to be certain; the promise of grace is fittingly reestablished and certain,

[1] CR 15:897.
[2] Ibid.
[3] CR 15:898.
[4] Ibid.

therefore the promise of grace does not depend on the
condition of the law, but is gratuitous and received by
faith."[1] So fundamental is this doctrine for Melanchthon,
that it grounds the necessary difference between law and
Gospel.[2] If the gratuitousness of the promise depended on
the conditions of works there would be no difference
between Church and "the gentiles" (ethnicos).[3]

The law does not provide the promise. On the
contrary, the law brings wrath because our depraved nature
never fulfills that which the law prescribes.[4] Therefore,
the law is always accusing and bringing the wrath of God.
It brings dread, a sorrowful dullness in the heart, and a
pernicious distress in the sense of the judging and the
wrath of God.[5] Just as Nathan reproved David, the law
accuses and reveals our sins.[6]

The minor proposition is established in that the
law does not announce the remission of sins. Rather, it
always accuses and does not provide the means for salvation.
The gratuitous promise of the remission of sins and the

---

[1] CR 15:898.

[2] Ibid.

[3] Ibid.

[4] CR 15:899.

[5] Ibid.

[6] Ibid.

restitution of righteousness and eternal life is surely proclaimed in the Gospel.[1] "Thus the Lord says: God so loved the world that he gave his only begotten Son etc."[2] The promise of God through the mission of the Son is established and sure as are its benefits "on account of the truth of God and not because of any human worth."[3] The monks have taught and still teach, says Melanchthon, that we ought always to doubt as to whether sins are remitted and we are pleasing to God, and they say this doubt is pious.[4] For Melanchthon, the doctrine and teaching of the Church cannot leave man in doubt, for this would be to remove the very promise of the Gospel.[5]

Within the Commentary on Romans of 1532 particular emphases in Melanchthon's doctrine of works are taking shape.

The new obedience that is due to the new life or renovatio is necessary. Melanchthon is simply taking seriously the significance of the term nova and renovatio; if it is a new life there must be new obedience. The emphasis here is not on the moral mandate, but on the necessity of the effect which derives from the novitas.

---

[1] Ibid.

[2] Ibid.

[3] Ibid.

[4] CR 15:899-900.

[5] CR 15:900.

Faith, for Melanchthon, still bears much the same significance and characteristics as it had in the Apology. Within the Commentary faith is defined as an assent and trust (fiducia) in the promise of God. Faith "looks to" the promise of God on account of Christ.[1] The word intuens or "looking to" here provides Melanchthon with a philological tool for establishing a doctrine of righteousness that is extra nos and not intra nos. Therefore, faith is not able to be a quality or habitus within.

As in the Apology the affirmation that we are justified by faith is understood as a correlative proposition. According to Melanchthon, faith is reckoned as just on account of the justice or righteousness of another, namely, of God.

An important shift in emphasis takes place here as a result of Andreas Osiander. He taught that the renovation of the Christian was due to the outpouring of the Holy Spirit. Melanchthon was concerned that this inner renovatio would be understood as a cause for the remission of sins. As a result, he began to enhance the imputatio of God's righteousness to the sinner and the likened non-imputation of sins.[2]

---

[1]The word Melanchthon uses is intuens. See CR 15: 892-898.

[2]CR 15:895. Melanchthon's shift came primarily from his correspondence with Osiander. For information on Osiander see: M. Möller, Andreas Osianders Leben und-

The Doctrine of Good Works in the Loci of 1533

After the feast of Ephphany in January 1532
Melanchthon began a series of lectures on Paul's letters
to the Romans. After this series he began in April to
lecture on the fifth books of Aristotle's Ethics.[1] In
light of his various lectures, notably those on Paul a
revised Loci was produced in 1533.[2] There he again

---

ausgewählte Schriften, Väter und Begründer der Lutheri-
schen Kirche, vol. 5 (Eberfeld, 1870); Gottfried Seebass,
Das reformatorische Werk des Andreas Osiander. Anhang:
Portraits von Andreas Osiander. (Nuremberg: Verein für
Bayerische Kirchengeschichte, 1967), and Bibliographia
Ossiandrica. Bibliographie der gedruckten Schriften
Andreas Osianders d. A. (1496-1552). (Nieuwkoop: B.
de Graaf, 1971); Emanuel Hirsch, Die Theologie des
Andreas Osiander und ihre geschichtlichen Voraussetzungen.
(Göttingen· Vandenhoeck und Ruprecht, 1919); ADB 24:473-
483; W. Moller and P. Tschackert, Herzog-Hauck PRE[3] 14:
501-509; E. Bizer, RGG[3] 4:1730-1731; P. Meinhold, LTK[2]
7:1261-1263.

[1]See Melanchthon's Annales Vitae CR 28:41-42

[2]CR 2:661, the critical text of Bretschneider's
which is made up only of fragments of the manuscript if
found in CR 21:253-332. All subsequent references to
CR 21, unless otherwise indicated, refer to the Loci of
1533. Authors cited by Melanchthon include: Arians:
261, 262; Augustine: 253, 285, 290, 297; Anselm: 286;
Bonaventure: 286; Cherinthus: 259; Cicero: 276, 291;
Cyprian: 253, 297; Ebion: 259; Hesiod: 269; Irenaeus:
263; Isaiah: 265; James: 323; Jeremiah: 265; John:
255, 258, 259, 261, 262, 264, 265, 268, 269, 284, 288,
307, 308; Jerome: 281; Matthew: 259, 264, 270; Origen:
253, 264, 297; Paul: 254, 256, 259, 268, 272, 277, 278,
279, 280, 281, 282, 283, 284, 289, 291, 292, 293, 294,
295, 296, 300, 301, 304, 305, 306, 307, 309, 310, 311,
312, 314, 315, 316, 317, 320, 321, 324, 325, 326, 327,
328, 329, 330; Paul of Samosata: 261, 262; Plato: 291;
Pomponius Atticus: 291, 292; Servetus: 262, 263; Stoics:
292; Tertullian: 263; Themistocles: 291, 293, 317;
Valentinians: 258, 261, 268, 269; Xenophon: 291, 293.

examined good works by use of both an asystematic and a
systematic method.

Melanchthon states quite clearly in the _Loci_ of
1533 that good works are fitting (_oportet_) and "God requires this _disciplina_, even if we are not righteous before God because of it.[1] Indeed, _poenitentia_ is necessary.[2]
The law, however, is unable to accomplish anything without
Christ, it is necessary first to lay hold of (_apprehendere_)
the remission of sins by trust (_fiducia_) in Christ.[3]
This trust does not contribute to our dignity. The
remission of sins is bestowed because of faith and the
honor that is Christ's, even though _poenitentia_ is
necessarily added. For Melanchthon, this necessity of
penance must not be seen as providing the remission of
sins because of the dignity or worth of that penance.[4]
"Christ did not say that [our sins] are forgiven because of
our offering but he requires our obedience."[5] The Gospel
of Christ is always added to the law.[6]

---

[1] CR 21:279-280.

[2] CR 21:318.

[3] Ibid.

[4] Ibid.

[5] Ibid.

[6] Ibid.

In this treatise Melanchthon does assert that "the
law is necessary but not pleasing without Christ. Obedience
toward the law is necessary, etc., because no one satisfies
the law.[1]

The law is considered to be pleasing only in the
reconciled, for the end of the law is Christ.[2] "We do
say that good works are necessary, but it is always fitting
(oportet) for reconciliation to precede."[3] Reconciliation
is due to faith and "not to our dignity."[4] Works are not
pleasing "unless the person first has been freed of doubt.
Consequently, it is necessary first to be justified by
faith."[5]

As noted above Melanchthon insists that the Gospel
of Christ be added (addendum est) to the law for no one
is able to fulfill the law. This is so because sin
always "inheres in us."[6] Therefore, it is fitting that first
of all we be reconciled by Christ through faith. Only
afterwards is "that beginning and incomplete obedience"
pleasing.[7] The Christian is just not because of the

---

[1]
CR 21:318.
[2]
CR 21:319.
[3]
Ibid.
[4]
Ibid.
[5]
Ibid.
[6]
Ibid.
[7]
Ibid.

obedience but on account of Christ and trust in the imputed mercy which does fulfill the law.[1] Even though Christ alone fulfills the law, Melanchthon declared that "obedience to the law is necessary."[2] We require "obedientia ac poenitentia."[3]

Reward and Punishment in the Loci of 1533

In addition to the requirement of good works or obedience to the law, Melanchthon also asserted the need for new spiritual motives or inclinations (motus). Among these are the "fear of God, trust, prayer, love," and other motives which our adversaries "do not teach nor are they able to understand."[4] As in the Apology, Melanchthon poses, in the Loci of 1533, the obvious question concerning why one is able to obey the law or require new motives if all we do is sin. Is not one maintaining that more sinful acts be performed, even though God certainly does not approve of sin?[5] For us, says Melanchthon, the answer is easy (facilis est responsio).[6] Even if the obedience is

---

[1] Ibid.
[2] CR 21:326.
[3] CR 21:327.
[4] CR 21:308.
[5] CR 21:292.
[6] Ibid.

imperfect the person pleases, and "this obedience has, in those who truly believe, its corporal and spiritual rewards in and after this life."[1]

Melanchthon says, we are not Stoics "who maintained that all sins are equal," for Nero certainly sinned more than Pomponius Atticus. Even if the judgment of God (dei iudicium) is granted according to the "degree of interior defect" that "certainly ought not to diminish" the judgment itself, which is of a God who requires good works.[2] For God "requires external respectable works which are called works of the law."[3]

Another reason, argued by Melanchthon, for requiring works of the law is human peace and tranquility among one another in addition to discipline as is provided by the Gospel.[4]

Paul refers to the law in Galatians 3:24 as a "tutor" (paedagogus). "The doing of this law (haec Paedagogia) God adorns with excellent corporal reward" and the external violation of the law "he punishes with grave corporal and eternal penalties."[5]

---

[1] Ibid.

[2] Ibid.

[3] Ibid.

[4] Ibid.

[5] Ibid.

God punishes shameful matters (flagitia) in so far
as he desires a proper discipline to exist among men.[1] This
is witnessed to even by the law of nature (lex naturae).[2]
For to know that law is to recognize (sentire) that God
"grants rewards for good deeds and penalties for evil deeds."[3]
Even the heroic deeds of the ancient Greeks were noteworthy
and were certainly not evil. This "justice of the flesh
(iustitia carnis) has its praise."[4] Further, we must teach
"that God requires it and grants rewards for it."[5]

God no doubt requires works. For Melanchthon,
however, the works men do turn out to be sins because
they are done by a fallen, sinful person. God requires
good works and not evil works or sins. Such works, performed by a sinful person, are not done out of fear and the
proper trust in God. As a consequence, such a "work is
not obedience towards God."[6] Further, sinful works are
not able to console the conscience terrified of God's wrath.
Instead, what is needed is a mediator. Even if "man has,

---

[1] CR 21:292-293.

[2] Ibid.

[3] Ibid.

[4] CR 21:293.

[5] Ibid.

[6] Ibid.

without faith, some knowledge of God and illustrious
virtues still they do not vivify (vivificant) in the
judgment of God."[1]

Even though God requires this "paedagogia or justice
of the flesh, even if he grants corporal rewards," our
adversaries err, says Melanchthon, when they maintain that
"works merit the remission of sins either de congruo or
de condigno."[2] They even teach, he continues, that "works
merit the remission of sins without trust in Christ (fiducia
Christi)."[3]

For Melanchthon the legitimate and proper rewards
granted for acts of justice are effective only to the
degree to which the fallen nature of humankind received
them. That nature still sins with and without rewards,
the iustitia carnis can still only be righteous before
God on account of Christ, the mediator, and his Spirit.
The nature of man "is not pleasing to God without the
Holy Spirit, for it does not have justice or eternal life."[4]
As Paul says (Romans 8:14), "all that are led by the
Spirit of God are sons of God."[5]

---

[1]
 Ibid.
[2]
 CR 21:294.
[3]
 Ibid.
[4]
 CR 21:278.
[5]
 Ibid.

That which is pleasing to God is so because of Jesus Christ. Even if "the remission of sins, the justification of a person, and the promise of eternal life were given, it would not depend on the condition of our worth."[1] Nevertheless, works "in those who are reconciled have some worth (dignitas) and are meritorious."[2] This worth both professes and honors the glory of God. These people are pleasing to God not "because of their own perfection but because the person is in Christ."[3] It is fitting (oportet) that reconciliation precede so that we are made sons of God and thereby, or consequently, works are pleasing.[4]

Good works are not pleasing to God unless they come from a reconciled person.[5] After being reconciled and pronounced righteous those who do works in an attempt to fulfill the law provide works that "are pleasing to God and merit promised rewards, not because they fulfill the law" but on account of Christ.[6]

---

[1] CR 21:313.

[2] CR 21:314.

[3] Ibid.

[4] Ibid.

[5] Ibid.

[6] Ibid.

The Meaning of Faith in the Loci of 1533

As earlier, Melanchthon is concerned to remove
righteousness far away from the individual person. He
takes his lead from Paul's discussion of the faith of
Abraham as depicted in Romans 4. Paul "clearly affirms"
that "Abraham is pronounced righteous because he believed,"
therefore God renders him favorable, not on account of
"personal worth but on account of the promised mercy."[1]
Melanchthon understands Paul to say that faith means trust
in mercy (fiducia misericordiae) and it opposes the
worthiness of human effort.[2] Faith is intended to exclude
our worth (dignitas nostra). Abraham was justified by
faith, that is, by trust in mercy. Therefore, he was
not justified "on account of personal worth."[3]

If, says Melanchthon, the promise of justification
depended on the condition of the fulfillment of the law,
that promise would then be uncertain.[4] It is fitting
(opportet) for our conscience, however, that this promise
be certain. Thus, it is necessary (necesse est) that
justification be promised by grace and that it be accepted

---

[1]CR 21:305.

[2]Ibid.

[3]Ibid.

[4]Ibid.

"by faith and not on account of our worth."[1] The doubtful
or unsure conscience is not consoled if the promise depends
on the degree to which the law is fulfilled. That is, we
are not pronounced just until we have satisfied the law
or when a certain number of works have been performed.[2]

   The significance of the emphasis on righteousness
apart from, or from outside of the person is clarified by
Melanchthon's observation that it is not in a personal
quality (qualitas) or in the worth of a work that we are
able to be pleasing to God.[3] It is, rather, in "regard
to the promise and mercy extra nos" that we are pleasing
"through mercy because of Christ and [God's] grace."[4]

Person and Work in the Loci of 1533

   An important development for Melanchthon's defense
of his understanding of righteousness and works appears
within the Loci of 1533. That development is the distinction between a "person" and the "work of a person." He
states quite specifically in regard to those who teach merit

---

[1]
 Ibid.
[2]
 Ibid.
[3]
 CR 21:317.
[4]
 Ibid.

that they "ought to distinguish between 'person' and
'work'."[1]

His argument runs in this fashion, even if Saul
has many notable works he sees that sins remain within and
that those works are not able to make that person pleasing
to God.[2] Thus, the conscience always remains in doubt,
for there will always be sin no matter how small. It is
fitting, however, that this doubt be removed, but no
matter how many works or attempts to satisfy the law are
performed "sin remains in us."[3] The person therefore "is
pleasing to God by grace on account of Christ."[4]

Obedience follows (sequens) when one is pleasing
to God and a person is pleasing on account of another,
namely Christ (scilicet propter Christum).[5] The obedience
itself is not pleasing unless the person is first freed
from doubt.[6]

The distinction between person and work is important
for Melanchthon since work itself does not and cannot
establish the person as righteous, but only leaves this

1
CR 21:310.
2
Ibid.
3
Ibid.
4
Ibid.
5
Ibid.
6
Ibid.

doubt about righteousness. A "person is not pleasing because of the law or the dignity of a work."[1] Before works it is necessary that the person be pleasing "by grace on account (propter) of Christ."[2]

How is it possible, however, for works to be in any way pleasing to God? Since works are done by a fallen human nature, they are not done out of proper fear and trust in God, and so how can they be pleasing? Melanchthon responds that this problem can be solved if "faith pertains to the person and law pertains to the work."[3] A work is pleasing if it is a command of God and the person is pleasing to God on account of Christ (propter Christum)."[4] A work is pleasing to God not because it satisfies the law, but due to the fact that it is offered to God because of or through Christ.[5]

---

[1] Ibid.

[2] CR 21:310-311.

[3] CR 21:316.

[4] Ibid.

[5] Ibid.

The Loci of 1533 and the Sinful Human Condition

In a person justified by faith obedience "to the law necessarily ought to follow (<u>necessario</u> <u>sequi</u> <u>debet</u>)."[1] The Gospel preaches penance and therefore "requires obedience to the law."[2] With the new life comes a new obedience and works.[3] Even though works must be done, Melanchthon is careful to point out how ineffective they actually are, for sin is always present. Even if works of the law are done, nevertheless "there remain (<u>haerent</u>) in the soul the ignorance of God, doubt, contempt, diffidence" and like faults.[4] Further, all "works of unbelievers are sins."[5] Because a person without fear and trust in God does works of the unbeliever, these are impious and condemned fruits.[6] For this reason Melanchthon rejects the teaching of the scholastics that "the honest and civil works of the unbeliever are not sins but merit the remission of sins . . ."[7]

---

[1] CR 21:308.

[2] Ibid.

[3] Ibid.

[4] CR 21:277-278.

[5] CR 21:290-291.

[6] Ibid.

[7] Ibid.

Paul, says Melanchthon, maintained that "all that is not from faith is a sin," that is, a "thing (res) damned to eternal death."[1] Faith (fides) is that which signifies trust in God's mercy; it makes us "pleasing to God on account of Christ even if works are unworthy (indigna)."[2]

Since Melanchthon considers works unworthy, no matter how abundant, they do not provide justification or fulfill the demands of the law.[3] It is important to note that Melanchthon repudiates justification by the law, not because of the law, but because of unworthy works. He states that Paul does not disparage "the justification of the law because the law itself is evil, but because no one satisfied the law."[4]

Paul states in Galatians 3:18 that "if the inheritance is from the law, it is not from the promise."[5] If the law were able to vivify (vivificare), then surely the inheritance would be by the law. If the "moral law vivified, i.e., freed from eternal death, the work of the Gospel would

---

[1]
CR 21:291.
[2]
Ibid.
[3]
CR 21:306.
[4]
Ibid.
[5]
CR 21:307.

be nothing."[1] The moral law not only does not free us
from an eternal death, but it even stands as accuser.

The function of the law, in the _Loci_ of 1533,
reveals an emphasis on extrinsic justification. He agrees
with Paul, who "asserts everywhere that men are not able to
be justified by the law. That is, they are not able to be
pronounced (_pronunciari_) just on account of the fulfillment
of the law."[2] This is simply due to the fact that we are
unable to satisfy the demands of the law.

Faith, however, is able to fulfill the law.
Melanchthon understands this in two ways; imputatively, and
effectively.[3] It is imputative "when we believe that
Christ's justice is imputed to us (_imputatur_ _nobis_)"
and we thereby fulfill the law.[4] It is effective because
"the law is not able to be fulfilled unless doubt is first
removed by faith."[5] The law does not teach that we are
pleasing to God by grace, rather "it requires the condition
of perfect obedience."[6] The Gospel, however, does teach

---

[1] Ibid.

[2] CR 21:281.

[3] CR 21:313.

[4] Ibid.

[5] Ibid.

[6] Ibid.

that we are pleasing to God by grace on account of Christ, thereby "faith is able to exist and is the beginning (inchoatio)" of a new obedience and love of God.[1]

Melanchthon sums up his understanding of the role of the law and the mode of justification by saying that no one is able to satisfy the demands of the law.[2] "No one is righteous on account of the fulfillment of the law. No one is without sin," but all are "pronounced righteous (pronunciator iusti) by trust (fiducia) in [God's] mercy on account of Christ."[3]

The Christian as Pronounced Just in the Loci of 1533

To be pronounced righteous by God is crucial for Melanchthon, but he does not rule out obedience, even if imperfect. "[Good] works are necessary," he states, but "works do not satisfy the conscience."[4] If obedience to "the law is necessary, when no one fulfills the law in what way is one pleasing to God by this imperfect obedience?"[5]

1
  Ibid.
2
  CR 21:326.
3
  Ibid.
4
  CR 21:309.
5
  Ibid.

How are we to be saved when obedience is far from the "perfection of the law, when we know that sin remains in us?"[1] It must be known, says Melanchthon "that even in the saints there exist an imperfect and only nascent (inchoatio) obedience . . . ."[2]

The condition of these works is the very reason for the "pronouncing just." The imperfect obedience is unable to fulfill the law due to that which remains in human nature. There "remains in the saints the residue of sin, namely concupiscence . . . ."[3] This very sin must not be weakened or diminished because by its nature it is a fault and worthy of death.[4]

The promise of the remission of sins must be added to works. No one can properly assert, says Melanchthon, that the remission of sins depends on the state of our worth and works.[5] In order to have the remission of sins the soul itself would have to be "free from all offenses."[6] This is clearly not the case for Melanchthon, therefore the

---

1
 Ibid.
2
 Ibid.
3
 CR 21:309-310.
4
 Ibid.
5
 CR 21:318.
6 Ibid.

promise to come and the gracious "pronouncing just"
must be accepted.

The Loci of 1533 and the Function of the Law

As in the earlier Loci and the Apology, the inter-
posing or mediating role is inserted here by Melanchthon
because imperfect obedience necessitates being pronounced
righteous. The Gospel calls a person to recognize the
fault of corrupt human nature and the debilitating nature
of works. The Gospel, consequently, preaches Christ and
offers us "righteousness (iustitia) or being pronounced
righteous not, to be sure, because of our moral purity
(mundicies) or qualities but because of mercy through
Christ."[1] Our corrupt nature is such that it cannot be
responsible for the proper obedience and love for which we
were created, and which God requires.[2]

According to Melanchthon, the division between
law and Gospel is not ineffectual. Rather, it is most
important for him that we realize we are not able to satisfy the demands of the law. This incapacity brings us to
the point where being "pronounced just" is necessary. This
is precisely what the Gospel does, "proclaim that men are

---

[1] CR 21:275. On mundiciem see Niermeyer, Lexicon,
p. 709.

[2] CR 21:275.

pronounced righteous on account of Christ, not due to our fulfillment (_impletio_) of the law"[1]

For Melanchthon, a Christian is not able to fulfill the law. In baptism "guilt (_reatus_) is remitted, but the disease (_morbus_) still remains."[2] The disease (_morbus_) which remains, however, is not imputed to those who believe.[3] Furthermore, when "the Holy Spirit is given" a new spiritual and moral life is begun.[4]

Augustine, according to Melanchthon, defends the notion of the remission of sin. When Augustine speaks of the remission of original sin in baptism, "sin . . . is remitted (_remittitur_) not so that it will no longer exist, but so that it may not be imputed (_imputetur_)."[5] For Melanchthon, the disease, or fault, or sickness, or aversion, still exists within the believer, but (due to a mediator) it is not imputed, charged, reckoned, credited to the one who believes.

The judgment of God which considers our sins is

---

[1]
  CR 21:279.
[2]
  CR 21:290.
[3]
  Ibid.
[4]
  Ibid.
[5]
  CR 21:290.

that before which or under which the conscience of the
believer is not able to stand or assume a place (consistere).[1]
The law becomes the means whereby God's judgment and wrath
are revealed. Melanchthon demonstrates this from Romans
4:15 "the law brings wrath . . ." and 1 Corinthians 15:56
"the sting of death is sin, and the power of sin is the
law."[2] No matter how many works we perform, he says, "we are
not able to oppose the judgment of God because we are not
able to come near (accedere) to God without the mediator
Christ."[3] Thus, imperfect obedience, a corrupt nature,
inability to fulfill the law, and the imputation of God's
righteousness call for one who is able to intercede for
that righteousness and the non-imputation of the sins of
that faulty nature.

Syllogistic Arguments within the Loci of 1533

As in the Commentary on Romans, Melanchthon con-
structs, through syllogisms, a series of seven arguments
which propose, analyze and answer specific theses related
to the doctrine of good works. The topics included are:
the meaning of faith, the significance of love as a virtue,

---

[1] CR 21:293.
[2] Ibid.
[3] Ibid.

love as the fulfillment of the law, righteousness of the
law, doubt concerning the remission of sins, the certainty
of eternal life, and the necessity of obedience.

Firstly, if I have all the faith etc., says Paul,
therefore "we are not righteous by faith alone."[1]
Melanchthon answers that Paul does not speak here of the
antithesis, that we are righteous by love or charity. His
statement is only that "we also affirm . . .[that]love is
necessary."[2] Penance and obedience to the law "are necessary
(necessaria est), and even if the cause of justification is
other than the worth (dignitas) of penance" or our charity.[3]

In addition to Paul's requiring charity, it is
known, remarks Melanchthon, "from other places how works
and virtues are pleasing to God not because they satisfy
the law," but rather because the person is first reconciled
to God by faith.[4] It would be absurd to assert that
nothing would be accorded to the person unless perfect
charity were obtained; if so no one would be saved.[5] Our
worth is not able to oppose the terrors of sin and death.[6]

1
 CR 21:320.
2
 Ibid.
3
 Ibid.
4
 Ibid.
5
 CR 21:321.
6
 Ibid.

For Melanchthon, therefore, it is clear that "we do not
have the remission of sins due to our love (dilectio)."[1]

       Secondly, charity or love (dilectio) is "the high-
est (maxima) virtue, therefore on account of it are we
righteous."[2] Melanchthon regards the inverse of the conclusion to be true. "Charity is the greatest virtue;
therefore it justifies [all lesser ones]."[3] This is due to
the great length "we are removed from the perfection of the
height of the law and virtue."[4] This, according to
Melanchthon, is the reason the Gospel teaches, "that on
account of another (extra nos), namely, because of mercy
we are pronounced righteous" not because we are able to
fulfill the law.[5] When the Gospel teaches that "we are
pronounced righteous because of another" it is not due to
the "exercise of reasoning powers (ratiocinandum) regarding
justification" from the magnitude of virtues.[6] The state
or condition of virtues cannot, Melanchthon contends, be
the quia or the "on account of" or the why we are pronounced

---

[1] Ibid.

[2] Ibid.

[3] Ibid.

[4] Ibid.

[5] Ibid.

[6] Ibid.

righteous. He does not wish to deny charity as the greatest virtue, but merely, to assert that we are not righteous
by that virtue. For we are righteous by faith (quia fide
iusti sumus).

Thirdly, Melanchthon proposes the proposition that
since charity is the fulfillment of the law, therefore, "we
are righteous because of charity."[1] But Melanchthon denies
that righteousness comes from charity as the fulfillment
of the law. "Righteousness by faith is taught because we
are not righteous by the law."[2] It is written that Christ
fulfills the law for all those who believe.[3]

Faith, for Melanchthon, is the fulfillment of the
law, as well as of charity. Faith imputatively fulfills
the law, that is, "on account of Christ we are reputed to
be righteous just as if we had fulfilled the law."[4]

When speaking of charity as fulfilling the law,
Melanchthon notes that true charity is the fulfillment of
the law formally (formaliter).[5] Each mark of the law is

---

[1]
CR 21:322.
[2]
Ibid.
[3]
Ibid.
[4]
Ibid.
[5]
Ibid.

charity, both as righteousness according to the law and in its kind (species).[1] Melanchthon compares the fulfill- ment of the law with singing. Even though the "fulfillment of music is to sing," the fulfillment of the law cannot be provided by our obedience, since we neither love perfectly nor fully satisfy the law we must be justified because of another.[2]

Melanchthon mentions that Paul does speak of charity or love as the plenitudo legis, but that Paul does not mean we are righteous because of the fulfillment of the law.[3] He intends to preach "works and obedience to the law which ought to follow faith (quae sequi fidem debet)."[4] Here again he repeats that if justification were a matter of fulfilling the law no one would be justified.[5]

"Not hearers, but doers of the law are pronounced just, therefore we are justified by works," goes the fourth thesis.[6] Melanchthon responds that this directs us only to works pertaining to the law. Paul accuses "the Jews and

---

[1] Ibid.

[2] Ibid.

[3] Ibid.

[4] Ibid.

[5] Ibid.

[6] Ibid.

those who argue by reason that they are not justified by
the law because they do not satisfy the law."[1] For
Melanchthon, it is true that one who fulfills the law is
just and one who does not is not, in so far as the justice
of the law is concerned. The Gospel, however, "proposes
another justice (alia iustitia) which pronounces us righteous
(iusti) by mercy even if we do not satisfy the law."[2]

The Gospel also teaches that "obedience to the law
is as pleasing as if it satisfied the law."[3] Therefore,
doers of the law are justified. If after they are justified by faith they are reputed to have fulfilled the law,
such "doers of the law are pronounced righteous."[4]

Melanchthon's fifth thesis concerns James 2:24
"You see that a man is justified by works and not by faith
alone." Melanchthon points out that James notes the
importance of works and praises them, "he praises works
following faith and requires a living faith . . ."[5] What
James means, in Melanchthon's opinion, is that not only is
a "righteousness by faith required, but also a righteousness

---

[1]
  Ibid.
[2]
  Ibid.
[3]
  Ibid.
[4]
  CR 21:323.
[5]
  Ibid.

by work."[1] For "good works and righteousness by faith are necessary in those who believe."[2] Melanchthon qualifies the role of this righteousness when he says, "we have the remission of sins on account of Christ" and works are "pleasing not because they satisfy the law but because the person who does them is pleasing on account of Christ."[3]

"Man is justified by faith and works," that is, pronounced righteous because "of faith and work."[4] Melanchthon considers this righteousness of works to be righteousness only if the person is righteous because of another. Righteousness and reconciliation are due to the benefits of Christ, which make works pleasing.[5] Thus, Melanchthon is interpreting James as saying works are necessary and pleasing in those who are reconciled by faith.

"Eternal life is referred to as 'reward,' therefore it is given because of works," reads the sixth thesis, "and it is not granted by grace."[6] Here Melanchthon relies

---

[1] Ibid.

[2] Ibid.

[3] Ibid.

[4] Ibid.

[5] Ibid. This alien righteousness means that we receive righteousness from outside ourselves. It is granted to us due to the benefits procured by someone else, namely, Christ.

[6] CR 21:324.

on the experience of his readers. He argues that the
refutation of the thesis is apparent in the present
conscience of each person. No experienced or knowledgable
person would maintain that his good deeds are worthy of
eternal life or that they bear a dignity worth eternal
life.[1] It is obvious, for Melanchthon, that doubt as to
worthiness or holiness is what each conscience experiences
when it looks within. It is necessary, however, that the
"hope of eternal life be certain, as it is necessary that
the faith which believes we are forgiven our sins is
certain."[2] In order for faith or hope or trust to be
certain, the object of that hope or trust cannot be self
worth or dignity. Trust and hope are certain and sure
when transferred to the gracious promise of Christ, but
are not secure in our own dignity.[3]

The seventh thesis, which Melanchthon refutes,
concerns those who fail to do good works. It is held that
those who do good works will be saved, while those who fail
to do good works will not be saved.[4] Therefore, the smallest

[1]
Ibid.
[2]
Ibid.
[3]
Ibid. The manuscript available is cut short here
and continues with the next argument. The original premise
concerning reward is postponed for analysis to another work.
[4]
CR 21:325.

good deed performed becomes an important part which contributes causally to justification.[1] Melanchthon's response is a concession that "obedience is necessary, but it does not justify a person."[2] No matter how many good deeds or works a person performs, those works are not able to compare to or outweigh even one sin.[3] For obedience in and of itself is imperfect and is unable to compensate or make expiation for sins. Therefore, it is necessary that justification or being accepted as righteous be on account of or because of another.[4]

Conclusion

From the appearance of the Apology in 1531 until 1534 Melanchthon reformulated and adapted his teaching regarding good works as conflicts or conditions provided the need.[5] As his letters, written to Brenz during 1531, indicate Melanchthon was quite concerned with an over-emphasized teaching on the newness (novitas) provided to

---

[1] Ibid.

[2] Ibid.

[3] Ibid.

[4] Ibid.

[5] Persons with whom Melanchthon was involved in debate include: Eck, Cochlaeus, Campeggio, Carlstadt, and Schwenckfeld.

the Christian by the Holy Spirit. He maintained that any
novitas, of which Brenz spoke highly, was not sufficient
in itself, but faith is required as that which apprehends
and receives righteousness offered. Rather than employ
faith as medium Melanchthon is disposed toward that distance between Christ and ourselves and the consequent
need for our being reputed righteous.

          A further circumstance of this period which bore a
marked influence on his thinking was that of the stars.
An impeding celestial crisis or catastrophe, according
to Melanchthon's estimation, might well have conveyed
the imperative of imputare in as much as glory is that
extra nos and the evanescent nature of theological
reflection is brought to light by those very astrological
signs. The significance of cosmic portents for Melanchthon
is akin and corresponds to the frightened conscience and
God extra nos acting.[1]

          A development during these years pertaining
notable to methodolgy is that of including syllogisms.

1

          See CR 11:261-266; CR 2:530-537; Hans Blumenberg, Die
kopernikanische Wende. (Frankfurt am Main: Suhrkamp Verlag,
1965), pp. 7, 12, 14, 16, 55, 57, 59, 60. See also Wilhelm
Maurer, "Melanchthon als Humanist," Philipp Melanchthon:
Forschungsbeiträge zur vierhundertsten Wiederkehr seines
Todestages dargeboten in Wittenberg 1960. (Göttingen:
Vandenhoeck und Ruprecht, 1961), pp. 116-132; Charles Leander
Hill, "An Exposition und Critical Estimate of the Philosophy
of Philip Melanchthon" (Ph,D. Dissertation, Ohio State Univer-
sity, 1938).

Melanchthon adopts syllogisms as a means to explicate, and clarify positions bearing upon the doctrine of good works.

Particularly within the 1532 commentary on Paul, Melanchthon reveals a shift from the moral mandate to that of works being a necessary result deriving from our novitas. The shift is that from a moral ought characteristic to that of a causal is characteristic.

In the Romans Commentary of 1532 Melanchthon also attends to Osiander's desire to underscore the importance of renovatio. It is not denied by Melanchthon, but he cautiously reinforces the imputatio of God's righteousness by stressing the intuens of faith. Moreover, Melanchthon refines his definition of faith in the commentary by declaring the proposition, fide iustificamur, to be correlatively understood. The righteousness achieved by faith (fide) is relative to the cause on account of which it is granted, namely, Christ the mediator.

Even though the Loci of 1533 incorporates, clarifies, and augments the doctrine of works as found in the Apology, the following are specific notions in the Loci which are peculiar to it, though not exclusively, and elucidate the slow shift in Melanchthon's thought: 1) Obedience to the law is necessary, even if works are unworthy (indigna). 2) God rewards works of the law, though not with salvation. Those who do works "merit" rewards on account of Christ. 3) Righteousness is distinct from any personal worth or dignity of the individual, properly speaking it is <u>extra</u> <u>nos</u>. 4) The distinction between person and work must be made; hence, works are incapable of making a person pleasing to God. 5) The law is not evil, in and of itself; men are simply unable to fulfill its demands. 6) The conscience, terrified by God's wrath, is unable to be pacified by any amount of works. 7) Christ as mediator "aligns" imperfect obedience and being pronounced righteous. 8) Sin always remains in human nature. 9) Works are pleasing to God after the person is reconciled by faith in Christ as mediator. 10) Faith imputatively fulfills the law in that we are reputed to be righteous on account of it as if the law had been fulfilled.

CHAPTER III

THE DOCTRINE OF GOOD WORKS
IN THE <u>LOCI</u> OF 1535

Not Without Works

On April 29 and 30, 1534 a conference was held in
Leipzig in an attempt to reconcile the Catholic and
Evangelical parties in regard to matters such as good works
being necessary for justification and the practice of private
masses. The elector of Mainz and Duke George of Saxony were
moderators, while Melanchthon and Brück attended in the name
of the Saxon Elector. The position regarding justification
and works professed by the Evangelicals is found in the
<u>Corpus</u> <u>Reformatorum</u>.[1] The Evangelicals clearly reiterated
the <u>sola</u> <u>fide</u> position and the fact that righteousness is
procured by faith in Christ.[2] The doctrine of works went
through several forms, but did appear as one acceptable to
both sides (for the time being).[3]

Righteousness, the Evangelicals declared, is obtained
through faith in the grace of God. That righteousness is
received because of the work of God and no other work.[4] The

---

[1]CR 2:722-726. The text is a copy of the report
corrected by Melanchthon.

[2]CR 2:722.

[3]See CR 2:723. It was acceptable to Melanchthon
even though he felt that <u>diese</u> <u>Form</u> <u>für</u> <u>leidlich</u> <u>bleiben</u>
<u>lassen</u>.

[4]Ibid.

proper exposition is "der Glaube allein gerecht mache" and not "ander Werk."[1] It is imperative, however, that " ... gute Werke von Gott gebothen muss man thun ..."[2]

The attainment of righteousness and the presence of faith were conjoined by the Evangelicals. They asserted that "... Gerechtigkeit und Glaube nicht bleiben kann ohne gute Werke ..."[3] Good works cannot be the means whereby righteousness is acquired, yet that very same righteousness cannot be maintained without them.

During August, 1534 in an attempt to explain his conciliatory actions with the Catholics, Melanchthon wrote a deliberation on the controverted topics.[4] There, he grants papal and episcopal authority for the sake of unity insofar as sound doctrine is not distorted.[5] He proposes common worship rites, but desires that such matters be seen as adiaphoristic, namely, indifferent matters. Confession may be preserved. The doctrine of meritorious sacrifice of the mass, private masses, communion in only one kind, and worship or invocation of the saints are all to be abolished.

When Melanchthon comes to the controversy surrounding

---

[1] Ibid.

[2] Ibid.

[3] Ibid.

[4] Cr 2:741-762.

[5] CR 2:744-746

justification and works he points out the fact that "good
works are not excluded, but another sure and sufficient
cause is sought for the remission of sins."[1] The cause
does not lie in faith or _fiducia_ in our works, but _fiducia_
in Christum.[2] Even the _saniores_ among the adversaries would
have to admit that men are righteous principally by trust
in the promised mercy due to Christ. It is not works or
the attempt to fulfill the law that saves or reconciles, but
"persona est reconciliata in Christo."[3]

One cannot become pleasing to God on account of the
worth of works, but by faith on account of Christ (_sed_ _fide_
propter _Christum_).[4] Works do possess a certain dignity and
are pleasing to God, not because they satisfy the demands of
the law, but because the person believes in and professes
Christ.[5]

The remission of sins is achieved by faith _propter_
Christum.[6] As a result, works performed are pleasing to
God, not in that they are able to satisfy the law, but due

---

[1] CR 2:749-750.

[2] Ibid.

[3] Ibid.

[4] Ibid.

[5] Ibid.

[6] Ibid.

to the fact that the person believes in Christ.[1] All
those who agree, asserts Melanchthon, that "the righteousness
of good works or of the good conscience is necessary" wish
to teach and strengthen, for the desperation of pious minds,
the fact that our obedience is pleasing.[2] Further, we ought
to mortify the old man (veterem hominem) and profess that
the Holy Spirit does not remain in those who commit mortal
sins, namely, deeds performed against the conscience and the
law of God (legem Dei).[3]

Introduction to the Loci of 1535

In Wittenberg in 1535 appeared the second edition of
Melanchthon's Loci Communes Theologici. The breakdown of
method remained much like the 1521 edition, but the 1535
edition was to undergo thirteen revisions up to the year 1541.
During those years disputations concerning the doctrine of
good works were to force Melanchthon to refine his own understanding of the issue as he did in the second edition of the
Loci.

The two primary controversialists were Conrad
Cordatus and John Agricola. Caspar Cruciger had delivered
lectures in Wittenberg during 1536 using notes on the Gospel

---

[1]Ibid.

[2]Ibid.

[3]Ibid.

of John prepared by Melanchthon. During the course of his lectures he was heard to say that good works are a "causa sine qua non" of salvation. A preacher in Niemegk who attended the lecture, Conrad Cordatus, challenged Cruciger. When Cruciger defended himself by stating that the lecture notes were prepared by Melanchthon, Cordatus went to Luther accusing Melanchthon of heresy.

In a letter to Cordatus dated September 10, 1536 Cruciger defended his position.[1] He reiterated the teachings of Paul that we are justified by faith and that Christ is the cause of our justification.[2] The grace that justifies, however, does "not exclude contribtion, but it is necessary in the justified man, and our contrition is called 'causa sine qua non,' because faith is not able to exist without it."[3]

Melanchthon was not in Wittenberg at the time, but as soon as he heard of the controversy he composed a letter explaining his position.[4] This letter, dated November 1, apologizes for the unfortunate controversy, and Melanchthon wishes all including Jonas and Luther, to understand that

---

[1]
On Cordatus see Tagebuch über dr. Martin Luther geführt von dr. Conrad Cordatus 1537. Zum ersten male hrsg. von dr. H. Wrampelmeyer. (Halle: M. Niemeyer, 1885).

[2]
 CR 3:160.

[3]Ibid.

[4]CR 3:179-181.

his position does not deviate from theirs.[1] He says that
at the beginning of their endeavors much was said of the
inner newness of the Christian, which God infuses into the
soul. As a result, Melanchthon felt that it was necessary,
"to transfer [in the Apology] the matter to an imputative
grace" and make it more distinct.[2] "Then questions arose,
as you know, that if we are received by mercy" then why is
a new obedience required?[3] This explains the repeated
emphasis Melanchthon considered necessary in order to have
an ethical mandate without providing works as a cause for
salvation. Indeed, he goes on to say that no matter how
much praise he heaped on good works, he never extolled
(ornavi) them with a false praise. For no one earns or merits
eternal life.[4]

Melanchthon arrived in Wittenberg on November 5 and
sent a cordial and conciliatory letter to Cordatus asking
for unity among the theologians in regard to this matter.[5]
Nevertheless, Cordatus was still concerned and ultimately
referred the matter to Jonas, the rector of the university,

---

[1]CR 3:179-180.

[2]CR 3:180.

[3]Ibid.

[4]Ibid.

[5]CR 3:181-182.

for his decision.[1]

The controversy continued throughout the succeeding
months when certain remarks published, by Melanchthon, in
the Loci of 1535 (discussed below) were considered by some
of his contemporaries to be unorthodox. At the request of
Melanchthon, Cruciger wrote to Veit Dietrich on July 10, 1537
in an attempt to explain the rather surprising statement of
Melanchthon: "new obedience is necessary for salvation"
(nova obedientia sit necessaria ad salutem).[2]

Cruciger maintained that the significance of the
proposition had been misunderstood. It does not propose
merit, but simply that the proper effect follows justification.
As Melanchthon attests, not works, but God, achieves salvation. Melanchthon himself, states Cruciger, responded that
the obligation to the law has been abrogated, "not only with
respect to justification and condemnation has the law no
force, but even that owed to obedience has been annulled."[3]

Cordatus, in a letter of April 17, to Jonas and
Melanchthon, reveals the principle reason for his direct
attack on Melanchthon. The proposition concerning works

---

[1]Cordatus wrote Melanchthon on December 16, 1536
telling him that he felt the matter must be pursued. See
CR 3:203-204.

[2]The systematic treatment of Melanchthon's arguments
will be expounded later. See CR 21:429. Cruciger's letter
is found in CR 3:384-387.

[3]CR 3:385.

brings about two causes for justification and this, he says, "I am not able to tolerate."[1] There can only be found one cause for justification and that is Christ. This is the case even if we ought to have contrition, for there cannot be a duality of cause.[2] The same sentiment is expressed in a letter of April 17 to Brück in which Cordatus laments the unfortunate suffering being caused at Wittenberg: "Plura non possum scribere quam hoc, dass die zwei Caussae mehr Leides zu Wittenbergk haben angerichtet denn gut ist."[3]

Melanchthon writes to Bucer on April 23 discussing Cordatus, whom he calls sycophanta, and his attack on Melanchthon's position, "Bona opera necessaria esse ad salutem."[4] Melanchthon rhetorically asks who is able to deny the proposition that a new spirituality is necessary for eternal life? "This is what I mean when I say a new obedience is necessary for eternal life."[5]

In a treatise written during 1537 in an attempt to clarify the position on justification and good works vis-à-vis the Catholic position, Melanchthon repeats his emphasis on

-----

[1] CR 3:350.

[2] Ibid.

[3] CR 3:353.

[4] CR 3:356.

[5] Ibid.

a new obedience.[1] The difference from the Catholic position
is that "we exclude the condition of merit, even if faith
ought (oportet) to be followed by other virtues ..."[2] It is
fitting for there to be a nova obedientia in the justified.[3]
The mandate provided here by Melanchthon is more than a mere
suggestion, for he states that it is "always necessary for
there to be an inchoate obedience in the justified."[4]

This obedience to the law is salutary and the law
"has its rewards and would merit eternal life, if we were
without sin."[5] Since we are not without sin, eternal life is
given on account of another. Nevertheless, there is recompense
(compensatio) for attempts to fulfill the law and that
"necessarily accompanies faith and is the beginning of a
new future" in the eternal life.[6] The pious person realizes
that eternal life is granted propter Christum, that he is
freed from eternal death by the Son of God.[7] He also knows
that "obedience is necessary" and is duly rewarded.[8]

---

[1]The treatise is found in CR 3:430-437.

[2]CR 3:433.

[3]Ibid.

[4]CR 3:435.

[5]CR 3:437.

[6]Ibid.

[7]Ibid.

[8]Ibid.

The emphasis on this new obedience was not lightly undertaken by Melanchthon. He was quite resolute as to its place in Evangelical teaching, notably as expounded in his Loci of 1535. The earnestness of his devotion to that particular work and its doctrines is revealed in his own last will and testament. It was written sometime in or just before November 1539, when Melanchthon was forty-two. He had apparently been suffering from insomnia and the burden of incessant controversy. Believing that his last days were upon him he composed a will which he intended to be a profession of faith.[1] He sounds quite distraught with the innumerable controversies in which he was embroiled. He exhorts the reader in such a manner as if to decree that the Loci (which will be examined in the next section) is his final word on theological matters. Melanchthon says the Loci of 1535 ought to suffice as a "declaration" of Evangelical doctrine.

"I declare," he states, "that I affirm the Apostles' and the Nicene creeds, and concerning the entire Christian doctrine, I maintain what I have written in the Loci Communes and in the last edition of the Commentary on Romans in which I explain in every article what I hold without ambiguity."[2]

-----

[1] CR 3:825-828.

[2] CR 3:826: "Secundo affirmo me vere amplecti symbola, Apostolicum et Nicaenum, et de tota doctrina Christiana sentire, ut scripsi in locis communibus, et Romanis postremae editionis, in quibus explicare de singulis articulis sine ambiguitate conatus sum dicere, quod sentio."

Henry VIII, after becoming the head of the Church
in England in 1534, moved toward a tolerance of Protestant
ideas by twice inviting Melanchthon to make a trip across
the channel. Melanchthon chose not to accept the invitations;
so in March 1535 the King sent Robert Barnes as an imperial
legate to Wittenberg to consult with the Evangelicals in
regard to Henry's second marriage and to the possibility of
introducing the continental reforms in England. Melanchthon
welcomed Barnes and wrote to the King advocating the Evangelicals' positions. He even dedicated the 1535 edition of
the Loci to Henry. The King was most thankful and sent a
laudatory letter of gratitude to Melanchthon as well as a
gift of two hundred florins.[1]

---

[1]After being discouraged over the King's intentions,
Melanchthon removed this dedication from succeeding editions
of his Loci. Bretschneider's critical text is entitled: Loci
Communes Theologici Recens Collecti et Recogniti a Philippo
Melanthone. Authors Melanchthon cites include: Ambrose: 500,
505, 510; Aristotle: 403, 404, 413, 420, **534**; **Augustine:** 334,
379, 383, 423, 430, 434, 452, 459, 468, 473, 488, 504, 508;
Athanasius: 505; Basil: 356, 376; Bonaventure: 380; Celsus:
543; Cicero: 385, 401, 416, 534; Cyprian: 334, 473, 504;
Euripides: 337, 346; Gregory: 460; Gerson: 464; Hesiod:
338, 367, 387, 401; Homer: 413; Irenaeus: 359, 363, 545;
Isocrates: 413, 547; James: 439; John: 351, 352, 354, 356,
357, 358, 359, 360, 361, 365, 366, 367, 371, 376, 378, 382,
402, 415, 417, 420, 426, 432, 435, 442, 447, 452, 458, 469,
475, 481, 482, 484, 487, 488, 490, 494, 497, 501, 505, 507,
520, 521, 524, 533, 537, 538, 557; Jerome: 430; Peter Lombard:
335, 342, 346; Luke: 365, 415, 433, 434, 442, 469, 486, 495,
498, 503, 509, 515, 521, 522, 529, 533, 537, 539, 549, 553;
Mark: 434, 471, 498, 507, 516, 531; Matthew: 352, 355, 356,
361, 365, 368, 396, 397, 407, 411, 412, 428, 429, 430, 433,
434, 438, 463, 465, 466, 471, 472, 474, 475, 477, 483, 486,
487, 488, 490, 493, 494, 498, 501, 503, 505, 506, 509, 513,
514, 517, 518, 519, 520, 521, 522, 524, 527, 528, 529, 533,

The Loci of 1535 on Works as Necessary

The terms incorporated by Melanchthon in his exposition on good works vary, but the fact that works are "necessary" is most often employed in the 1535 Loci. Works are considered necessary especially as the function of the law becomes more integrated for Melanchthon. He is of the opinion that the law teaches those who are justified by faith those matters concerning good works and in what way works are pleasing to God. Additionally, the law informs them of those works which actually "carry out obedience to God."[1] Even though we are free from the law insofar as it pertains to justification, nevertheless the "law remains

---

537, 539, 540, 545, 558; Origen: 334, 335, 360, 457, 473; Gregory Nazianzen: 354, 505, 509; Peter: 462, 469, 482, 495, 497, 503, 505, 521, 529, 531, 532, 540, 544, 557; Paul: 334, 338, 341, 343, 351, 354, 363, 366, 369, 371, 375, 376, 377, 378, 381, 382, 387, 389, 390, 394, 401, 402, 405, 406, 407, 410, 411, 412, 414, 415, 417, 420, 421, 422, 423, 425, 426, 427, 428, 429, 430, 431, 432, 433, 434, 436, 438, 439, 442, 443, 445, 446, 447, 448, 449, 450, 451, 452, 453, 454, 456, 457, 458, 459, 460, 461, 463, 464, 465, 468, 469, 470, 471, 472, 474, 476, 477, 479, 481, 483, 485, 486, 488, 489, 490, 492, 493, 495, 496, 497, 498, 499, 501, 502, 503, 505, 506, 507, 508, 510, 511, 512, 513, 514, 515, 516, 517, 519, 520, 521, 522, 524, 527, 528, 529, 530, 531, 532, 533, 535, 537, 539, 540, 541, 542, 544, 546, 548, 549, 550, 551, 552, 553, 555, 556, 557, 558; Phidias: 336, 337; Plato: 335, 346, 404, 410, 462, 547, 548; Paul of Samosata: 358; Servetus: 359; Scotus: 346; Tertullian: 359; Thomas: 343, 346; Valentinus: 367; Virgil: 536; Wycliff: 503, 508; Xenophon: 336, 370, 387, 401, 416; Zeno: 373.

[1]CR 21:406. All subsequent references to CR 21, unless otherwise indicated, will refer to the Loci of 1535.

insofar as it pertains to obedience."[1] The law, then
provides the means and directive for that which is necessary.
For the justified "it is necessary (necesse est) to obey
God."[2]

As in the earlier Loci Melanchthon also uses the
phrase sequi debet. Once the Holy Spirit is received a new
life, a whole new attitude is begun, and this renovatio is
called regeneration. Consequently, "a new obedience ought
to follow (sequi debet)..."[3] Therefore, "I clearly state;
our obedience, that is, the righteousness of the good conscience or of works" which God enjoins upon us "necessarily
ought to follow reconciliation (necessario sequi debet
reconciliationem)."[4] Paul says (Romans 8:12) that we are
debtors and that we do not live according to the flesh.
Christ himself says (Matthew 19:17) that if you wish to enter
into life you must keep the commandments. We who are justified "live a new and spiritual life which is obedience to
God ..."[5] According to Ephesians (2:10): We are "created
for good works."[6]

---

[1]CR 21:406.
[2]Ibid.
[3]CR 21:428.
[4]CR 21:429.
[5]Ibid.
[6]Ibid.

One of Melanchthon's more surprising positions
follows. First, he endorses the fact that eternal life is
"not given because of the dignity of good works, but by grace
propter Christum."[1] Then he adds, "Nevertheless good works
are necessary for eternal life (bona opera ita necessaria
sunt ad vitam aeternam), because they necessarily ought to
follow reconciliation (quia sequi reconciliationem necessario
debent)."[2] Not only are external civil works required, but
even "a spiritual attitude, the fear of God, trust, invocation,
love" and similar attitudes.[3]

When David says (Psalm 143:2) that no one living is
justified before God, "he teaches that justification is to
be obtained by mercy, not because of our dignity."[4] The
acts or works performed, says Melanchthon, by those who are
reconciled to God by faith are only inchoate, but they are
pleasing to God. Obedience "pleases God."[5]

Obedience is pleasing to God not "because it is
perfect," but due to the fact that the person is reconciled
by faith and his infirmities are pardoned.[6]

---

[1] Ibid.

[2] Ibid. A 1539, and three 1541 editions have "Et tamen
haec nova spiritualis obedientia ita necessaria est..debet."

[3] CR 21:429.

[4] CR 21:431.

[5] Ibid.

[6] CR 21:431-432.

Even if a person has the remission of sins "by
mercy propter Christum and is received or accepted," says
Melanchthon, nevertheless righteous works "necessarily ought
to follow."[1] The reason for insisting that works ought to
follow is the "command of God, so that we maintain this
obedience because Christ clearly preaches: Do penance."[2]

This obedience even means obedience to the law.
No one is able to fulfill the demands of the law because of
sin which remains, yet obedience to the law is necessary.[3]
Consequently, "the law is added to the Gospel of Christ."[4]
It is fitting (oportet), first of all, that we be made sons
of God by mercy on account of Christ.[5] "Thereafter our
obedience ought to follow (sequi debet obedientia nostra)"
even if it is imperfect. The person is pronounced righteous,
that is, received because of another, videlicet propter

---

[1]CR 21:432. Maurer interpreted Melanchthon as saying
that the enlivened faith was the primary reason for doing good
works and Anscombe sees it as depending primarily on the "ought"
characteristic for the Reformers. See Wilhelm Maurer, Der
junge Melanchthon zwischen Humanismus und Reformation. vol. 2.
(Göttingen: Vandenhoeck and Ruprecht, 1969), pp. 381-385.
G. E. M. Anscombe, "Modern Moral Philosophy." Philosophy 33
(January 1958):6. At this point, however, Melanchthon considers
works as integral to the state of being reconciled. If one
is reconciled one will do good works. This is more than a moral
exhortation or the vivifying of faith through external acts.

[2]CR 21:432.

[3]CR 21:438-439.

[4]Ibid.

[5]Ibid.

<u>Christum</u>.[1] Due to this other, the person is pleasing to
God and even this inchoate obedience is pleasing.[2]

The Worth of Works in the Loci of 1535

Even though Melanchthon maintains that works are
necessary and, in one section, that they are necessary for
salvation, he takes pains to transfer the causal significance
for salvation to Christ and away from works. When speaking
of the first epistle of John (5:10) Melanchthon states that
the "condition of our dignity is excluded" and the cause of
favor or benefit is transferred from us to Christ.[3] It is
not our obedience that Melanchthon wishes to exclude. Rather,
Melanchthon wishes "to transfer the cause of benefit from the
dignity of our obedience to Christ" so that the benefit is
made certain.[4] The Gospel urges penance, "but in order that
reconciliation be certain it teaches that sins are remitted"
and that we are pleasing to God "not on account of the
dignity of penance or our <u>novitas</u>."[5] Melanchthon is of the
opinion that this principle must be maintained for the
consolation of pious consciences.[6]

---

[1]CR 21:439.

[2]Ibid.

[3]CR 21:415.

[4]Ibid.

[5]Ibid.

[6]Ibid.

When Melanchthon says that we are reconciled by
grace (gratis), he means that "gratis" is an exclusive
particle (exclusiva particula). This means that the remission
of sins and reconciliation are given by grace (gratis) alone.[1]
This "exclusive particle" does not exclude, says Melanchthon,
our "penance and good works, but it only excludes the condition of dignity" and transfers the cause to the benefit of
Christ so that it will be certain.[2]

Not only linguistics, but even common psychological
experience reveals the worthlessness of works for Melanchthon.
As he indicated in the Loci of 1521, he repeats here that
"never would any experienced conscience maintain that its good
deeds are worthy of eternal life" or that eternal life be
granted on the basis of the worth of works.[3]

Melanchthon quotes the Gospel of John in explaining
the transfer of merit from works to Christ. As Jesus says
in John 6:39: "This is the will of my Father who sent me,
that all who see the Son and believe in him have eternal
life."[4] John also writes (3:15) that whoever "believes in
the Son has eternal life."[5] Thus, for Melanchthon, it is

---

[1]CR 21:423.

[2]CR 21:423-424.

[3]CR 21:441-442.

[4]CR 21:442.

[5]Ibid.

quite clear that eternal life is expected "because of Christ, not because of personal worth (dignitas propria)."[1]

That which is applied to us on account of the benefit or favor of Christ is not dependent on a tertium quid. That is, there is no mediation of the Mediator. In particular, the "benefit of Christ does not depend on the worth of an alien human work."[2]

It is not just the worth of a single task or work that Melanchthon wishes to avoid, but any and all states, attitudes, or offices that are considered worthy of grace or the remission of sins. Sins are remitted, in his view, by grace because of Christ and "not on account of the worth of contrition, love or any other work."[3] Of particular concern to Melanchthon was the "trust of monks who vainly think they more merit the remission of sins and justification by their celibacy" than other men.[4] Much more do they err who assert that "celibacy is the perfection of the Gospel."[5]

---

[1]Ibid.

[2]CR 21:485.

[3]CR 21:421.

[4]CR 21:412.

[5]Ibid.

Causes For Doing Good Works
in the Loci of 1535

If no single work, nor any number of works, merits
the remission of sins and justification, then why maintain
works as necessary? Melanchthon provides four reasons:
1) they are necessary, 2) they maintain a certain worth
(dignitas), 3) they are deserving of rewards, 4) they exercise
the faith of the individual.[1] He adds to those causes the
remark that "however imperfect obedience is, nevertheless it
is pleasing [to God] in the reconciled."[2]

The ability to pursue the good of these causes comes
from the aid and powerful protection of the Holy Spirit who
does not allow the Devil to "lead us astray into pernicious
errors or to shameful things, as it is written (John 14:18):
I will not leave you orphans."[3] Thus, we do good works
because an "inchoate obedience is pleasing and help is
promised to us."[4]

To reflect on these causes it is worthwhile, says
Melanchthon, to consider how much injury and evil we have
caused by our malicious works. It is important to remember

---

[1]CR 21:435.

[2]Ibid.

[3]Ibid.

[4]CR 21:436.

that "they merit God's wrath and eternal damnation."[1]
Further, they deform "the Gospel and the glory of God."[2]
Thirdly, those suffer greatly who are under the power of the
Devil and are forced into "all kinds of errors and shame."[3]
His influence results in physical punishments, wars, and
innumerable other calamities. Fourthly, "all spiritual
exercises are hindered (impediuntur) and faith is destroyed
in those who indulge" in lustful things.[4] Finally, that
which is worst of all, "sins merit (merentur) the hardening
and the punishment of sins as Paul indicates in Romans 1."[5]

Considering these reflections on our evil and the
causes for doing good works "we learn to fear God's wrath
and to incite ourselves to the performance of good deeds."[6]
It might be added, says Melanchthon, that "works are required
of Christians" and God does exhort us to follow through.[7]

Four other reasons for the maintenance of good works
are to be found in three printings of this Loci which appeared

---

[1] Ibid.
[2] Ibid.
[3] Ibid.
[4] Ibid.
[5] Ibid.
[6] Ibid.
[7] Ibid.

in 1541.[1] The first is that "God demands it" and all ought
to obey.[2] Secondly, penalties are rendered for evil deeds
because "God punishes the impious with perpetual torment
after this life, but even in this life he punishes the wicked
with terrible means."[3] God will bring the murderer to suffer
for his crime even if such a person thinks he has escaped the
hands of the magistrates. All kinds of evil and human
wickedness is daily punished even if persons are not humanly
judged and imprisoned.[4] As the Psalmist (32:9) teaches: We
must "be curbed with bit and bridle (chamo et freno)."[5]
Even though philosophers have questioned the causes for
misery the Psalmist proposes an answer. "Men are subjected
to these calamities because [their] nature is fallen" and as
a result they are forced to suffer this daily misery.[6]

Even the pagans who consider the value of works
possess insight into the inadequacy of evil works. For
even they understand that "murder, perjury, and incest"
result in cruel penalties.[7]

---

[1]
To be found in Cr 21:386. Note 76.
[2]
Cr 21:386. Note 76.
[3]
Ibid.
[4]
Ibid.
[5]
Ibid.
[6]
Ibid.
[7]
Ibid.

The third reason proposed by Melanchthon for
discipline is simply stated: that society in common will
be tranquil.[1] That is, good works are to lead to order
and peace and the establishment of a tranquil society.

The fourth reason for doing good works and following
a discipline lies in what Paul calls the pedagogical law
(legem paedagogiam) in Christ.[2] The believer in Christ
follows a discipline and obedience, for those who entertain
their foulness and continue to sin are "not members of
Christ."[3] Further, those who do that which is against the
conscience do not remain members of Christ.[4]

Natural Law as a Cause
for Doing Good Works
in the Loci of 1535

An anthropological reason or, more properly speaking,
an epistemological reason for doing good works, as enunciated
in the Loci of 1535 is found in the extent to which the human
mind perceives and understands the natural and divine laws.

Paul states in Romans 1:20 that the divinity is
perceived in nature. Just as philosophers testify to a
divinity from a consideration of nature, so all affirm from

---

[1]Ibid.

[2]Ibid.

[3]Ibid.

[4]Ibid.

the entire universe, which acts as a witness, that "there
is a God, that there is wisdom, goodness, and justice."[1]
Even the celestial bodies in motion provide us with knowledge
as to their conservation, their end, and their coming into
being. The most important and most perfectly expressed
"vestige of God (vestigium Dei) is the human mind" and the
knowledge impressed on the mind "that of honesty, justness,
and the terrors of the conscience."[2] It is necessary for
there to be "another mind from which human minds and that
knowledge are born."[3] When the human mind grasps (teneat)
the difference "between justice and injustice it is necessary
for there to be wisdom and justice in that eternal mind."[4]
In the human mind, then, are images of the divinity or "as
I say, mirrors (specula) in which we ought to contemplate
the divinity."[5]

In addition to the knowledge of God there is for
Melanchthon the knowledge of the law of God (notitia legis
de Deo).[6] This law is most perfectly clear if it is present
in a mind unmarred by original sin. That divine light is not

---

[1] CR 21:369.

[2] Ibid.

[3] Ibid.

[4] Ibid.

[5] Ibid.

[6] CR 21:370.

extinguished in our souls "for there remains some knowledge
of the law of nature," but it is darkened by the cover of
original sin.[1]

As God has impressed his knowledge and wisdom on the
human mind we are able, says Melanchthon, to know the law
that has been imposed on nature. Just as light is imposed
or placed upon the eyes, so knowledge has been imposed upon
the human mind, a light by which it knows and judges.[2] The
philosophers call this light the "knowledge of principles
or κοινὰς ἐννοίας and προλήψεις ."[3] Further, just as
they teach that there are speculative principles whereby men
recognize and understand natures with certainty, there also
exist practical principles whereby the lex naturae is known.[4]

No matter how much the law of God has been obscured
in the souls of men, nevertheless there remain of it traces
(vestigia).[5] For the reason of nature or the conscience
proclaims and asserts that there is a God, creator of all

---

[1]Ibid.

[2]CR 21:399. Dilthey was quite correct in saying
that: "Die Lehre vom lumen naturale ist die fundamentale
philosophische Lehre im Gedankenzusammenhang Melanchthons.
Sie ist gleicherweise das philosophische Fundament seiner
wissenschaftlichen Lehrbücher und das seiner Glaubenslehre."
(Gesammelte Schriften, 2, p. 171).

[3]CR 21:399.

[4]Ibid.

[5]CR 21:400.

nature, "who blesses the just and punishes the unjust."[1]
Cicero (De natura deorum) and Xenophon, as well as the
Fathers of the Church, attested to the existence of a law
of nature or a knowledge of such a law.[2] From the ancient
period up to our day the judgment has been passed on and on
that "God blesses the just and punishes the unjust."[3]

Paul in Romans 1 accuses the Gentiles of excusing
themselves from this first law of nature "which acknowledges
and glorifies God, namely, to fear and to trust in him."[4]
It is this first of the natural laws which "we see comes
together with the first precept of the Decalogue, which God
revealed ..."[5]

Although our perception has been blurred by original
sin, the law of nature is renewed by the divine voice. That
divine voice testifies in the Word of God that "this natural
knowledge of nature is the law of God."[6]

The law that pertains to national or political categories may or may not be the natural law Melanchthon speaks
of here. For the natural "law actually signifies the natural

---

[1] Ibid.
[2] CR 21:401.
[3] Ibid.
[4] Ibid.
[5] Ibid.
[6] Ibid.

judgment of reason" or, as the philosophers call it, the _ius naturae_.[1] This distinction applies to the works we ought to do as specified by the Decalogue. The Decalogue is made up of two tables, the first five commandments and the second five. The first applies to works which we do before God, namely, "the true interior and exterior worship of God."[2] The second contains works done for our neighbors, "interior and exterior."[3] Thus, the different ends of works are distinguished: the "first pertains to the spiritual life and the second to the political life."[4]

Even if there is a knowledge impressed on the mind whereby we can distinguish between justice and injustice, even if we do perceive that there is a law of nature which may be called the law of God, and even if we do understand how "law" may be of God or man, still why should we do works? Even if there exists a law in nature, created by God, why should it be followed? To explain what _is_ is not to explain what _ought_ to be.

---

[1] CR 21:403.
[2] CR 21:392.
[3] Ibid.
[4] Ibid.

The Loci of 1535 and
the Moral Law as Necessary

If the natural law comes together with the
Decalogue, then does our freedom from the law (due to the
Gospel) actually mean a freedom from this natural law and
the Decalogue? No, says Melanchthon, for the "Gospel does
not abolish the law of nature ..."[1]

Yet, we are promised by the Gospel salvation and
freedom from the law. Quite so, says Melanchthon; we are
indeed free from the law; it has been entirely abrogated.[2]
Furthermore, our justification is assured, but "the moral
law which pertains to obedience remains, because surely the
Gospel submits us to obedience before God."[3] Insofar as
this obedience is pleasing, "it is necessary to keep the
moral law (necesse sit retinere legem moralem)."[4]

The Gospel is concerned with a spiritual and eternal
life, says Melanchthon, and does not require the external
rules of Mosaic regulations which pertain, more specifically,
to the physical life.[5] Yet, because the Gospel conveys "a
new and a spiritual life, it requires obedience to God, it

---

[1]CR 21:408-409.

[2]CR 21:459.

[3]Ibid.

[4]Ibid. This does not amount to two kinds of law,
but two functions of the law.

[5]CR 21:461.

proclaims penance" and it condemns the wicked nature and represses concupiscence.[1]

Spiritual works, as taught in the Decalogue, are required of us. For there "remains in human nature a natural knowledge of the Decalogue or moral law" which directs us to obey.[2]

Indeed, says Melanchthon, when one speaks of works and the Gospel it is not thought to bear on Mosaic prescriptions, but on moral and spiritual ends. The Gospel does not require Mosaic rules and yet it does not "abolish arithmetic or eloquence, nor indeed the love of nature," that is, the natural judgment concerning moral and civil life.[3] For Melanchthon, the Gospel "does not establish a new body politic," but brings us to apply our own "natural judgment."[4]

We are free from the law, says Melanchthon, however, "we are not free from obedience to the moral law, only from the curse of that law."[5] As he noted earlier, we are not able to satisfy the law, but due to another (Christ) "we have the remission of sins and the imputation of righteousness

---

[1]Ibid.

[2]Ibid.

[3]CR 21:461-462.

[4]CR 21:462.

[5]CR 21:459.

(iustitia)."[1] Further, the remission of sins is granted
just as if we had satisfied the law. We are free from the
law that condemns (sub lege), but we are still "sub gratia,"
and this means that it is necessary to retain the moral law.[2]
What is now "owed" is because of another and that which
accuses cannot condemn.[3]

Rounding out the position that the moral law is
necessary and that it must be followed is the declaration
that "men are not able to satisfy the law of God."[4] Actually
the moral mandate of Melanchthon is impossible to fulfill.
He means that the "divine law not only requires external acts,
but inner purity, fear, trust, and love of God" that amounts
to a perfect obedience.[5]

The constitution of the law is such that it requires
a perfect obedience to God, and it will not remit our sins by
grace nor pronounce us righteous "unless the law is satisfied."[6]
No matter what is promised it requires a complete fulfillment

---

[1]Ibid.

[2]Ibid.

[3]Ibid.

[4]CR 21:375. Melanchthon did not hold, as Bring
(Verhältnis, pp. 59-60) maintains: "Der Mensch wird in der
Rechtfertigung von der Anklage des Gesetzes befreit, und er
erhält danach Kraft, das Gesetz zu erfüllen." See Bring, Das
Verhältnis von Glauben und Werken ..., pp. 59-60.

[5]CR 21:375.

[6]CR 21:414.

of its demands. On the other hand, the Gospel, even though it stresses penance and good works, contains the promise of the benefits of Christ which actually frees us from the law. Sins are forgiven, then, by grace, and "we are pronounced righteous even if we do not fulfill the law."[1] The Gospel equally teaches penance and the fulfillment of the law, yet the promise of remission of sins is entirely gratuitous.[2]

Melanchthon reminds us that we are able to follow the moral law, but need not despair of its fulfillment, for the consummation of those demands is due to another. Christ is the consummatio legis and through his benefits we are able to begin to love and fear God properly.[3] Even the first precept of the commandments is impossible for us until we are relieved of the condemnation of the law. Insofar as we are pronounced just because of Christ, says Melanchthon, are we truly able to love and fear God. Therefore "the first precept is imputative."[4] The initial trust in Christ allows, indeed permits and enforces, the initial precept of loving God.

The incapacity or inability to fulfill the demands of the law upon us must be kept in mind at all times. Sins are forgiven, we are justified, we are reconciled "because of

---

[1] Ibid.

[2] Ibid.

[3] CR 21:393.

[4] Ibid.

Christ not because of a ceremonial dignity or moral work."[1]
Our fallen and infirm condition is not able to satisfy the
moral law, even if "an inchoate obedience is both required
by and pleasing to God in the reconciled."[2]

The law of God, says Melanchthon, requires the
perfect obedience of human nature. When human nature is
not able to provide this perfect obedience, it follows that
"men are not pronounced righteous before God because of the
law for sin always remains in [human] nature."[3] God does not
require us to sin but he does require works.[4] It happens
that those very works, required by God, are sins per accidens
because the person is corrupt.[5] God requires that which is
good, but human good deeds are contaminated because of a
corrupt nature.[6]

Psalm 130:3 states that "if you should observe
iniquities, Lord, who could stand?"[7] It is clear for
Melanchthon that concupiscence remains even in the saints and
it "by its nature is sin and worthy of death for it is not

---

[1]CR 21:426.

[2]Ibid.

[3]CR 21:405.

[4]CR 21:387.

[5]Ibid.

[6]Ibid.

[7]CR 21:430.

indifferent ..."[1] Therefore, the corruptness, according to Melanchthon, of that which should provide the required perfect obedience necessarily prevents that very exercise.

Corrupt Works as Pleasing to God
in the Loci of 1535

The corrupt works of corrupt minds are not pleasing to God, as Paul says (Romans 8:6): "The mind of the flesh is dead."[2] Even though a man without faith has some knowledge of God and praiseworthy virtues, still "in the judgment of God they do not vivify (vivificant)."[3] Even if God requires this paedagogia or righteousness of the flesh or rewards it with physical rewards, nevertheless "our adversaries are wrong," says Melanchthon, when they affirm that "such works merit the remission of sins either de congruo or de condigno."[4]

In Melanchthon's mind it is not the work that establishes the person's worth, but the person the work. Even if a person has innumerable good works if that person is not reconciled or is one of the impii those works are not pleasing to God due to the corruptness of the person.[5] This is even

---

1
  Ibid.
2
  CR 21:387.
3
  IBid.
4
  CR 21:387-388.
5
  Cr 21:385.

the case with people like Cicero, who did not acknowledge
the Gospel and the fact that God remits sins by grace. This
forgiveness is had only by faith and faith means "trust in
[God's] mercy."[1] Just as Paul states in Romans 14:23:
"Whatever is not from faith is sin."[2]

This does not mean that external works of the law
cannot be performed by those not possessing renovatio, for
many philosophers rightly attribute the role of free will
in such matters.[3] Even sacred Scripture recognizes this,
declares Melanchthon, that there is a righteousness of the
flesh, and works of the law can be done by those who are not
reborn or those without renovatio.[4] The point to be made,
moreover, is that renovatio is not procured by means of those
works, and that is why Melanchthon calls it iustitia carnis.[5]

Obedience is necessary "and it pleases God, but in
the reconciled."[6] It is also "righteousness, not because
it satisfies the law," but on account of the person.[7] The
inchoate obedience that follows a person being reconciled is

---

[1]Ibid.

[2]Ibid.

[3]CR 21:374.

[4]Ibid.

[5]Ibid.

[6]CR 21:430.

[7]Ibid.

pleasing "because the person on account of another is
pleasing, i.e., on account of Christ (propter Christum)."[1]

The person, not the work, is acceptable to God and
pleasing due to the mediator. That inchoate obedience,
states Melanchthon, no matter how far removed from the perfection of the law, is nevertheless "approved because the
person" is reconciled by faith in Christ (in Christum).[2]

The function of the mediator for Melanchthon is not
only paramount here, but quintessential. Neither the person
nor the works are pleasing or acceptable to God without the
mediator. Those who do not believe in Christ are not forgiven
their sins. The impious or those who "do not obtain
(apprehendunt) the remission of sins through trust in Christ
(fiducia Christi) have mortal sins and are condemned
(damnantur), even if they do not have disgraceful external
action."[3] For Melanchthon, Scripture is clear on this point,
for John 3:18 states that he who "does not believe is condemned because he has not believed in the name of the only
born Son of God."[4] Further, John 3:36 states that he who
believes in the Son has eternal life, whereas he who does
not believe "will not see life, but the wrath of God remains

---

[1]Ibid.
[2]CR 21:425.
[3]CR 21:447.
[4]Ibid.

upon him.[1] Thus, the sole mediatorship of Christ is guarded
by Melanchthon to the end.

Works are necessary and are pleasing to God, but
they contribute nothing towards justification. Melanchthon
reiterates that the condition of fulfilling the demands of
the law in no way brings about the promise of the Gospel.
That promise is not due to the fulfillment of the law, but
rather to "grace on account of Christ."[2] It is the "promise
of the remission of sins or of reconciliation or of justification" which the Gospel proffers.[3] The benefits offered are
certain or assured, which would not be the case if the
benefits promised were contingent on our works' fulfilling
the law. Therefore, remission, reconciliation, or justification
is conferred (donatur) "not because of our worth (non propter
nostram dignitatem)."[4] It is fitting (oportuit), nevertheless,
that there be some "victim (victima) for us."[5] Therefore,
Christ was given to us and made a sacrifice (hostia) on account
of whom we surely would stand pleasing before God the Father.[6]

---

[1]Ibid.

[2]CR 21:414.

[3]Ibid.

[4]Ibid.

[5]Ibid. On victima see Niermeyer, Lexicon, pp. 1096-
1097.

[6]CR 21:414.

Corrupt works can be pleasing to God. On account of
the sacrifice of Christ for us and the gratuitous favor of
God, those who receive the assured remission of sins may do
works that, while corrupt, are acceptable to God. Even he
who does good works can anticipate an increase in spiritual
gifts. Melanchthon says that he agrees with Augustine when
he states that love "merits an increase in love."[1] The keynote
pertaining to these good works, for Melanchthon, is that they
are works of the righteous.[2] For one must first receive "by
faith the remission of sins, reconciliation and the
acceptance in eternal life" and those are granted by mercy
propter Christum.[3]

Those corrupt works can be pleasing to God, not due
to any amount of works, but "after we are reconciled by
faith."[4] It is therefore "necessary for the reconciliation
of the person to precede" works that are acceptable.[5]
Because reconciliation is due to the mercy of God and not
our own personal worth obedience that is pleasing follows
"because we are in Christ" (quia sumus in Christo).[6]

---

[1] CR 21:434.

[2] Ibid.

[3] Ibid.

[4] CR 21:431.

[5] Ibid.

[6] Ibid.

The Meaning of Faith in the Loci of 1535

The meaning of faith, as expounded in the Loci of 1535, becomes clear when Melanchthon explains what he means by justification. By the term "justification," Melanchthon intended to signify, in the Loci of 1535, "the remission of sins, reconciliation, or the acceptance (acceptatio) of the person to eternal life (ad vitam aeternam)."[1] That which is "received" comes from without, therefore justification, Melanchthon defines as essentially a forensic act. For the Hebrews "to justify is a forensic word," just as Scipio, when reprimanded by the tribune, was "absolved or pronounced just" by the Roman people.[2] In like manner, the righteousness of the Christian comes from without and our "worth or purity is no cause of the remission of sins."[3]

If works or personal worth do not contribute to justification, then with Paul, states Melanchthon, faith "signifies without a doubt trust in the promised mercy propter Christum."[4] Melanchthon does not rule out the historical-knowledge interpretation of faith, but he does side with Paul's understanding.[5] A trust in the promised

---

[1] CR 21:421.

[2] Ibid.

[3] CR 21:422.

[4] Ibid.

[5] Ibid.

mercy on account of Christ readily refers to that article
of faith, says Melanchthon, which recalls the historical
Christ and the benefits due to his deeds.[1]

Paul, says Melanchthon, actually brings together
"the promise of grace and faith and requires faith, which
apprehends the promise."[2] Further, this "faith is a trust
(fiducia) in mercy."[3] The nature of the trust is, however,
that its object is not personal worth, but the "trust in
benefits from outside, namely, those of Christ."[4] Faith,
therefore, "has its correlative in mercy just as if it were
its object."[5] When it is stated that we are justified by
faith (fide iustificamur), then the relation of faith to its
correlative is understood. That is, we are justified by the
promised mercy due to Christ, "but this mercy is apprehended
by faith."[6]

Paul's understanding of faith, for Melanchthon,
pertains specifically to that which is received, that
accepted from the gratuitous giving of God through the promise
of Christ. The Scholastics, says Melanchthon, do not speak

---

[1] Ibid.

[2] Ibid.

[3] Ibid.

[4] Ibid.

[5] CR 21:423.

[6] Ibid.

of a person being justified by grace in this manner. They
do not speak of a trust in mercy, but "they idly think that
a man is pronounced righteous on account of personal worth,
that _novitas_, or personal purity."[1]

Abraham's faith, as described by Paul in Romans 4:3,
is indicative of the nature of faith Melanchthon attempts to
propose. There, Paul states that Abraham believed in God and
it was reckoned (_imputatum est_) to him as righteousness.[2]
Melanchthon notes then that Scripture affirms that Abraham
was pronounced righteous because he believed "not on account
of personal worth," but because of the mercy promised.[3]
Melanchthon further quotes Paul (Romans 4:5) as saying that
it is not one who does work, "but he who believes in him who
justifies the impious, whose faith is reckoned as righteousness."[4] For Melanchthon, the ready conclusion is that "faith,
that is, trust in mercy, opposes our worth" or dignity.[5]

Even though fully examined in a later section dealing
with systematic arguments of Melanchthon on good works, a
definition of faith is touched on that may be brought up here.
Melanchthon responds to the view that faith is a work and so

1
  Ibid.
2
  CR 21:425.
3
  IBid.
4
  Ibid.
5
  Ibid.

we are actually justified by works. He agrees that faith
is a work.[1] He states, however, that like other works or
virtues (love, patience, chastity), faith is imperfect.
Therefore, it is not due to the dignity of faith that we are
righteous, but due to the mercy of God received.[2] Faith itself
then, is "an instrument" by which the mercy of God promised
because of Christ is apprehended.[3]

In the previous Loci and in the Apology, Melanchthon
turned his attention to the well-disputed definition of
faith as affected by the passage James 2:24 concerning works.
Once again he considers the matter, and here in the Loci of
1535 he treats the passage and provides his own understanding
of faith.

The passage in James (2:24) states that man is not
justified by faith alone but by works. Melanchthon attacks
the controversy head on when he states that if James means
"faith" to signify the knowledge of history and the meaning
of faith in verse 19 is that demons believe, then there is
no controversy.[4] James does speak of the righteousness of
works, but never in connection with the remission of sins.
Paul understands faith to be "the trust in mercy which

---

[1] CR 21:443.

[2] Ibid.

[3] Ibid.

[4] CR 21:439.

receives the remission of sins" and frees the conscience
from the terrors of sin.[1] This kind of trust one cannot
attribute to the Devil. If James understands faith as Paul
then there is no problem, for _fiducia_ is not the same as
notitia.

Melanchthon admits that both kinds of righteousness
are necessary, "the righteousness of faith and the righteousness of works."[2] The latter, the justice or righteousness
of good works, is not that righteousness which is able to be
set against the wrath of God and "it is not pleasing unless
it is in the reconciled."[3]

First, we receive the remission of sins and become
justified persons, accepted by mercy on account of Christ,
because of faith and not because of any dignity or worth of
our obedience.[4] Afterwards follows obedience that is
righteousness which is, "pleasing to God."[5] There is no
confusion when the saying in Romans 4 concerning faith and
works is understood in this manner.[6] We "are justified by

---

[1]Ibid.

[2]Ibid.

[3]Ibid.

[4]Ibid.

[5]Ibid.

[6]Ibid.

faith and works," that is, "both _iustitia_ are required."[1]
This means that the righteousness of faith and the righteousness
of works are both required.

Melanchthon finds James' phrase easy to understand;
it depends upon the meaning of "being justified." James
does not speak of faith and works as if "the remission of
sins or reconciliation" follows.[2] We are justified, and
"having faith and works is to have righteousness and both
are required."[3] Paul, he says, clearly speaks of the
remission of sins and by this he understands justification
to be the remission of sins, and reconciliation or that
receiving or acceptance before God. People are accepted
before God and this depends on his mercy.[4] Works do not
establish acceptance; rather, that depends on God's
gratuitousness. Such a position leaves the conscience
unsettled, destroys faith and obscures the glory of Christ.[5]

Melanchthon readily professes that there is a need
for contrition. Contrition, however, no matter how worthwhile,
does not merit the remission of sins. One must have faith

---

[1]CR 21:439-440.

[2]CR 21:440.

[3]Ibid.

[4]Ibid.

[5]Ibid.

that sins are forgiven by grace propter Christum.[1] The
faith Melanchthon proposes is not that which believes
something is so. It is not enough to believe (credere); the
Devil believes that God exists and that "there is in the
Church the remission of sins."[2] Melanchthon intends faith
as trust (fiducia) in another, a special faith to which is
applied the benefit of Christ (beneficium Christi).[3]

The Gospel preaches penance and promise which the
mind is not able to grasp by natural means.[4] Due to God's
Son sins are remitted and we are pronounced righteous, that
is received, and given the Holy Spirit and eternal life. If
we merely believe (credamus), the remission of sins is ours,
and we can be assured (confidamus) that this will be granted
us propter Christum.[5]

Finally, Melanchthon comes to his understanding of
faith by its relatedness to the active conscience of the
person. Faith "is not able to exist with an evil conscience
because faith is trust (fiducia) that God" is gracious towards
us.[6] The evil conscience is the one which judges precisely

---

[1] CR 21:491.

[2] Ibid.

[3] Ibid.

[4] CR 21:415.

[5] Ibid.

[6] CR 21:432.

the contrary, that trust is not there. Those "who do not
do penance," but indulge in wicked pursuits "do not retain
faith."[1] The faith Melanchthon speaks of "seeks the remission of sins, it does not delight in sin."[2] The Holy Spirit
does not remain in those who submit to wicked affections
"for as John (1 John 3:8) indicates: 'He who does sin is of
the Devil.'"[3]

For Melanchthon faith is: a trust in the promised
mercy of righteousness which comes from without. It is not
simply an historical knowledge, correlatively related to
mercy as though its object. Faith is opposed to our worth
or dignity, an instrument by which God's mercy is apprehended,
an assurance that God's mercy will be granted to us on account
of Christ. This type of faith does not exist in sinners.

Rewards for Works in the Loci of 1535

Even if we do honest works, they amount to sins. If
such works are sins, asks Melanchthon, why do them? If works
are necessary, then is doing evil necessary? The answer is
that God desires us to be obedient to his will and he even
rewards our labors. God grants to "those who truly believe
corporal and spiritual rewards in this life and after this

---

[1] Ibid.

[2] Ibid.

[3] Ibid.

life."[1]

When it comes to the unbelievers we "are not Stoics,"
says Melanchthon, who held that "all sins are equal."[2]
For Nero sinned more than Pomponius Atticus even if we
understand that God is properly judge. God "does require
external honest works which are called works of the law."[3]
He requires them on account of human tranquility among ourselves and for the purpose of discipline.[4] As Paul indicates
in Galatians 3:24: "The law is a pedagogue (paedagogus)."[5]
God rewards or honors this pedagogue or custodian with
"excellent corporal rewards, and on the other hand he punishes
a violation of the external law with serious corporal and
eternal penalties."[6]

The heroic virtues of unbelievers witnessed down
through the ages, as those of Xenophon, Themistocles, Fabio
and Scipio, are great acts of the spirit. Even though they
are not the most true and proper works of God, they "certainly
are not a thing of evil."[7] Therefore, this righteousness of

---

[1]CR 21:386.

[2]Ibid.

[3]Ibid.

[4]Ibid.

[5]Ibid.

[6]Ibid.

[7]CR 21:387.

the flesh (iustitia carnis) has its own reward and men
should know, says Melanchthon, "that God requires it and
provides it with rewards."[1]

The various precepts of the Ten Commandments show
us that God desires obedience and indicates that he punishes
those who abuse his commands and desire to live a wicked
life. Punishments are verified by "the law of nature and
experience."[2] The law of nature itself recognizes that God
"imparts rewards for good deeds and penalties for bad."[3]
This judgment "abides among all people."[4]

The works Christians do, for Melanchthon, are more
than rewarded by God, for they act as beacons of witness to
the faith. Melanchthon even calls them "true and most
praiseworthy sacrifices."[5] Perhaps the Christian would be
more zealous and courageous in works if he knew that his work
was a "most gracious sacrifice to God."[6] This could provide,
says Melanchthon, a means whereby one is able to judge one's
calling or vocation.

Christ himself admonishes us when he says (Matthew

---

[1]Ibid.

[2]Ibid.

[3]Ibid.

[4]Ibid.

[5]CR 21:433.

[6]Ibid.

5:16) "Let your light shine before men so that they may glorify your Father, who is in heaven."[1] Christ not only exhorts us to pursue good actions which will stand out to others, but he even praises our employment (officia) and says that by it we glorify God.[2]

Good deeds are actually the gifts of the Holy Spirit, and it is the impious person who fails to recognize and give thanks for works to the author and source. The pious person readily makes it known that good works, which stand out for all to see, are gifts of God and gives praise to God. Melanchthon likens them to the "plants of the Lord set out" for glorifying, as told in Isaiah 17:10.[3]

Being from God, good works, says Melanchthon, may even be called "sacraments, that is, signs of the will of God."[4] As such they even merit, not eternal life, but they "merit corporal and spiritual rewards."[5] Even though rewards are imparted in this life, they are also granted after this life. Christ says: (Matthew 5:12) "your reward is great in

---

[1] Ibid.

[2] Ibid. On the meaning of officia see Niermeyer, Lexicon, Pp. 737-738. Various meanings from Niermeyer include: household ministry, personnel, retinue, craft, craftguild, and official.

[3] CR 21:433.

[4] Ibid.

[5] Ibid.

heaven."[1] Further, Paul states (1 Timothy 4:8) that "piety
holds the promise for the present life and the life to come."
Therefore, God praises and rewards our works in this life
and fittingly praises and bestows honors in the future life.[2]

God honors each according to his works, but he "does
not approve works unless they are of the righteous."[3]
Melanchthon understands praiseworthy works to come from those
who are righteous by God's grace. Those who are justified
before God by faith can provide good works that are pleasing
to God and "merit favor (merces)."[4] God calls for us to do
good works often, and those works "in the pious are a true
worship of God."[5]

A problem arises, for Melanchthon, when one speaks
of the reward of eternal life as though it were owed due to
some act.[6] To refer to eternal life as reward is not, however,
to say that it is granted because of "the dignity of our
works."[7] The promise of eternal life is not offered because
of the worth of works, nor because of the fulfillment of the

---

[1] Ibid.

[2] CR 21:433-434.

[3] CR 21:434.

[4] Ibid.

[5] CR 21:544.

[6] CR 21:442.

[7] Ibid.

law, but because of Christ (_propter_ _Christum_), to those who
"embrace [God's] mercy by faith."[1] Wherefore, when eternal
life is called "reward, the manner [intended] is taken from
the law."[2] For the law speaks of the justice or righteousness
of our worth and promises reward based on work and merit.
Yet, for the Gospel, justification and the gift of eternal
life are received due to the mercy of God _propter_ _Christum_
and by faith, not on account of the worth of our works.[3]
Even when Scripture indicates that evil is punished and worthy
moral works are rewarded, eternal life is dependent on another
cause [Christ] as reward.[4]

Melanchthon holds that our works do not act as cash
on hand which is readily spent to purchase a treasure, for
even if works are a duty, they are duly compensated. It is
just like the son of a family who attains his inheritance
because of another cause (_propter_ _aliam_ _causam_), and yet his
duty (_officia_) is rewarded.[5] This is not to interpret the
meaning of reward so that the benefit of Christ is transferred
to our works; that would simply leave the conscience in a

---

[1] Ibid.
[2] Ibid.
[3] Ibid.
[4] CR 21:442-443.
[5] CR 21:443.

state of desperation.[1]

Syllogistic Arguments in the Loci of 1535

Melanchthon introduces his section of syllogistic arguments on justification and works by presenting the contention that we are righteous by faith: "Faith is a work, ergo we are righteous by works."[2] Melanchthon responds to the major proposition by indicating that we are righteous by faith, "not because it is a work or qualitas in us, but because it receives (accipit)" the mercy of God.[3] This is more intelligible, says Melanchthon, when the correlative of faith is used.[4] We are righteous by faith, that is, "we are pronounced righteous by [God's] mercy," but it is received or accepted by faith.[5] The minor proposition is true to the extent that "faith is a work."[6] It is like other works or imperfect virtues, such as charity, patience, and chastity; thus "faith is imperfect."[7] This does not mean that it is due to the "worth of faith that we are righteous,

---

[1]Ibid.

[2]CR 21:443.

[3]Ibid.

[4]Ibid.

[5]Ibid.

[6]Ibid.

[7]Ibid.

but because faith accepts [God's] mercy."[1] Faith "is an
instrument, by which the mercy promised propter Christum is
taken hold of (apprehenditur) ..."[2]

The second syllogism proceeds as follows:
Righteousness is obedience to the whole law; good works are
the [perfect] obedience to the law; therefore good works are
righteousness (iustitia).[3] The minor proposition here is
denied by Melanchthon; for good works are not perfecta
obedientia to the law because, as Paul states, the nature
"of the flesh is not able to obey perfectly the law of God."[4]
We would be righteous and justified, if "we perfectly obeyed
the law."[5]

The major proposition states that the righteousness
of the law is "obedience to the entire law, but because of
this we do not distinguish ourselves," therefore the Gospel
graciously offers us justification.[6] This means an "imputation
of righteousness" which we receive by God's mercy and not due

---

[1]Ibid.

[2]Ibid.

[3]The editor must have omitted perfecta from: Bona
opera sunt obedientia erga legem for that is the crux of
Melanchthon's argument. See CR 21:443.

[4]CR 21:443. The editor indicates this to be Romans
7:8, but there is little doubt that it is little more than a
paraphrase of Paul's theology.

[5]Ibid.

[6]Ibid.

to the "worth of virtues."[1] In Paul, states Melanchthon, and in other places, righteousness is perceived in like manner.

The third syllogism pertains to the proper meaning of righteousness and of faith. "Righteousness (iustitia) is in the will; faith is not in the will; ergo faith does not justify."[2] Melanchthon agrees with the major proposition in that the righteousness of the law, which means our obedience and virtues, is in the will. When one speaks, however, of the righteousness of or by faith, "righteousness means the imputation of righteousness or the receiving," for God graciously receives or accepts us not because of our qualities or worth, but because of Christ.[3] This faith is not only a knowledge, but "even the wish for and the accepting of (velle et accipere)" the promised mercy.[4] Moreover, this trust or fiducia is "a habit of the will by which we anticipate and accept the promised help."[5] Faith (fides) is then this trust (fiducia).[6]

The fourth syllogism proceeds as follows: "Works

----

[1] Ibid.

[2] CR 21:444.

[3] Ibid.

[4] Ibid.

[5] Ibid.

[6] Ibid.

against the law are sins, therefore good works are just.
Consequently, those who do good works are justified."[1]
Melanchthon's response is that the conclusion, "they are
justified who do good works," would be true "if we were
able to satisfy the law. Good works, then, would be righteous
and justify."[2] Since, however, men do not satisfy the law
and are not without sin, then it is necessary "to seek
another, namely, the mercy [of Christ], by which we are
pronounced righteous."[3]

The contention of this syllogism is that the
remission of sins "depends on the condition of penance, therefore it is conditional."[4] Melanchthon, however, denies the
outcome of considering the remission of sins as being conditional, for when we speak of conditional here "we understand
the condition of our worth."[5] Otherwise, we do concede, he
states, "that the promise has the condition of penance and
that an actual change from sin is necessary."[6] The condition
of that change, however, does not alter our worth. No matter
how many works we perform, that certain disposition adheres

---

[1] CR 21:444.

[2] Ibid.

[3] Ibid.

[4] Ibid.

[5] Ibid.

[6] Ibid.

to the soul. The promise is made uncertain if it depends
on the change in our worth. Sins are remitted even if
concupiscence and the state (<u>affectus</u>) of our corruption
adheres to and remains with men.[1]

As Paul states in Romans (4:15), the law brings
wrath.[2] It should be clear, says Melanchthon, that we
cannot attribute justification to our contrition because
contrition itself can bring eternal death unless we are
freed by faith from the terrors it sets up for us.[3] "If the
remission [of sins] depended on the worth of contrition,
more and more would the conscience" be hurled into a death,
because it would see that no matter what it did it would never
make itself worthy of the remission of sins.[4]

Contrition is required by Melanchthon, but any inherent
dignity possible is transferred to another. Such is the case
as "we consider the nature of law and work."[5] Any given
precept of the law has its place in condemning and hating
sin; it does not justify but brings death. There are a
great number of witnesses to the fact that the law does not
justify nor vivify men, but a "work is a consolation which

---

[1]Ibid.

[2]CR 21:445.

[3]Ibid.

[4]Ibid.

[5]Ibid.

faith brings."[1] Even so, that which faith brings to bear, namely, contrition and mortification, "is a sacrifice and pleasing to God."[2]

Melanchthon's use of syllogisms, certainly indicates that he is developing a Christian philosophy. This is revealed by a comparison between the number of lectures he gave on scriptural and philosophical topics between the years 1518-1521 and 1534-1541.[3] This may clarify the development of the doctrine of works between these two periods.

From 1518 to 1521 Melanchthon lectured on Paul's letter to Titus once, Matthew once, Romans three times, Corinthians twice, Colossians once, the Psalms once, Homer twice, Plutarch once, Pliny once, Lucian once, and logic and rhetoric once.[4] Thus, scriptural topics were examined nine times during lectures, while "philosophical" topics were examined six times.

From the period of 1535 to 1541, covered by the Loci of 1535, Melanchthon lectured on Romans three times, Colossians once, Cicero five times, Sophocles once, logic three times, Quintillian once, Ptolemy four times, Homer

---

[1]Ibid.

[2]Ibid.

[3]The earlier dating is that of the Loci of 1521 and the second is that of the Loci of 1535. Note that in the Loci of 1521 Melanchthon condemns syllogisms, whereas he later develops extensively that method of argumentation.

[4]See CR 28:6-76; Karl Hartfelder, Philipp Melanchthon als Praeceptor Germaniae. (Berlin: A. Hoffmann and Co., 1889; reprint ed., Nieuwkoop: B. DeGraaf, 1964), pp. 555-557.

once, Livy once, Isocrates twice, Euripides twice, Aristotle twice, Demosthenes twice, and Ovid once.[1] Thus, scriptural topics were examined in lectures four times, while philosophical or classical topics and authors were examined a total of twenty-five times.

Drawing on Melanchthon's increased interest in philosophy, it is easy for us to see why syllogisms have become (in the period 1534-1541) a more important part of Melanchthon's theologizing on the doctrine of good works.

Conclusion

During the period of 1534 to 1541, controversy was a major impetus in the shaping of Melanchthon's doctrine of good works. In 1534 Melanchthon still held that remission of sins is achieved by faith *propter Christum*, that the righteousness proper to good works is necessary, that obedience is pleasing to God, and that the Holy Spirit does not remain in those who commit mortal sins.

The impact of the controversy with Cordatus shows the importance of the understanding of faith, for Cruciger

---

[1]Hartfelder, idem., pp. 560-561. On the relationship between philosophy and theology see Siegfried Wiedenhofer, *Formalstrukturen humanistischer und reformatorischer Theologie bei Philipp Melanchthon.* (Frankfurt/M. und München: Peter Lang GmbH, 1976), pp. 110-129. He was particularly anxious about the antinomian positions of John Agricola and James Schenk. See CR 3:390-391, 410-411, 416-417, 419-421, 426-427, 428-430, 447-448, 452-454, 458-459, 459-460, 462-463. Melanchthon was very concerned about the possible influence of the Anabaptists. See CR 2:710-713, 889-890, 955, 1003-1004, 1005-1006; CR 3:11, 14-17, 201-202, 214-215; CR 4:734-735.

maintained that "our contrition is called <u>causa</u> <u>sine</u> <u>qua</u>
<u>non</u>, because faith is not able to exist without it."[1]
Melanchthon was careful to explain his own involvement.
He readily described how so much was being said about that
newness infused into the soul; as a result, he even more
emphasized an imputative grace. The causal significance
between works and salvation had been removed. As a result,
the constant repetition of an ethical mandate involving
works became necessary in order to avoid the possibility
that works might be abandoned altogether.

The most unexpected statement of a follower of Luther
comes when Melanchthon states that good works are necessary
for salvation. Throughout this period others were interpreting Melanchthon as espousing two causes for salvation,
Christ and works. For Melanchthon, there is still only one
cause, Christ, but once a person is justified it would be
unthinkable for him <u>not</u> to develop a new spirituality and
obedience. It is not that the consequential character of
works provides any cause for salvation, but that the state
of being justified <u>necessarily</u> brings about those consequences;
otherwise it would not exist. Being justified is a cause of
works, but works are not a cause of being justified.

The doctrine of works, in the <u>Loci</u> of 1535, is most
accurately characterized by enlisting the aid of the following

---

[1]CR 3:160.

categories: the necessity of works, the worth of works,
causes for doing good works, the natural law as cause, the
moral law as necessary, corrupt works as pleasing, the
meaning of faith, the significance of rewards, and analytic
or syllogistic arguments.

Accentuating the importance of the natural means
of knowing, even to calling it a "vestige of God" is no small
development in Melanchthon's thought.   Just as mirrors or
images of the divine are present to the human mind, he says,
so is a knowledge of the law of God.   Even though darkened
by original sin the perception of that law is still possible,
and the mind still perceives with certainty practical principles whereby the lex naturae is known.

Melanchthon brings to the defense of natural reason
such distinguished witnesses as Cicero, Xenophon, and Hesiod.
The natural reason, or the judgment of reason, which the
philosophers call the law of nature, Melanchthon equates
with the Decalogue.   We are freed by the Gospel from the law,
but the moral law remains, and it calls us to obedience
before God.   A natural law or moral law directs the person
to obey God.   We are freed from the curse of the law, but
not from obedience to the moral law.

The establishment of natural reason, natural
judgment, or natural law is an important correlative to the
increased emphasis on imputative justice and the moral
mandate.   The reasons for the moral mandate Melanchthon now

reveals from reason and natural knowledge.

Melanchthon did not deny the existence of a natural
law in earlier works, but he was more wont to consider man
"depraved."[1] He stated that the virtues derived from
natural reason are outer masks and that "our pseudo-theologians
tricked by a blind natural judgment have commended us to
philosophic studies, virtues, and the merits of external
works."[2] In an earlier work, Melanchthon while despairing
of the influence of philosophers and the incapacity of reason,
even attacks Aristotle. "The teaching of Aristotle is
universally a fanciful dispute, so that it would not be
proper to count him among the lowest together with the horta-
tory writers."[3]

The denial of the possibility of merit gave cause
for Melanchthon to push the necessity of works or they might
have been considered totally superfluous. Concurrently the
increase in Melanchthon's interest in classical thinkers,
natural knowledge and natural law gave rise to the unifica-
tion of the Decalogue and the moral mandate. In both
instances there exist juxtaposed, concurrent, interrelated
themes which bring Melanchthon from philosophy to works,
and from the doctrine of imputation to works. In the first

---

[1] CR 21:101: "... hominem pravum esse." This is from
the Loci of 1521.

[2] CR 21:100.

[3] CR 21:101.

case Melanchthon goes from philosophy to natural law,
then to moral law, then to moral mandate, followed by works.
In the second case Melanchthon goes from the doctrine of
imputation to the denial of merit, then to moral mandate,
and he finally arrives at works.

Within this 1535-1541 period the definition or
refinement of justification as the imputation of righteousness
and the nonimputation of sins appears to have been more
settled than in the previous Loci, the Commentary on Romans,
and the Apology. The shift is not away from the doctrine
of imputation, but with that doctrine the necessity of good
works is emphasized.

Along with this shift, the differentiation between
person and works is not as fully treated as in the previous
works. The inability of works themselves to establish the
person as righteous is not taken for granted, but once
accepted the causes for doing those very works are examined
more thoroughly within this period.

The pacification of the terrified conscience gives
rise to the softer exhortation that works, though unable
to justify, can be and are pleasing to God.

Finally, Melanchthon's understanding of reward is
further defined within this later period. Rewards, in and
after this life, are freely granted as an inheritance to
a son. The son's deeds did not merit the rewards, but they

are granted, graciously given on account of the deeds and
sacrifices of another.

CHAPTER IV

THE DOCTRINE OF GOOD WORKS IN
THE INTERIMS AND THE LOCI OF 1559

Introduction

From 1541 through 1550 Melanchthon was to undergo
his most difficult years in his relations with the Catholics
in conciliatory colloquia, but more especially because of
the attacks he suffered from within the Evangelical party.
Throughout these years, even up to his death, Melanchthon
served in two capacities: one was a mediator attempting
to establish unity and peace, the other was a theologian
attempting to systematize what he considered to be the
essence of the Evangelical position. The Diet of Worms (1541),
the Regensburg Diet (1541), the Augsburg Interim (1548), the
Leipzip Interim (1548), and the assembly at Celle (1548),
all reveal Melanchthon's understanding of "works" in controversy. Even though twenty-five editions of the Loci of 1559
were printed between 1543 and 1559, a concurrent, and some-
times varying, exposition of works is found within these
colloquia. When forced into a conciliatory role with
Catholics, Melanchthon accepted positions that would not be
integrated into his more systematic treatsies composed during
these years.

During a Diet held in Worms in January 1541 a number

176

of issues, notably the sacraments and original sin, were
debated by Eck and Melanchthon without any real evidence
of agreement. As a consequence, discussion of these
issues was deferred to another meeting to be held in Regensburg. The emperor selected Eck, John Gropper, and Julius
von Pflug to represent the Catholics and John Pistorius,
Martin Bucer, and Melanchthon to represent the Evangelicals.
Their task was to discuss particular articles of religion
in an attempt to arrive at some agreement. Shortly after
the proceedings began on April 27, Granvella, acting on
the part of the emperor, presented the delegates with the
Regensburg book, which they were to use in establishing
principles to be agreed upon.[1]

---

[1]After the Edict of Worms of 1521 the emporer took
a more conciliatory tact and attempted to negotiate a unity.
He pursued peaceful means, but eventually he became frustrated
and decided to use force. One reason he had not used armed
force soon after 1521 was the formation of the potentially
powerful Schmalkaldic League. On the Regensburg Diet see
Peter Matheson, Cardinal Contarini at Regensburg. (Oxford:
Clarendon Press, 1972). Theodor Brieger, Gasparo Contarini
und das Regensburger Concordienwerk des Jahres 1541. (Gotha:
Perthes' Buchdruckerei, 1870). Hubert Jedin, A History of the
Council of Trent. Translated from the German by Dom Ernest
Graf O.S.B. 2 vols. (London: Thomas Nelson and Sons Ltd.,
1957-1961). Walter Lipgens, Kardinal Johannes Gropper
(1503-1559) und die Anfänge der katholischen Reform in
Deutschland. (Reformationsgeschichtliche Studien und Texte,
No. 75. Münster in Westfalen: Ashendorff, 1951). Manfred
Rosenberg, Gerhard Veltwyck: Orientalist, Theolog und
Staatsmann. (Wiesbaden: Friedmann, 1935). W. Schenk,
Reginald Pole: Cardinal of England. (London: Longmans,
Green and Co. 1950); Robert Stupperich, "Der Ursprung des
'Regensburger Buches' von 1541 und seine Rechtfertigungslehre,"
(Archiv für Reformationsgeschichte, 36, 1957), pp. 88-116.
Eva-Maria Jung, "On the Nature of Evangelism in Sixteenth
Century Italy." (Journal of the History of Ideas, 14 1953),
pp. 511-527.

For discussion on the most important issue between the two camps, de iustificatione hominis, both Eck and Melanchthon decided not to use the book given them as a directive, but to debate openly the nature of justification. They did come to an agreement on the article which proposed the gratuitous nature of justification and the unity between faith and love.[1]

The document attempts to mediate both the Catholic and Evangelical positions, and propose something in between. It attests to the fact that we are reconciled by only one mediator, Christ. Additionally it asserts that we are freed from slavery to sin and "made sharers of the divine nature and sons of God (efficimur consortes divinae naturae et filii Dei)."[2] Being an adopted son means, not only the remission of sins, but the imputation of righteousness (imputationem iustitiae) as well.[3] What is actually proposed, then, is a theory of double justice.[4]

---

[1] The text is found in CR 4:198-201.

[2] CR 4:199.

[3] Ibid.

[4] The doctrine of double justice was a theory of justification which combined the notion of an inherent righteousness with that of an imputed righteousness. The inherent righteousness is imperfect and must be complemented with imputed righteousness. The imputed righteousness of Christ perfects any inherent righteousness. K. Rahner, LThK[2] 3:514-515. H. Jedin, Papal Legate at the Council of Trent: Cardinal Seripando. Trans. by F. C. Eckhoff. (St. Louis: B. Herder Book Co., 1947). Hubert Jedin, Studien uber die schriftstellertatigkeit Albert Pigges. (Munster i.W.,: Aschendorff, 1931), Josef Henninger, S. Augustinus et doctrina de duplici justitia. (Saint Gabriel: Sanckt

Faith and charity are not separated. However, to
be justified by faith (accepted by and reconciled to God)
means that "righteousness is imputed to us on account of
Christ and his merits not because of the work or perfection
of that righteousness imparted to us by Christ."[1] That
righteousness which is _imparted_ is not perfect without that
righteousness which is _imputed_. Thus, the sharing of the
divine nature, by participation, does not justify.

The righteousness the Christian receives from Christ
is even something that inheres with him. We are justified
by faith in Chrsit or "reputed righteous, that is, received
because of his merits and not because of our worth or works."[2]
Further, "we are said to be righteous because of this inhering
righteousness" since we are just who do just works as John
said: "He who does righteous things is righteous."[3]

In the reborn there should always be an increasing
"fear of God, penance, _humilitas_, and other virtues . . ."[4]
Those who do true penance by faith will stand most certainly
pleasing to God on account of Christ the mediator.[5]

Gabrieler Studien, 3, 1935). P. Pas "La Doctrine de la double
justice au concile de Trente," (Ephemerides Theologicae
Lovanienses 30, 1954), pp. 5-53. Carl E. Maxcey, "Double
Justice, Diego Laynez, and the Council of Trent," Church
History 48 (1979):269-278.

[1]CR 4:200.

[2]CR 4:200.

[3]Ibid.

[4]Ibid.

[5]Ibid.

Good works, the document states, "both internal and external are commanded and praised by God. Further, throughout Scripture, God promises rewards (mercedem) on account of Christ . . ."[1] God bestows goods, both corporal and spiritual, in this life, and after this life in heaven (post hanc vitam in coelis).[2] Those who do greater and more works do so "because of an increase in faith and charity," and they believe those works to be the very exercise of their faith.[3]

Whoever maintains, states the document, that "we are justified by faith alone (sola fide iustificamur) should also propose the doctrine of penance, of the fear of God, of the judgment of God, and of good works" so that the proclamation of penance and the remission of sins will continue in Christ's name.[4]

On June 24, Melanchthon presented an assessment of the overall conference and the Regensburg book.[5] He confesses that the treatise on justification is actually pleasing neither to Eck nor himself.[6] After a period of reflection

---

[1] CR 4:201.
[2] Ibid.
[3] Ibid.
[4] Ibid.
[5] CR 4:413-419.
[6] CR 4:414.

he composed an opinion on the book which appeared in October

1541.[1] Therein, he states that for the reasons given "I

conclude upon the Word of God and with good conscience that

I cannot and will not receive this book, and I pray God

the Father of our Lord Jesus Christ that he will grant

us good counsel and help . . ."[2]

The Interims

In addition to the dissolution of the Schmalkaldic

League, during the Schmalkald war, the hope for any unity

over doctrinal principles was vanquished. The emperor,

however, asked John Agricola, Julius von Pflug, and Michael

Helding to prepare a document which would, at least tempor-

arily, unite the Catholics and Evangelicals. The Diet at

Augsburg accepted the document in May 1548, and it came to

be called the Augsburg Interim.[3] Among its twenty-six

articles it granted the chalice to the laity, and the

marriage of priests, but it enforced episcopal rule, the

seven sacraments, the pope as interpreter of Scripture,

---

[1]
CR 4:419-431.

[2]
CR 4:430. "Aus diesen erzählten Ursachen schliesse
ich auf Gottess Wort und mit gutem Gewissen, dass ich diess
Buch nicht kann, auch nicht will annehmen, and bitte Gott,
den Vater unsers Herrn Jesu Christi, er wolle uns allen
guten Rath and Hülfe verleihen, und seine Kirchen, die er
durch seinen Sohn zum ewigen Leben erlöset, und wunder-
barlich erhält, schützen und regieren."

[3]
Melanchthon's judgments are found in CR 6:839-842;
842-845.

transubstantiation, and the invocation of saints.

Melanchthon was open to accepting certain adiaphoristic principles of the document, but no more. Even so, Christopher von Carlowitz, one of Elector Maurice's counselors, demanded that he accept it. Melanchthon answered on April 28, 1548.[1] He stated that he is open to certain issues within the Interim, but he does not want to be involved in any basic alteration of Evangelical doctrine. Within the text was a remark that was to lead to innumerable disagreements and questions regarding Melanchthon's intentions. He said: "Formerly I bore an almost unseemly servitude, since Luther often gave way to his temperament, in which there was no small amount of quarrelsomeness, and he did not adequately consider his personal dignity and public welfare."[2] Carlowitz showed the letter to some of his friends, who made copies and allowed the contents to become public knowledge. The Catholics were happy because it seemed to show that dissension existed within the parties of the Evangelical camp. For the Evangelicals it was an affront to Luther and to the leaders of the Schmalkaldic League.

---

[1] See CR 6:879-885.

[2] CR 6:880. "Ego, cum decreverit princeps, etiamsi quid non probabo, tamen nihil seditiose faciam, sed vel tacebo, vel cedam, vel feram, quidquid accidet. Tuli etiam antea servitutem paene deformen, cum saepe Lutherus magis suae naturae in qua φιλονεικια erat non exigua, quam vel personae suae, vel utilitati communi serviret. Et scio, omnibus aetatibus, ut tempestatum incommoda, ita aliqua in gubernatione vitia modestis arte ferenda et dissimulanda esse. Sed non modo silentium a me flagitari dicis, verum etiam suffragationem."

On December 17, 1548 the next Interim, the Celle
Interim, was accepted by Maurice of Saxony and Joachim of
Brandenburg as the norm of doctrine whereby the teaching
of their churches would stand. The Saxon theologians were
informed that they were to abide by it, but Melanchthon and
Bugenhagen both rejected it.[1] It dealt primarily with
authority in the Church, the role of the bishop, the baptism
of children, confirmation, penance, the mass, fasting, and
anointing.[2] This Interim was called the Recess of Celle
and its resolutions were presented to the deputies at the
opening meeting of another gathering in Leipzig on December
21.

These resolutions, with the addition of an article
on justification and good works composed in July by Melanchthon, became known as the Leipzig Interim.[3] Concerning the
doctrine of justification the document states: "God does
not make man just by the merit of the work which men do, but
from [God's] mercy without human merits, consequently, the
glory is Christ's and not man's; it is through Christ's
merit alone that we are freed from sin and made righteous.[4]

---

[1]
For the text see CR 7:198-221. Melanchthon's response
is found in CR 7:232.
[2]
CR 7:215-221.
[3]
See CR 7:48-64, 215-221, 258-264.
[4]
CR 7:51.

Of good works it declared that "they are necessary, for God has commanded them" as is so in the Ten Commandments, and the exhortations of the apostles to obedience.[1] Whoever lives according to faith does not sin against the conscience; whereas if one sins against the conscience, God's anger remains and one is not converted to God.[2] This is the language used by Paul when he enumerated specific sins (Galatians 5:21): "I have said to you and I say now, whoever does such a thing shall not inherit (erben) the kingdom of God (Reich Gottes)."[3] If conversion is necessary (Bekehrung nöthig sei), then one must live a converted life.[4] Where there is "no conversion, there is no grace (da ist keine Gnade)."[5] For "new virtues and good works are extremely necessary (hoch vonnöthen)" or there would not have been an awakening of the heart or the acceptance of divine grace.[6]

The document presents a dialectic between works and salvation. On the one hand it affirms that virtues, such as faith, hope, and charity "are necessary for salvation

---

[1]
 CR 7:61.
[2]
 Ibid.
[3]
 Ibid.
[4]
 Ibid.
[5]
 Ibid.
[6]
 CR 7:62.

(zur Seligkeit nöthig seyn)."[1] Good works are pleasing to
God and they obtain spiritual and temporal rewards in this
life and a further reward in eternal life.[2] On the other
hand, the error of the monks, whereby it is held that
"eternal salvation is merited through the worth of our
works" is rejected.[3] In other words, works are necessary
for salvation, but their worth does not establish or
bring about salvation.

As such, the document, along with discussions of
the mass, anointing, fasting, and the role of the bishop
in ordinations was presented for acceptance to the diet.
Melanchthon provided a qualified acceptance for he states
that in light of humanity to all and the need for moder-
ation, he approves.[4] The document was not well received
by the Evangelicals, and Melanchthon, who wrote the section
on works earlier in the year, came under severe attack.
Matthias Flacius Illyricus (1520-1565) became one of
Melanchthon's fiercest opponents. Flacius had studied
at Venice, Basel, and Tübingen. While in Wittenberg he

1
 Bretschneider's note indicates: "[zur Seligkeit]
Pez. (Christoph Pezel's edition) praetermisit, haud dubie
consilio."
2
 CR 7:63.
3
 Ibid.
4
 CR 7:291-292.

received an M.A. in 1546. During the 1547 dispersion of
the university because of the war he spent his time in
Braunschweig, but after returning to Wittenberg he again
left in protest, in 1549, over the "compromising" positions
of the Leipzig Interim. From Magdeburg, he and others,
including Amsdorf, Schnepf, Otto, and Gallas, carried
on an attack regarding those matters Melanchthon considered
adiaphoristic. As a result of this division the Gnesio-
Lutheran camp was established. Flacius accused Melanchthon
of selling out to the papists, restoring the papacy, and
installing anew the Anti-Christ.

Melanchthon insisted that there was room for interpreting adiaphoristic matters, but that the Leipzig Interim
had not basically altered any Evangelical doctrines. He
only began publicly to defend himself against the attacks
of Flacius in late 1549. He wrote to George of Anhalt in
September stating that he could more easily "bear exile
and death than this union of vipers."[1] Further, he says
that Flacius lies (mendacia) for: "I have never stated,
never written, nor ever thought what he says I said, that
this proposition sola fide iustificamur is a precise
and subtle quibbling over words (ἀκριβολογίαν καὶ
λεπτολογίαν)."[2] Flacius had attacked Melanchthon by stating

---

[1]CR 7:658.

[2]Ibid.

that Melanchthon held that it was not worth while disputing
the little word sola in the doctrine of justification.

As a result, in another September 1550 letter to
John Mathesius, one of those words Melanchthon defends
when he refers to the manifesta mendacia of Flacius is sola
fide.[1] He confesses that he has written much more in
"regard to the meaning of the exclusive particles [such
as sola] than others."[2] Not without "labor have I corrected
the opinion of others, who have not correctly interpreted
the particle sola . . ."[3]

Melanchthon was to continue to defend his part in
the Interims, but his reputation had been tarnished and he
was considered by the Gnesio-Lutherans to have colluded
with the Catholics. Violent pamphlets continued to be
sent out from Magdeburg railing against the Wittenberg
theologians, and against Melanchthon in particular.[4]

During the years 1552-1553 a controversy, revolving
around George Major, the superintendent of Mansfield, was
to surface in regard to good works. Major maintained, as
Melanchthon had done, and partly as a consequence of the

---

[1]Ibid.

[2]CR 7:658-659.

[3]CR 7:659.

[4]Even Calvin wrote to Melanchthon complaining about
the adiaphoristic controversy. See Calvin, Opera, CR 41:
593-596.

Interims, that good works were necessary for salvation.[1]
Major stated: "I have previously taught and still teach
and want to teach my whole life, that good works are
necessary for salvation; and I say openly and with clear
and plain words, that no one will be saved without good works
. . ."[2] His intent and meaning here is to hold, as
Melanchthon did, that it would be impossible for one to
have faith, and not to do good works. Faith is conjoined to
works or faith is dead.

Initially, Melanchthon chose to avoid the controversy
raging around Major, but since Major was identifiable as
well within the ranks of Melanchthon's followers he eventually had to respond. Finally, in 1553, he wrote an opinion
or sententia on the proposition that good works are necessary
for salvation.[3] When it is said "that a new obedience is
necessary for salvation," remarks Melanchthon, the papists
understand this to mean "that good works merit salvation."[4]
This proposition is false and yet it is commonly said that
"the new obedience is necessary by reason of formal cause;

---

[1]
See Robert Kolb, "Georg Major as Controversialist:
Polemics in the Late Reformation." (Church History 45, no.
4, Dec. 1976), pp. 455-468.

[2]
From: Auff des Ehrenwirdigen Herren Niclas von
Ambsdorff schrift, so itzundt neulich Mense Nouembri Anno
1551 wider Georgen Maior oeffentlich im Druck ausgegangen.
Antwort George Maior (Wittenberg: Rhau, 1552), lvs. Cv-Cijr.
Quoted by Kolb, "George Major . . ." (Church History 45, no.
4, December 1976), p. 459.

[3]
CR 8:194.

[4]
Ibid.

as for example, when I say the wall is necessarily white
by reason of whiteness."[1] Paul, being reborn, "living by
a new life, lives formally by this very newness."[2]
The parallel for Melanchthon is that the "form" of whiteness
is what makes the wall white ; the "form" of newness is what
makes Paul reborn.

"Necessary can mean [good works] are demanded by
force. Good works in the angels and in Mary, however,
are not to be understood as being demanded by force.
Further, this meaning is not intended in the statement that
good works are necessary. This understanding would be a
farmer's explanation [i.e. naive]."[3]

To clarify the necessity of works, and yet
to distinguish his position from Osiander's emphasis on our
newness (novitatem), in 1553 Melanchthon writes concerning
our obedience and our newness.[4] Man's righteousness
is that new obedience which the Holy Spirit effects
in us through charity and other virtues.[5]

---

[1]
Ibid.
[2]
Ibid.
[3]
Ibid.
[4]
CR 8:195.
[5]
Ibid.

Osiander maintained that there was a righteousness from God
that inhered in us. Melanchthon conceded that this
novitatem is present in the saints (*sanctis*), and that God
causes his righteousness to dwell within the Christian
(*inhabitationem*).[1] Because of this newness, however,
"man does not have the remission of sins and reconciliation";
first, that remission and reconciliation must be received
by faith, because of the mediator between God and man.[2]

During the years that the *Loci* of 1559 was being
composed, and then going through various printings, and
while Melanchthon was involved in various colloquia, the
shape or tone of his doctrine of works did not actually
move away from the proposition that works are necessary
for salvation.[3] On the one hand, he was willing to grant
this proposition for conciliatory purposes, but he would
not relinquish his theory of imputative righteousness, nor
would he permit the theory of merit. He was of the opinion
that, by reason of formal cause, one could hold that works
are necessary for salvation, without interpreting this
as merit. He did say that the expression "necessary for
salvation" was not used in the churches because of that

---

[1] Ibid.

[2] Ibid.

[3] As has been the opinion of some, see: Kolb,
"Georg Major: Polemics . . ." (*Church History* 45, no. 4,
December 1976), p. 459 note 13. Martin Greschat, *Melanchthon
neben Luther. Studien zur Gestalt der Rechtfertigungslehre
zwischen 1528 und 1537.* (Witten: Luther-Verlag, 1965)

interpretation, namely, merit. He did not maintain that
the proposition could not be held, but that a certain meaning
must be avoided.[1] In December 1557, or early 1558, he wrote
that the expression "new obedience is necessary" was to be
held, but that the "for salvation (ad salutem, zur Seligkeit)"
was not needed because of its misinterpretations as merit.[2]
He did not maintain that the ad salutem was incorrect
doctrinal teaching, but only that it would be prudent to
avoid it because of its misinterpretations. On the other
hand, his Evangelical cohorts could see that by insisting
on the necessity of works, Melanchthon was actually
moving closer to just such an idea as merit. Although
people like Flacius were heavily burdened with the
concern for doctrinal purity, Melanchthon could see the

---

[1]See CR 8:411-412. "Aber diese Proposition:
gute Werke sind nöthig zur Seligkeit, ist in unsern
Kirchen nicht gebraucht. Denn diese Deutung ist zu
fliehen; gute Werke sind verdienst der Seligkeit."

[2]CR 9:407. "Wiewohl nun diese Proposition
festzuhalten ist, nova obedientia est necessaria, wie
gesagt ist: so wollen wir gleichwol diese Worte: ad
salutem, zur Seligkeit, nicht daran hängen, weil dieser
Anhang gedeutet wird auf das meritum, und würde die
Lehre von der Gnade verdunkelt; denn dieses bleibe wahr,
dass der Mensch vor Gott gerecht und Erbe ewiger Seligkeit
sey au Gnaden, um des Herrn Christi willen, allein durch
Glauben."

problem in his own imputative doctrine, which would not need any works at all.[1] As a result, Melanchthon was developing a doctrine of good works somewhere between merit and imputation with no works.

Introduction to the Loci of 1559

Along with colloquia, battles with Eck, arguments with Agricola and Flacius, during the years 1543 until his death in 1560, Melanchthon was busy with the systematizing of his thinking in twenty-five editions of a Loci. These editions have come to be known simply as the Loci of 1559.[2]

---

[1] Melanchthon does say the expression "necessary for salvation " pertains particularly to antinomian thinkers. CR 9:405: "Von dieser Proposition: Gute Werke sind nöthig zur Seligkeit, zu reden, haben erstlich Ursache geben die Antinomer, das ist, die Lästerer, welche schreyen, dass der Mensch könne Glauben haben und gerecht seyn, wenn er gleich in Sünden wider Gewissen, in Ehebruch, Todtschlag lebt." For Melanchthon it is a matter of cause and effect: "Zum andern, dass auch neuer Gehorsam nöthig sey von wegen der Folge causae et effectus, ist klar; denn der heilige Geist wird in dass Herz darum gegeben, dass dieser Gehorsam angefangen werde im Herzen und äusserlich." In a 1559 letter to John Matthesius Melanchthon remarks that: "Id detorquet Islebius (John Agricola) ad alia, quae in praeceptis mandantur. Addit horribilia epiphonemata: ex Diabolo ortam esse hanc vocem, Bona opera sunt necessaria. Tales furores puniet Deus." CR 9:902.

[2] See CR 21:562-563. The critical edition of Bret- schneider's is found in CR 21:601-1050. It is entitled: Loci Praecipi Theologici. Nunc Denuo Cura et Diligentia Summa Recogniti, Multisque in Locis Copiose Illustrati, Cum Appendice Disputationis De Coniugio. Per Philippum Melan- thonem. The treatise on marriage was published by itself in 1551, and from 1552 was appended to the later Loci. Among the authors Melanchthon cites in this Loci are: Aristotle: 729, 740, 745, 784, 934, 1011, 1018; Basil: 617, 632, 633, 658, 748, 837, 838, 851; Augustine: 669, 675, 748, 837, 841, 858, 881, 882, 918, 1039; Bernard: 748, 798, 837; Bonaventure:

669; Chrysostom: 658, 970; Cicero: 614, 648, 713, 732, 735,
763, 764, 785, 833, 834, 951, 996, 1007, 1038; Cochlaeus:
601, 1032; Cyprian: 858, 909; Eck: 601, 606, 1032; Epiphanius:
837; Eusebius: 620, 878; Gerson: 1021, 1024; Gregory of
Nazianzus: 823, 841, 1002; Gregory Neocaesariensis: 620,
836, 845; Hesiod: 745; Homer: 732, 767, 902; Hugo: 669;
Irenaeus: 622, 626, 836; James: 759, 766, 785, 786, 791;
Jerome: 663, 664; John: 604, 608, 609, 612, 615, 617, 618, 619
620, 621, 622, 623, 624, 625, 626, 627, 628, 630, 631, 632, 633
636, 638, 645, 648, 657, 658, 660, 661, 664, 666, 671, 677,
680, 682, 685, 691, 694, 698, 717, 731, 732, 734, 735, 738,
741, 743, 746, 749, 751, 753, 754, 760, 762, 764, 766, 767,
769, 770, 775, 776, 780, 782, 783, 788, 790, 792, 796, 798,
814, 820, 821, 824, 833, 837, 845, 846, 848, 850, 856, 860,
872, 873, 875, 885, 899, 900, 903, 913, 914, 915, 916, 920,
921, 922, 925, 939, 948, 956, 957, 959, 974, 982, 984, 1022,
1037, 1040, 1043; Lombard: 610; Luke: 648, 656, 660, 664,
666, 674, 675, 697, 700, 707, 711, 734, 741, 744, 747, 761,
768, 796, 799, 824, 836, 840, 849, 850, 863, 865, 875, 876,
880, 884, 891, 899, 911, 916, 917, 922, 923, 948, 958, 959,
964, 973, 993, 1004, 1012, 1014, 1027, 1036, 1037, 1048;
Marcion: 606, 634, 635; Mark: 605, 676, 719, 754, 778,
854, 863, 963, 1013; Matthew: 616, 618, 624, 628, 630, 639,
648, 660, 676, 685, 686, 690, 691, 693, 696, 699, 702,
707, 708, 720, 721, 723, 724, 726, 727, 744, 747, 749, 760,
761, 770, 773, 778, 782, 792, 793, 797, 808, 811, 815, 820,
824, 835, 839, 840, 841, 849, 851, 856, 858, 859, 861, 863,
867, 868, 869, 878, 879, 880, 881, 885, 892, 893, 894, 895,
900, 911, 915, 916, 919, 921, 923, 925, 937, 939, 943, 945,
946, 958, 959, 961, 970, 976, 997, 1014, 1015, 1020, 1027,
1031, 1032, 1033, 1034, 1036, 1037, 1040, 1042, 1044, 1047,
1048, 1049; Occam: 673; Origen: 622, 623, 741, 748, 857,
858, 932, 933, 1002, 1007; Paul: 602, 606, 607, 608, 613,
615, 616, 618, 621, 624, 625, 626, 631, 632, 639, 641, 645,
646, 647, 648, 649, 654, 655, 656, 657, 658, 659, 662, 663,
667, 669, 670, 672, 673, 675, 676, 678, 682, 683, 686, 687,
692, 693, 694, 700, 703, 705, 707, 708, 710, 712, 713, 716,
717, 718, 719, 720, 724, 725, 728, 730, 733, 734, 735, 736,
738, 740, 741, 742, 745, 746, 747, 749, 750, 751, 752, 753,
754, 755, 756, 757, 758, 759, 760, 761, 762, 763, 764, 765,
767, 769, 771, 772, 773, 775, 776, 778, 780, 781, 782, 783,
784, 785, 787, 789, 790, 791, 792, 793, 798, 800, 801, 804,
807, 808, 811, 812, 816, 817, 818, 819, 820, 821, 822, 824,
825, 827, 833, 834, 837, 838, 839, 841, 842, 844, 846, 847,
850, 853, 856, 857, 858, 859, 860, 863, 864, 866, 868, 869,
874, 875, 878, 879, 880, 881, 882, 883, 884, 885, 889, 890,
891, 892, 902, 903, 904, 906, 907, 909, 910, 911, 912, 813,
914, 915, 916, 917, 918, 921, 922, 923, 926, 928, 930, 931,
932, 933, 935, 937, 939, 940, 944, 947, 948, 949, 950, 951,
954, 955, 958, 959, 960, 961, 964, 969, 970, 975, 976, 980,
982, 984, 991, 992, 993, 999, 1001, 1004, 1007, 1009, 1010,
1013, 1014, 1017, 1019, 1020, 1021, 1022, 1023, 1024, 1026,

This is the largest of the three _Loci_ treated here and the most systematic. In the _Loci_ of 1559, the predominant themes pertaining to the doctrine of good works are: 1) obedience is necessary; we are created for good works, and inchoate obedience is necessary in the reborn, and the reborn life is to be one of outward confessions of faith; 2) three causes of work are necessity, dignity, and rewards; 3) remission of sins is not due to our worth or merit; 4) the human condition is sinful; 5) there are two kinds of righteousness, human and divine; 6) works of the reborn are pleasing to God; 7) because of man's good works, God grants him rewards both during and after this life; 8) the meaning of faith is correlative; 9) the personal response to natural knowledge is one reason for doing good works; 10) good works are required by natural law; and 11) the largest, most thorough section is the one in which Melanchthon sets up eighteen syllogisms to deal with particular themes pertaining to the doctrine of good works.

1027, 1028, 1031, 1032, 1035, 1036, 1038, 1039, 1041, 1043, 1044, 1045, 1046, 1048, 1049; Photiorus: 619, 623; Plato: 610, 650, 715, 744, 764, 784, 834, 951, 952, 957, 987, 996 1003; Plutarch: 732; Pygius: 606, 1018; Samosatenus: 619, 620, 623, 634; Servetus: 619, 622, 623, 837; Sophocles: 745; Tertullian: 622; Theodosius: 848; Valla: 652; Xenophon: 642, 705, 713, 735, 834. All subsequent references to CR 21, unless otherwise indicated, will refer to the _Loci_ of 1559.

The Necessity of Good Works in the Loci of 1559

The initial question concerning the status of works Melanchthon answers primarily in five ways: 1) obedience is necessary, 2) works necessarily ought to follow reconciliation, 3) the Christian is created for good works, 4) an inchoate obedience is necessary in the reborn, 5) the Christian life is an outward confessing of the faith.

Both natural philosophers and the Church, testify that God "is eternal mind (mens), and the cause of good in nature."[1] In addition, says Melanchthon, it is known that God is of a spiritual essence; he is understanding, eternal, wise, good, righteous, and the creator.[2] As creator of all good things, God has created order in nature, and in human nature "a fixed order, that is, for a proposed obedience."[3] Philosophers, prophets, and apostles verify the existence of a mandated obedience. Samuel (1 Samuel 15:22) tells us that "it is better to obey than to sacrifice."[4] Hosea (6:6) has it: "I desire

---

[1]CR 21:610.

[2]Ibid.

[3]Ibid.

[4]CR 21:690.

mercy more than sacrifice."[1] Further, for Christ to say
(Matthew 22:39) that we are to love one another, and this
is like the first command to love God is "to demand a
necessary obedience," just as obedience is demanded in
the first command.[2] Works, then, are a "true worship of
God"; additionally, all works of the commandments, in a
sense, refer back to the first precept of loving God above
all things.[3]

Whatever the precepts, Melanchthon understands
the new life to be just that, a new life, a new attitude,
a real conversion. So this regeneration is not present
as John (3:3) says, unless one is born anew.[4] For this
conversion or new life, "it is necessary for a new obedience
to follow . . ."[5] This new obedience Melanchthon postulates
immediately after (postquam) the exposition of the doctrine
of reconciliation and faith; they cannot be separated.[6]
Our obedience, he says, or "the righteousness of a good

---

[1]Ibid.

[2]Ibid.

[3]Ibid.

[4]CR 21:760.

[5]Ibid.

[6]CR 21:702.

conscience, or works, which God enjoins upon us,
necessarily ought to follow reconciliation (necessario
sequi reconciliationem debet)."[1] Christ clearly preaches
penance and Paul says (Romans 8:12): "We are debtors, we
do not live according to the flesh."[2] He also tells us
(1 Corinthians 6:9) that fornicators, adulterers, idolaters,
etc., will not be able to inherit the kingdom of God.[3] Thus
philosophers, prophets, apostles, and Christ himself admonish
us to obedience.

Another reason for doing good works, Melanchthon
appropriates from Ephesians 92:10), where it is written
that we are God's work "created in Christ Jesus for good
works, which God prepared for us to walk in."[4] According
to Melanchthon, this passage provides both a doctrine
that is to be held as necessary and one that offers
consolation. First of all, it is "by necessity, when it
states that we are created for good works."[5] Secondly, God
prepares good works for the Church; he "calls and rules

---

[1]Ibid.
[2]Ibid.
[3]Ibid.
[4]CR 21:762.
[5]Ibid.

and preserves" the Church, and he works in us.[1] By God

preparing works in the Church, it is protected and made

stable. We "understand our calling" therefore, and the

fact that we ought "to do the works prepared by God."[2]

The external tasks prepared by God are to be ful-

filled, but interior tasks, or works are also to be fulfilled.

For instance, it is not only external works of the

Decalogue that are to be done, for even unbelievers do

like things.[3] Rather, we are also to possess an inchoate

interior obedience.[4] Such "interior works" pertain especially

to the first precept of the Decalogue: "To believe in the

Word of God, to fear God, and to trust in God."[5]

To follow the Decalogue and to abide by its precepts,

even though sin remains in the Christian, means "that it

is necessary for there to be an inchoate obedience in the

reborn . . ."[6] It would be almost impossible, according to

Melanchthon, for one who is reborn, and who lives this new

----

[1]
  Ibid.
[2]
  Ibid.
[3]
  CR 21:763.
[4]
  Ibid.
[5]
  Ibid.
[6]
  CR 21:768.

life, not to live it out in act. Human nature is so con-
stituted, that it must share with others. Interrelation-
ship is necessary. Consequently, in human life there is
conversation, communication, and confessing or proclaiming.[1]
So even if "we are righteous propter Christum by faith,"
that is accepted or received for eternal life, nevertheless,
"it is necessary for this novitatem to follow . . ."[2]
This is the very reason Paul states (Romans 10:10) that
man believes in his heart and is justified, confesses and
is saved.[3] For the righteous there is a conversion in this
life which, at the same time, is the inchoatio novitatis.[4]
When God intends for us to confess our faith, he means for
our "entire lives to be a confession."[5]

To be a member of the Church, one is to confess one's
faith, such a confession is desired by God. As a member
of the people of God, the Christian invokes God for himself
and others and offers sacrifices; "all kinds of good works
are ordered by God."[6]

---

[1] CR 21:773.

[2] Ibid.

[3] Ibid.

[4] Ibid.

[5] Ibid.

[6] CR 21:777.

A category used by Melanchthon in explicating the
performance of those good works is that of "the righteousness
of good conscience."[1] The person who does good work acts
according to a good conscience within whom is present the
Holy Spirit, and as one of the reconciled he acts out the
faith. This is so, for those who fall into wrongs (ruunt in
delicta) which are against the conscience, it is certain that
they do not remain in grace, nor retain faith, righteousness,
or the Holy Spirit.[2] The true invocation of God is not able
to exist with the bad conscience, which only flees from God.
Melanchthon quotes 1 John 3:21: "If our hearts do not condemn
us, we have trust in God."[3] The principle to be maintained,
then is "that it is necessary in the reconciled for there to
be a righteousness of the good conscience (bonae conscientiae)
as is said in 1 Timothy 1:5, the greatest "command is to love
from a pure heart, a good conscience, and by faith."[4] For
Melanchthon, one who does those good works will have a good
conscience; it can be no other way. Melanchthon also quotes
1 Timothy 1:18: "Wage an honest warfare, having faith and a
good conscience."[5] The good works performed by the reconciled
are the "testimony of our conscience" (2 Corinthians 1:12).[6]

---

[1] Ibid.

[2] Ibid.

[3] Ibid.

[4] Ibid.

[5] Ibid.

[6] Ibid.

As in the previous <u>Loci</u>, Melanchthon here uses the
language of fittingness (<u>oportere</u>) when speaking of the need
for works. In a passage dealing with the gratuitousness of
God's grace, he states that "it is fitting for there to
exist in us penance, and there ought (<u>debere</u>) to follow
good works"; however, the remission of sins is granted on
account of a mediator, and not because of our worth or
dignity.[1]

Another phrase Melanchthon uses with this "ought"
characteristic, which is stronger than the "fittingness"
of works, is the phrase "new obedience necessarily ought
to follow (<u>necessario</u> <u>sequi</u> <u>debet</u> <u>nova</u> <u>obedientia</u>) . . ."[2]
He does not wish to exclude penance, but at the
same time he does not want it to be held as causally
related to the remission of sins. For, "surely penance is
necessary, but the cause for the remission of sins is not
transferred to our <u>dignitatem</u>, but to Christ."[3] Thus, the
remission of sins is not due to our contrition, or the
condition of our works; as is written in Ephesians 2:8:
"By grace you are saved, it is a gift from God, it is not
from you."[4]

---

[1]
 CR 21:783.
[2]
 CR 21:877.
[3]
 CR 21:890.
[4]
 Ibid.

Finally, Melanchthon tells us that this necessary obedience should constantly increase, so that the true worship of God is differentiated from the purely human observations. The "call to good works and universal obedience are owed to God" and should increase with the confession of faith.[1] To confess the faith is to obey and that obedience which God deems necessary must be heeded. God commands this confession, says Melanchthon, as Matthew 10:32 indicates, Christ tells us that "he who confesses me before men, I will confess him before my Father in heaven."[2]

Three Causes for Doing Good Works in the Loci of 1559

Not only does Melanchthon tell us that works are necessary, but he points out, in addition to ancillary reasons three specific causes for doing good works. Of these causes for doing good works, Melanchthon singles out what he considers to be the most important three: necessity, dignity, and reward.[3] The first, necessity, bears many faces, for works are commanded (mandati), owed (debiti), revealed for the maintenance of faith (retinendae fidei), and performed

---

[1]CR 21:908-909.

[2]CR 21:1036.

[3]CR 21:775.

in order to avoid penalties.[1] It would not be proper,
says Melanchthon, to say that necessary means compulsion
or coercion, even though the _ordinatio_ of God concerning
works is eternal and immutable, and God desires that his
creatures obey.[2] This command is clearly present in the
Scriptures. Paul states (Romans 8:12) that "we are debtors
to God, not to the flesh."[3] Christ says (John 13:34) that
"you love one another," and in 1 Thessalonians 4:3 it is
written that "this is the will of God, your sanctification;
that you abstain from fornication, that you each take a
wife" in honor and sanctification, and not according to the
flesh as the heathens who do not know God. God "does not
call us to uncleanness, but to sanctification."[4]

The necessity of doing good works also applies to
the need of retaining faith. The Holy Spirit is rejected
when the Christian sins against the conscience.[5] 1 John
3:7 indicates that "he who sins is from the Devil."[6]
Romans 8:13 also shows that if you mortify the deeds of the

---

[1] Ibid.
[2] Ibid.
[3] Ibid.
[4] Ibid.
[5] CR 21:775.
[6] CR 21:776.

flesh with the Spirit you will live, while "if you live according to the flesh you will die."[1] Faith, then, is not able to exist in those who indulge in sins or do not follow penitence.[2] That which offers the conscience peace, namely, faith, cannot exist when things are done against the conscience, because the deeds of a good conscience are the very means whereby faith is retained.[3] As Paul says (Romans 14:23), all "that is not from faith is sin."[4]

Works are also held by Melanchthon to be necessary, in that they help in avoiding penalties for sins. The history of the world provides evidence for all to see, that sins are punished. Even though, says Melanchthon, we suffer currently for our present sins, this does not correspond to the "eternal anger of God," but acts as testimony of the coming judgment.[5] God reminds us to await the judgment of another when things eternal, not things perishable, will be considered. Our eternal judgment should be that which is evinced from the day to day sufferings that we bear.[6]

---

[1]
 Ibid.
[2]
 Ibid.
[3]
 Ibid.
[4]
 Ibid.
[5]
 Ibid.
[6]
 Ibid.

Worth or dignity is also a reason which Melanchthon
proposes for doing good works. This does not mean that
Melanchthon attributes worth to virtues, nor does he believe
that because of the worth of virtues a person obtains
the remission of sins, satisfies the law of God, and receives
the reward of eternal life.[1] He says that we stand pleasing
to God because of Christ (propter Christum) and by faith.[2]
Because of the mediator, God desires that there be a Church
in which he is invoked and where obedience, because of the
Son, is called sacrifice. This sacrifice is honored and
rewarded by God.[3] As Peter says (1 Peter 2:5): "offer
spiritual sacrifices."[4] The "worth [is] of a calling, not
of a person (dignitas vocationis non personae), just as a
magistrate or apostle, who does great works," ought to
know that works are great things by which God directs life
and "grants eternal life (dat vitam aeternam)."[5]

The third and final reason, in this section, for
doing good works is reward (praemia), which can be merited
by those works. Melanchthon says that the remission of

1
  CR 21:777.
2
  Ibid.
3
  Ibid.
4
  Ibid.
5
  Ibid.

sins and reconciliation is given through grace on account of
the Son of God (propter filium Dei gratis), and is assured.[1]
It is made uncertain, however, "if it depends on the condition of our merits."[2] After reconciliation, good works
are pleasing by faith on account of the mediator (propter
mediatorem), and "merit spiritual and corporal rewards in
and after this life (merentur praemia spiritualia et
corporalia, in hac vita, et post hanc vitam)."[3]

The scriptural evidence is there, says Melanchthon,
for in Matthew 25:29 it is clearly stated in a parable, that
to whomever has more more will be given. In 1 Timothy
4:8 it is said that "piety holds the promise for the present
and the future life."[4] Mark 10:30 indicates that some
"will receive a hundredfold in this life, but with tribulation, and after this eternal life."[5] Like reward is indicated by Matthew 10:42, when it is written that whoever gives
to the little ones a cup of water because he is a disciple
"will not lose his reward."[6] Further, Luke states (6:38),

---

[1] CR 21:777-778.
[2] CR 21:778.
[3] Ibid.
[4] Ibid.
[5] Ibid.
[6] Ibid.

that if you give, "it will be given to you."[1]

The Old Testament also makes known rewards for
good works, as when it states (Exodus 20:12) that one should
honor one's "father and mother, so that you may remain long
upon the earth."[2] Isaiah 33:16 also states, that his "bread
will be given to him, and his water made certain."[3] It is
seen, says Melanchthon, that God intends for there to be
order in the world. "For obedience and good works he [God]
grants a tranquil state" and an honest and peaceful governing thereof.[4] Thus, the Scriptures, both Old and New
are full of such testimonies "to the promise of spiritual
and temporal rewards."[5]

The giving of reward, however, must always be seen
in light of the gracious giving of God; it is a gift. All
gifts, more especially the gift of eternal life, are freely
given by God. Our virtues do not merit, or achieve the
reward of eternal life, for that is granted propter
mediatorem.[6] Christ said (John 6:40) that this is the will

---

[1]
  Ibid.
[2]
  Ibid.
[3]
  Ibid.
[4]
  Ibid.
[5]
  Ibid.
[6]
  Ibid.

of the Father, that "all who see the Son and believe in him have eternal life."[1] These words pertain especially to pious persons who practice true _poenitentia_, for eternal life is granted only because of the mediator.[2] "Just as the experienced conscience is easily able to judge, faith is not able to rely on two things, the mediator and our merit."[3]

Melanchthon's Refutation of Merit in the Loci of 1559

This experienced conscience recognizes the need for good works, nevertheless, it is fitting that it bear the burden of human sin. The burden, the accusation however, is such that the human conscience alone cannot bear it. That is why Paul tells us (Romans 4:16), that the promise rests on faith, "so that through grace the promise is assured."[4] It is necessary, says Melanchthon, to hear the gospel message proclaiming that our inability to fulfill the demands of the law will not condemn us, but that faith and grace will save us. "If the promise of reconciliation depended on the condition of the law," then the promise itself would be uncertain.[5] It is fitting, however, that

---

[1]
 Ibid.
[2]
 Ibid.
[3]
 Ibid.
[4]
 CR 21:754.
[5]
 CR 21:758.

this promise to our conscience be assured. Therefore, it
is necessary to understand that the promise through grace
of the remission of sins and reconciliation, received by
faith is not because of our worth.[1]

It is known, says Melanchthon, that there are two
promises in the holy Scriptures.[2] Both of these promises
appertain to the condition of or the fulfillment of the
law, thus, they are promises of the law. "The law teaches
that God is good and merciful, but to those who are without
sin."[3] The law and human reason both teach this, for the
natural reason has the same knowledge as the law. The use
of this reason enables some persons to judge, as does God,
concerning what is sinful and what is not, that is "those
who are without sin [are able to judge]."[4] Nevertheless,
human reason itself is not able to stand pleasing to God
because of its own unworthiness and impurity. Thus, "the
law and the promise of the law, which are conditional, leave
the conscience in doubt."[5]

The actual promise of the Gospel is otherwise. It
does not have the condition of the law, that is, "it does

---

[1]CR 21:758-759.

[2]CR 21:733.

[3]Ibid.

[4]Ibid.

[5]Ibid.

not promise because of the fulfillment of the law, but
through grace on account of Christ (<u>sed</u> <u>gratis</u> <u>propter</u>
<u>Christum</u>).[1] It is the "promise of the remission of sins
or reconciliation or justification" which the Gospel
preaches.[2] Its benefits are certain and do not depend on
the condition of the fulfillment of the law. If the
situation was such that we had to satisfy the law in
order to have the remission of sins, that remission would be
hopeless. Therefore, remission, reconciliation, or justification is granted to us by grace, and not due to our own
worth or dignity.[3]

It is to be understood, says Melanchthon, that the
promise of the Gospel is that which is received by faith.
Just as Paul teaches in Romans 4:16, it is "by faith
through grace that the promise is made firm."[4] The
"particle <u>gratis</u> does not exclude faith, but the condition
of our worth, and it transfers the cause of benefits from
us to Christ."[5] Our obedience is not excluded, "only the
cause of benefits is transferred from the dignity of our

---

[1] Ibid.
[2] Ibid.
[3] Ibid.
[4] CR 21:734.
[5] Ibid.

"worth to Christ, so that the benefit is assured."[1] The
Gospel does preach penance, but in order for reconciliation
to be assured, "it teaches that sins are remitted and that
we are pleasing to God, but this is not because of the worth
of penitence or of our novitatis."[2]

God so desires for us to know and love him and be
saved, that he sent his Son as a victim or sacrifice for us.
As a result, we are freed from the law, and sins are remitted
because of Christ. We know, then, that the gift of grace
is given to us because of the Son and "not because of our
worth or our merits."[3]

According to Melanchthon, those who would consider
merits or our worth as the cause of the remission of sins,
or transfer that cause to human work, sin in two ways.[4]
First, "the wrath of God and sin are diminished, and secondly,
they deprive the Son of God the honor due him."[5] Melanchthon
says that human "blindness and concern do not understand the
magnitude of God's wrath against sin."[6]

---

[1]Ibid.

[2]Ibid.

[3]CR 21:735.

[4]CR 21:753.

[5]Ibid.

[6]Ibid.

Those who maintain that grace is given because of human merits, Melanchthon considers to have destroyed the significance of the mediator. They would hold that human disciplines are pleasing, and they would understand Christ to be a teacher of that same discipline, or a legislator, whereas, he is actually a victim for sin. As John says (John 1:29), he is "the Lamb of God, who takes away the sins of the world."[1]

Yes, says Melanchthon, we must do good works. The condition they provide, however, is not that which would (depending on them as cause) provide us with certainty regarding the remission of sins. One of the reasons for this is God's anger at sin, and the subsequent need for a mediator. The remission of sins and reconciliation is available because of God's Son "the mediator by faith."[2] The magnitude and power of God's wrath we are unable to comprehend. Further, we are not able to sustain that wrath, "unless God mitigates it with his immense mercy because of his Son."[3] "Human nature is not able to bear the wrath of God and his righteous penalties," as Isaiah says (38:13): "Like a lion he breaks all my bones."[4] Likewise, it is

---

[1] Ibid.

[2] CR 21:770.

[3] Ibid.

[4] Ibid.

written in Job 9:13: "God, whose wrath no one is able to
withstand (cuius irae nemo resistere potest)."[1]

       According to Melanchthon, the Psalms provide adequate
evidence that works are not able to oppose the wrath of God.
Even as Paul cites from the Psalms, the Psalmist (31:5) says:
"I said, I will confess my injustice to my Lord, and he will
forgive the iniquity of my sin."[2] Psalm 142:2 indicates that
"no one living is justified in your sight."[3] Further, it is
stated in Psalm 50:4 that "Against you only am I a sinner,
so that you are justified in your judgment."[4] These
scriptural citations verify, for Melanchthon, the fact that
no personal worth enables us to approach God on our own.
No such righteousness of ours, or "our merits are able to
oppose the judgment and wrath of God," but we take refuge
in the mediatorem Christum, and are received as righteous
because of grace.[5]

       The function of the mediator is paramount for
Melanchthon, since our works are not worthy of eternal life

---

[1] Ibid.

[2] CR 21:891.

[3] Ibid.

[4] Ibid.

[5] Ibid.

and do not merit. Since the remission of sins is not capable

of being merited by human act, the honor due to Christ is

justly returned to him.[1] Because of Christ, then, and not

due to any inane trust in Mosaic prescriptions, or acts

intended to fulfill the law, are we justified. It is "because

of Christ the mediator that believers have the remission of

sins, are reputed to be righteous, and are heirs of eternal

life; it is not because of circumcision, any Mosaic ceremony,

or anything like it."[2]

That attempt to fulfill the law, and thereby receive

forgiveness, was the error of the Pharisees, and merit is

the error of the papists. The inability of our personal

worth or merit to receive the remission of sins, brings us

to the one mediator. Christ as mediator is the one who

frees us from the law that entrapped the Pharisees, this

Melanchthon calls the freedom of the Christian. " We are

therefore freed from sin, from the wrath of God, from eternal

damnation, from the law accusing us, and from the condition

of merit."[3] The Son of God, the mediator, is the reason

that we receive the remission of sins and are righteous,

that is, we are pronounced so by God. It is by the Son of

---

[1]
  CR 21:1019.
[2]
  Ibid.
[3]
  CR 21:1039.

God, not by the law or our merits, that "we are reconciled
and reputed to be righteous," even if "we are far from the
perfection of the law." It is "because of Christ by
faith (propter Christum fide) that we are pronounced righteous."[1]

The Loci of 1559 and the Sinful Human Condition

We are unable to merit, or fulfill the demands of
the law, says Melanchthon, due to the sinful condition of
human nature. The proper understanding of that human
condition, before and after baptism, is indispensable
to Melanchthon's theses regarding the inability of personal
worth to merit, and the distinction between human and divine
righteousness.

According to Melanchthon, in the beginning, human
beings were created in nature with integrated affections,
such as the love of God, of parents, of offspring, the
marriage partner, brothers and sisters, and of all other men.[2]
Along with such affections, we were created with the joy of
knowing God and his design in the world, a hatred for the
Devil, a hope for eternal life, and a pure love of God
and all his heavens.[3] The Scriptures testify that Jesus

---

[1]
 Ibid.
[2]
 CR 21:676.
[3]
 Ibid.

Christ shared these very affections and loves. For us,
however, something was to happen. Since the fall, these
affections have wandered about aimlessly without any design
or purpose and have become contaminated.[1] As a result of
the fall and faith in Christ there exists the differentiation between affections, present in those who are reborn by
faith, and those who are not.

"Heroic wrath in Achilles is a good thing, because it
is truly a work of God"; however, it is contaminated,
because of its failure to recognize God, and because it does
not "brightly bear invocation and trust in God."[2] These
defects are not to be considered light sins; even if good
things, they are to be rejected.[3]

"On the other hand a similar wrath is more pure in
David who practiced recognition, fear, invocation, [and]
trust in God."[4] We all know, says Melanchthon, that affections
(στοργαs) remain in the reborn, but because they are properly ordered and integrated, they are rendered more pure.
The question remains, however, what is the state of the
human condition, even if reborn, after the fall? Even after

---

[1]
  CR 21:677.
[2]
  Ibid.
[3]
  Ibid.
[4]
  Ibid.
[5]
  Ibid.

baptism, says Melanchthon, "it is properly stated that there is sin in infants, or that concupiscence is sin."[1] It follows, then, that "it is proper to say, that in the reborn adult, there is sin."[2] As John states in the first epistle of John 1:8 if "we say that we have no sin, we deceive ourselves, and the truth is not in us."[3]

Possessing sin means that we are unable to perfectly fulfill the demands of the law. It is necessary for us to do good works, and obedience ought to increase and flourish. Even if "obedience ought to increase, nevertheless, no one satisfies the law, not even the reborn."[4] The sins which remain are forgiven, and we are reputed to be righteous propter mediatorem Christum. Christ is the fulfillment of the law (consummatio legis).[5] Because of him, we are imputed to be righteous and our inchoate obedience is considered pleasing, even if it does not fulfill the demands of the law.

The inability to fulfill the demands of the law is due to that abiding residue of original sin. According to

---

1
  Ibid.
2
  Ibid.
3
  Ibid.
4
  CR 21:693.
5
  Ibid.

Melanchthon, "the burden of sin inhering even in the reborn is much greater" than any human is possibly able to comprehend.[1] "We do not take lightly," he says, "the saying: Who can comprehend [one's] sins?"[2] There are a great many "kinds of sins which remain in the saints."[3] This contrasts, says Melanchthon, with the false teaching of the monks, who hold that these sins do not exist and deny that such sins are "things conflicting with the law of God."[4] Further, they incorrectly assume that "the reborn satisfy the law of God."[5]

The testimony is quite clear, for Melanchthon, that "the reborn do not satisfy the law of God in this life, since mortal sins remain in this nature."[6] In addition to the previously cited 1 John 1:8, Melanchthon quotes Psalm 143:2: "Do not enter into judgment with your servant, because no one living is justified before you."[7] Melanchthon considers Romans 7:23 to be of particular significance: "I see another law in my members, which conflicts with the law of my mind and makes me captive to

---

[1] CR 21:769.

[2] Ibid.

[3] Ibid.

[4] Ibid.

[5] Ibid.

[6] Ibid.

[7] Ibid.

the law of sin which is in my members."[1] According to
Melanchthon, the sophists "allude to this passage and say
that there is a metalepsin in the world for sin and actually
it (Romans 7:23) signifies either the penalty for sin (rather
that sin itself), or an inclination born from the fall of
the first parents. Paul refutes this allusion when he
defines this as sin, and says it is an evil in our members
at war with the law of God."[2]

  This human "defect which remains in nature is a
thing which combats the law of God."[3] Although, human judgment detracts from the real depravity, Paul's use of language
reveals to us the condition, as it actually exists. The
security in carnal things, the unjust diffidence, the
arrogance, the inflamed lust, the desire for revenge, all
of these "are not unimportant evils (levia mala), as human
philosophy considers; moreover, they incessantly torment
the saints . . ."[4]

  Matthew 6:12 teaches the saints to pray: "Forgive
us our debts."[5] Even in the saints there are "sins throughout this entire life, for which pardon is sought."[6]

---

[1] Ibid.

[2] Ibid.

[3] Ibid.

[4] CR 21:769-770.

[5] CR 21:770.

[6] Ibid.

This is indicated by the saying that when you have done all things, you are still an unworthy servant. Paul states, in 1 Corinthians 4:4, that he is not aware of anything against himself, "but in that I am not justified."[1] According to Melanchthon, Paul does teach that we are to have that righteousness which comes from a good conscience. Nevertheless, Paul does say that it is not because of that good conscience that, "I have the remission of sins, and am reconciled to God, but God receives me because of his Son, the mediator, by faith."[2]

Paul also teaches that for one to boast (1 Corinthians 1:3) one should boast in the Lord.[3] We "are not able to boast that we are without sin" but we boast in the Lord and his promised mercy.[4] Paul also states in Romans 11:32, that God "has confined (conclusit) everyone to be under sin, so that he may have mercy on all."[5] Also from Romans 3:9 "We said that all are under sin."[6] That inability to merit or earn by our worth is due to our feeble and weak nature. Melanchthon acknowledges "that there are sins even in the reborn . . ."[7]

---

[1] Ibid.

[2] Ibid.

[3] CR 21:771.

[4] Ibid.

[5] Ibid.

[6] Ibid.

[7] Ibid.

The Distinction Between
Human and Divine Righteousness in the Loci of 1559

In light of this abiding sinful condition of the
human race, Melanchthon distinguishes between a righteousness or justice that can be established through the aid
of reason, and that righteousness which comes not from
human disciplines, but from God.

John 16:8 has it that when God comes, he will
convince the world of matters pertaining to righteousness.
The wise, says Melanchthon, "hold that righteousness is
any kind of discipline or universal obedience, as they call
it, [which is], according to the laws."[1] The Gospel, however, brings us another kind of righteousness. "For that
human discipline does not remove sin or death, but the
righteousness before God, in which God reputes us [to be]
righteous, accepted, and heirs of eternal life, does
destroy sin and death." [2] Thus, for Melanchthon, there are
two types of righteousness, one which can remove sin and
death, and one which cannot.

The difference between these two types of righteousness is not discernible in terms of the human discipline.

---

[1]
CR 21:666
[2]
Ibid.

Melanchthon uses the distinctiveness of both Cicero and
Jeremiah as an example.[1] Jeremiah fulfilled his responsi-
bility to the political realm as well as Cicero did. The
major difference, is that the works of Jeremiah are enlivened or brightened by faith.[2] By that faith, Jeremiah stands
pleasing to God, and he praises and serves God. Because of
his faith in God, the works performed by Jeremiah do not
become an end in themselves; therefore, he does not bear
any doubt because of them. Whereas, for Cicero, works as
objects overwhelm him in the darkness of his mind, and leave
him in eternal doubt.[3]

Melanchthon states that it is "fitting for there to
be [both] a true invocation, [namely,] that of the people of
God, and the invocation of the Jews or Muslims."[4] Faith
stands as the major difference between the two kinds of
invocation. The Christian believes in, and invokes, the
eternal God "who is the Father of our Lord Jesus Christ
[who was] crucified for us [and] who rose again."[5] This
"invocation particularly established the difference between

---

[1] CR 21:764.

[2] Ibid.

[3] Ibid.

[4] CR 21:767.

[5] Ibid.

the Church and the people who disagree with the Gospel
(_Ecclesiam_ _et_ _Gentes_ _pugnantes_ _cum_ _Evangelio_)."[1]

   In 2 Corinthians 3:6 Paul calls "the law the letter
and minister of death, [and] the Gospel the minister in
spirit."[2] Paul knows that "without a knowledge of the
Gospel you only have law, or a philosophical discipline, or
terrors."[3] Such a discipline, Melanchthon calls "the
righteousness of human reason (_iustitia_ _humanae_ _rationis_),"
which is the case with both Pomponius Atticus and a
"hypocrite who has neither a true fear of God" nor a true
invocation and witness to Christ.[4] Such discipline is more
like the letter, than the spirit; moreover, "a shadow does
not bring life."[5]

   The abiding sinful condition of the human race
prevents human disciplines which are able to remove
sin and death and provide righteousness. As a result,
just as there are two kinds of invocation, Melanchthon
distinguishes between human and divine righteousness.

---

[1] Ibid.

[2] CR 21:931.

[3] Ibid.

[4] Ibid.

[5] Ibid.

Even though there is a clear difference, for
Melanchthon, between human and divine righteousness,
Melanchthon holds that works are necessary, and that
God desires our obedience. Our infirmity is such, however,
that there is "mutilation, impediments, imperfections, and
contaminations."[1] As Paul says in Romans 7:15; "I do not do
what I want, but what I would not, that I do."[2] If we sin
and do those very things that we should not, how can our
works be pleasing to God?

For Melanchthon, it must first be understood that
the reborn stand reconciled to God on account of the Son
of God (propter Filium Dei), or "the person is received due
to grace, because of the Son of God by faith."[3] Secondly,
those who are reconciled know that "in this life infirmity
and sins remain in the reborn," and they bear the sufferings
of afflictions, depravity, and perverse inclinations against
the law of God (contra legem Dei).[4] Thirdly, no matter
how far one is from the perfection of the law, it is most
fitting for there to exist an inchoate obedience in the

---

[1] CR 21:767.

[2] Ibid.

[3] CR 21:771.

[4] Ibid.

reborn, and "the righteousness of a good conscience."[1]
Moreover, God is pleased with this obedience in the reconciled
"because of the Son, the mediator, who offers our invocation,
and our worship, to the Father, and conceals [our] infirmity."[2] Thus, it is "because of the Son that the person is
first reconciled [to God] and the following works are
accepted . . ."[3] As Peter says in the first epistle of
Peter 2:5: "Offer spiritual sacrifices, acceptable to God
through Jesus Christ."[4]

The faith spoken of, Melanchthon considers to
operate actually in two ways. It is by faith in the Son
that works are pleasing, and it is faith that asks for
help when it comes to performing those works.[5] David knew
that impediments and dangers existed which would threaten
his governing, "but he believed God was pleased with his
labors because of the promised mercy."[6] David asked for
help, and did the best he could in defense of his people
and directed civil morals as much as he could. It is when
the pious person attempts to obey God, and then sees the

---

[1] Ibid.
[2] Ibid.
[3] CR 21:771-772.
[4] CR 21:772.
[5] Ibid.
[6] Ibid.

problems, the privation, the darkness of nature, that he falls into desperation. Melanchthon endorses the saying of Paul (Romans 8:1) that there is "no condemnation for those who walk in Christ Jesus. This means that even if the reborn are not without sin, God accepts them and pronounces them righteous" because they believe in his Son.[1] As a result, God also "accepts their obedience because of [his] Son."[2]

Christ is referred to as the consummation of the law. Even if "the reborn have not yet satisfied the law, nevertheless, they are righteous and pleasing to God because of [his] Son."[3] Melanchthon says that there is reason for great rejoicing, because this inadequate, imperfect, sordid, and "contaminated obedience is received, not because of the worth of our virtues, but on account of the Son of God."[4]

Paul indicates in Romans 6:14 that you are "not under the law, but under grace."[5] Then is obedience pleasing when it does not satisfy the law? Paul responds

---

[1] Ibid.
[2] Ibid.
[3] Ibid.
[4] Ibid.
[5] Ibid.

that it is pleasing, "because we are not under the law, that is, not condemned by the law, but under grace, that is, reconciled or received in grace."[1] He also asks (Romans 8:34), "who can condemn us?"[2] "Christ died for us, rose, he is at the right [hand] of God, and intercedes for us, therefore, the saints are pleasing because of the intercession of Christ."[3]

The invocation of the heathen, the Jews, and the Muslims, Melanchthon also separates, as works, from the invocation of the Christian who believes and trusts in the promise. "For invocation does not please God, unless it is done by one who acknowledges, and has trust in Christ, the mediator, as it is written (John 16:23): Whatever you ask the Father in my name," that is, understanding that this naming is witness to the mediatorial function, "he will give to you."[4]

Contaminated works are not pleasing to God. For Melanchthon, the person is not considered pleasing, until received by God, because of the Son. Subsequently, works done by a person, cannot be accepted until that person is accepted. Only after the person is reconciled, through

---

[1]Ibid.

[2]Ibid.

[3]Ibid.

[4]CR 21:636.

Christ by faith, are works accepted, and in fact, are pleasing to God. Due to the intercession of the Son, contaminated obedience is accepted and pleasing to God.

The Loci of 1559 and the Possibility of Meriting Rewards

Obedience is acceptable, and even pleasing to God even if we remain far from fulfilling the demands of the law.[1] Not only does God accept or receive works, "but he even provides this sordid obedience with honor and rewards."[2] God advocates and admonishes us to do many good works, and he adds his promise of divine help and rewards.[3]

The ministry of the Church, Melanchthon considers to be spiritual, namely, the conversion of the heart to God, and true spiritual renovation.[4] "This merits the mitigation of penalties, for it is a worship pleasing to God."[5] Melanchthon does not mean that we are able to merit the mitigation of penalties without contrition and without faith; for works without fear and without faith are not the worship of God regardless of how wonderful they are.[6] As Paul tells us (Romans 7:6), we serve in a new

---

[1] CR 21:773.

[2] Ibid.

[3] CR 21:779.

[4] CR 21:910.

[5] Ibid.

[6] Ibid.

spirit, not under the old code; but according to a true
conversion of the heart, and not simply according to
external role and ritual.[1]

Christ had said, give and it will be given to you.
For Melanchthon, the promise is added to this saying of
Christ's for two reasons. First of all, "we know that the
generosity of the pious person merits rewards"; secondly,
we know that God insists on this officium in order that our
"faith be engaged in the expectation of rewards."[2] Thus,
the deeds of those who have faith, and are righteous, can
merit rewards.

The proper understanding of cause is most important
for Melanchthon. The remission of sins and reconciliation
are granted because of Jesus Christ, and not because of
works; therefore, reconciliation is assured. "It would be
uncertain if it depended on the condition of our merits."[3]
Works do not bring about reconciliation, but are subsequent
to reconciliation. When done by the reconciled, works are
pleasing to God, and they "merit spiritual and corporal
rewards in and after this life."[4]

---

[1]Ibid.

[2]CR 21:725.

[3]CR 21:777-778.

[4]CR 21:778.

Melanchthon substantiates his position concerning the
meriting of rewards by turning to Scripture. Matthew 25:29
indicates that to whomever has more will be given. 1 Timothy
4:8 states: "The pious have the promises of the present and
the future life."[1] Mark 10:30 has it, that they "receive a
hundredfold in this life, but with tribulation, and after
this eternal life."[2] Matthew 10:42 attests to the fact
that one who gives even a cup of water to one in need, will
not lose a reward. We are also told (Exodus 20:12) to honor
our fathers and mothers, "so that you may remain long on
the earth."[3] Thus, Scripture admonishes us to perform good
works; moreover, it is indicated that works merit both
present and future rewards. Scripture, says Melanchthon,
is full of references to the "promise of spiritual and
corporal rewards."[4] Both, he considers, to be necessary
in this life. One is not able to retain faith without its
exercise and one, namely God, cannot preserve the Church
without spiritual rewards. We are to exercise or practice
our faith, and we are invited to "earnestly work for rewards."[5]

---

[1]
Ibid.
[2]
Ibid.
[3]
Ibid.
[4]
Ibid.
[5]
Ibid. See also CR 21:946, 969.

Melanchthon states that the works we are to perform include the following: penitence, the fear of God, faith, invocation, confession, patience, chastity, temperance, and diligence in one's calling.[1] God wishes us to follow these virtues, which he "compensates and honors with great goods," such as more light or spiritual wisdom, the confirmation of faith, resoluteness, consolation, peace, and the necessities of life. Furthermore, after this life [these virtues] will be given eternal rewards (post hanc vitam praemia aeterna dabuntur)."[2]

The Meaning of Faith in the Loci of 1559

In order to understand why Melanchthon (in the Loci of 1559) defends rewards for good works, but denies merit, it is necessary to understand what he means by justification and especially what he means by faith.

According to Melanchthon, "justification means the remission of sins and reconciliation or the acceptance of the person for eternal life."[3] For the Hebrews "to justify (iustificare) is a forensic verb. As I said: the Roman

---

1
CR 21:1028.
2
Ibid.
3
CR 21:742.

people justified Scipio who was accused by the Tribune, that
is, [he was] absolved or pronounced righteous."[1] Paul takes
the meaning of the word justify from the Hebrew use meaning
"the remission of sins, and reconciliation or being received."[2]
Melanchthon does hold that when God remits sins, "at the
same time he gives the Holy Spirit [and] new inchoate virtues.
Nevertheless, the frightened person first of all seeks the
remission of sins and reconciliation."[3] In another place
within the Loci, Melanchthon also refers to this forgiven
state and concludes: " . . . that through grace because of
the Son of God is given the remission of sins, reconciliation,
justification or the imputation of righteousness, and the
acceptance for eternal life . . ."[4]

When Paul states that we are justified by faith, "he
wishes for you to look to the Son of God seated at the right
of the Father. The mediator [by] interceding for us, causes
your sins to be remitted so that you are made righteous,
that is, accepted, reputed, or pronounced[righteous] because
of that same Son who was victim."[5] The word faith does not

---

[1]
  Ibid.
[2]
  Ibid.
[3]
  Ibid.
[4]
  Ibid.
[5]
  CR 21:743.

simply mean, as indicated in the last _Loci_, "a knowledge of history, but it means a trust in the mercy promised because of Christ."[1] For Melanchthon, this proposition must always be "understood correlatively: By faith we are righteous, because of a trust in mercy, on account of Christ are we received, and not because of our virtues."[2] Thus, for both Paul and Melanchthon, faith corresponds to or is correlative to the function of a mediator or propitiator by means of whom, or on account of whom, we are accepted as righteous.

Faith, for Melanchthon, may have two primary meanings, a trust (_fiducia_) in promised mercy or a knowledge (_notitiam_) of history.[3] In both instances, faith is that which looks to Christ, who is acknowledged as the eternal Son of God, who was crucified for us and rose from the dead. Historical knowledge can avow the effect of the sacrifice of Jesus and state: _Credo remissionem peccatorum_.[4] The same statement of article can also be attested by a person with trust or faith (_fiducia_). For Melanchthon, the major difference is that the profession of the statement is essentially frustrated when one does not believe that one's

---

1
 Ibid.
2
 Ibid.
3
 Ibid.
4
 Ibid.

sins are remitted.[1] We are justified by faith, and to that now "I add that faith in the teaching of the Gospel means trust (fi ucia) in the promised mercy because of Christ."[2]

For Melanchthon, love and any number of worthwhile virtues exist in the reborn, but they do not effect reconciliation between God and men, only the mediator can do that. Therefore, Melanchthon is concerned to remove the doctrine of reconciliation away from our merits, our virtues, and any infused faith. Due to the intercession of the Son of God, we are accepted as righteous. Thus, just as love and fear are the names of relative realities, so faith is relative, or correlative, to the task of the mediator. It is by God's mercy because of another that we have the remission of sins. Our faith is correlative to that other, and this is the meaning of the proposition that we are justified by faith.

This fiducia or trust, Melanchthon also refers to as a movement in the will (motus in voluntate) which necessarily responds as an assent.[3] This faith or trust apprehends and applies the promise in order to quiet the heart, when justified by faith, we have peace before God through Christ.[4]

---

[1]
  Ibid.
[2]
  Ibid.
[3]
  CR 21:751.
[4]
  Ibid.

When we do assent to the promise, says Melanchthon, we
include all articles of faith. In the creeds he refers
particularly to: "I believe in the remission of sins and I
believe in eternal life."[1] This is the greatest promise and
the end to which the other articles refer. Indeed, 1 John
3:8 indicates that Christ was sent to "destroy the works of
the Devil, that is, remove sins and restore righteousness
and eternal life."[2]

If reconciliation and the remission of sins amounts
to a being received, or accepted, for Melanchthon, this
means that grace must primarily be something that comes
from without. Truly, grace is "the gratuitous remission of
sins and the imputation of righteousness."[3] For Melanchthon,
the word grace (gratia) means the gratuitous remission of
sins. But he complements this by acknowledging the
presence of the Holy Spirit in the Christian. He said: "We
condemn the errors of the Pelagians, who do not uphold the
difference between philosophy and the Gospel. Further, they
maintain that in philosophy men are able to satisfy the law
of God without the Holy Spirit" and that the gift of the
Holy Spirit is not necessary.[4]

1
 Ibid.
2
 Ibid.
3
 CR 21:752.
4
 Ibid.

This is "the definition of grace: the remission of sins, or the mercy promised because of Christ, or the gratuitous acceptance, which is necessarily accompanied by the giving of the Holy Spirit."[1] The Hebraic use of the term for grace Melanchthon considers pertinent, for it is employed in the sense of favor or a gracious giving. Paul tells us in Romans 4:4 that the rewards of one who does works are earned and are "not imputed as a gift."[2] In this case, says Melanchthon, "grace [gift] is understood as a gracious benevolence or imputation."[3] For those who believe, even if they do not contribute merits, nevertheless, they are granted "the gratuitous imputation of righteousness."[4]

Melanchthon defends the position that it is not by our worth, but through grace, by faith alone that we receive the remission of sins. The particle he refers to, sola of sola fide, does not exclude contrition or other virtues, "but denies that they are causes of reconciliation and transfers that cause to Christ alone."[5] The particles, of faith alone and grace alone, are correlatively understood.

---

[1] Ibid.

[2] Ibid.

[3] Ibid.

[4] Ibid.

[5] CR 21:755-756.

Melanchthon says that "by faith" means that "we are righteous by our trust (fiducia) in Christ, that is, because of Christ we are righteous, by grace, and not because of our worth."[1]

The emphasis on sola fide, for Melanchthon, is to avoid the doctrine that our worth establishes us as righteous. For Melanchthon, we are reconciled, we receive the remission of sins, and we are reputed to be righteous because of Christ. It is Christ whom God intends to act as propitiator and mediator. We are justified, then, in his blood, and God's wrath is placated by the death of his Son. It is fitting, says Melanchthon, that this benefit be applied to the believer by faith.[2] It is not because of our worth or personal dignity, but due to the act of propitiation of God's Son that God himself is propitious towards us.[3] "It is this faith (fides) that is trust (fiducia), which brings peace and life to the heart . . ."[4]

As in the previous Loci, Melanchthon attacks those who would maintain that faith must be considered a synecdoche, or a figure of speech by which part is used for the whole.[5]

_____

[1] CR 21:756.

[2] Ibid.

[3] Ibid.

[4] Ibid.

[5] CR 21:757.

His adversaries maintain that faith is fashioned and joined
to other virtues that are considered noteworthy. Since
they understand faith to be a knowledge of history they
conclude that "they know that men are not righteous by
faith, but by other virtues."[1] Melanchthon holds that this
interpretation contrasts with that of Paul, who considers
faith as well as grace to be a particle. He holds that we
do not have "reconciliation because of our virtues, but on
account of the mediator."[2] Paul has it, that we are
justified by faith because of the mediator; thus, not on
account of our virtues are we sons of God."[3] "This clearly
is in disagreement with the synecdoche of the adversaries."[4]

Such a synecdoche, says Melanchthon, yields to
perpetual doubt. "You are pleasing if you have enough
merits."[5] The teaching of Paul (Romans 5:1) clearly
contradicts this position: "Since we are justified by
faith, we have peace."[6] If doubt does remain it only
brings desperation and a hatred of God.

---

[1] Ibid.

[2] Ibid.

[3] Ibid.

[4] Ibid.

[5] Ibid.

[6] Ibid.

The true faith which Melanchthon intends, conquers
all manner of doubt, it is not that which condemns God or
flees from his wrath, and "does not truly invole [him]."[1]
The presence of this doubt in some, confirms the fact that
they "deny faith to be understood as trust in the mercy of
God. But for them faith only means a knowledge, of the
sort which is in the Devil."[2] Melanchthon holds faith to
be not only a knowledge of history, but also an assent,
"whereby we believe in the promise, or trust in the mercy,
which is offered in the promise."[3] James 2:19 indicates
that faith is not only this knowledge of history when it
states that demons themselves tremble and recognize the
Son of God, "but they do not embrace the promise."[4]

Melanchthon maintains the grace is something which
comes from without, it is a gratuitous acceptance, the
giving of the Holy Spirit, the remission of sins, but it
is primarily the gratuitous imputation of righteousness
to those who believe. The significance of the particles
(sola gratia, sola fide) is to transfer the cause of the

---

[1] CR 21:763.

[2] Ibid.

[3] CR 21:759.

[4] Ibid.

remission of sins and justification to Christ by insisting
on the correlative meaning of faith. Faith is a trust in
another (fiducia ad alterum), it is relational. According to
Melanchthon, this prevents us from seeing faith as simply a
knowledge of history or something infused into the soul, by
which we are made righteous.

The Role of Natural Knowledge in the Loci of 1559

For Melanchthon, one very important reason, yet
to be examined in this Loci, for doing good works is the
personal response to the natural or moral law. In order
for the natural law to be perceived, a principle of knowing that natural law must be established. In addition, God
wishes for man to know him (God) in and through his own
image. God wishes for man to be able to perceive his
signs (vestigia) in man. Furthermore, nature retains a
certain image of the divine that is not totally obscured.[1]

From the effects of the world at work one is able
to induce the order of natural things.[2] "It is impossible
for a perpetual order in nature to have been created by
chance and remain by chance," nor could it have been
created purely from matter.[3] Even all distinct parts or
particularities in nature are ordered. "So there remains a

---

[1] CR 21:615.

[2] CR 21:641-642.

[3] Ibid.

perpetual order in the movement of the heavens," and in all men there is a natural knowledge in the mind.[1] "Therefore, nature does not exist by chance, but its origin is due to some mi d, which comprehends (intelligit) order."[2]

In addition, when Melanchthon considers the nature of the human mind, he is of the opinion that brute, insensitive reality outside the mind is "not the cause of the nature of knowing."[3] The human mind has another cause for its being; it is not able to exist in and of itself, as its own cause, but has its beginning because of another.[4] "Therefore, it is necessary for there to be another understanding, which is the natural cause of the human mind. It is necessary for there to be a God."[5]

The existence of a natural cause (God) is important for Melanchthon in understanding those areas pertaining to natural knowing such as order and numbers, and the discernment between honesty and dishonor.[6] "It is impossible for there to be the difference between honesty and dishonor in the mind by chance, or to have arisen from matter. Just as it is impossible for the knowledge of order

---

1
  Ibid.
2
  CR 21:642.
3
  Ibid.
4
  Ibid.
5
  Ibid.
6
  Ibid.

and numbers to be accidental."[1]   Therefore, "it is
necessary for another mind to be the architect."[2]

It follows, for Melanchthon, that God has established
this light in the mind, which acts as a testimony in
nature, and provides us with natural knowledge. This is
what Paul meant (Romans 1:20) when he said that God had
revealed himself.[3]   God "imparted this knowledge to the
human mind, that there is a God, and at the same time he
imparted (indidit) the power to reason from effects."[3]
Not only the knowledge of God's existence, but the natural
knowledge of moral principles has been implanted in the
soul. The human mind, without this knowledge being
imparted from another mind, is unable to judge properly
between that which is morally right or wrong.[4]

Before Melanchthon discusses natural law, he does
assert that knowledge is possible; it is derived both from
within the mind and from without. The intelligibility of
causal relations shows us that there cannot be an infinite
series of efficient causes in nature, therefore it is
necessary that there be one first cause, thus God must

---

[1]
   Ibid.
[2]
   Ibid.
[3]
   Ibid.
[4]
   Ibid.
[5]
   Ibid.

exist.[1]   In addition to the fact that the intelligibility
of causes in nature are knowable, God by imparting knowledge
to the mind, has enabled us to differentiate between
morally right and wrong acts. For Melanchthon this
discrimination cannot arise from brute nature.

Natural or Moral Law and the Loci of 1559

Having established the existence of a natural
knowledge, Melanchthon, then, is able to attest to a
natural or moral law. This he refers to as a divine law
or the law of God. The law of God, says Melanchthon, applies
not only to external mores, but it is just as relevant to
the inner workings of the heart.[2] The law requires a
"full obedience of the heart," as it is written in
Deuteronomy 6:5, you shall love the Lord your God with all
your heart, with all your soul, and with all your might.[3]
The knowledge of God is obtained through the principle of
causality and is impressed upon the mind. Likewise, "the
law of God is the eternal and immutable rule of the divine
mind and is the judgment against sin, that was impressed on
the mind . . ."[4] According to Melanchthon, this is what
Christ intended when he said (Matthew 5:17), "I have not

1
 CR 21:642-643.
2
 CR 21:655.
3
 Ibid.
4
 CR 21:686.

come to abolish the law, but to fulfill it."[1]

This moral law of which Melanchthon speaks is the eternal judgment of God; it is a "rule that is not changed by times."[2] The moral law directs us to "the knowledge of God in the mind and the obedience of the heart toward God, and of virtues toward men, such as justice, chastity, truth, [and] temperance."[3]

Philosophers have often spoken of knowledge that is imparted to the human mind from divine being(s). They have referred to it as "this light, the knowledge of principles or κοινὰς ἐννοίας and προλήψεις."[4] Melanchthon maintains that the knowledge of these principles can be divided between those of a speculative nature (principia speculabilia) and those of a practical nature (practica principia).[5] The knowledge of speculative principles that are impressed on the mind includes "the knowledge of numbers, order, syllogisms, and geometric and physical principles."[6] For Melanchthon, these are imperative, "for what would life

---

[1]Ibid.

[2]CR 21:688.

[3]Ibid.

[4]CR 21:711.

[5]Ibid.

[6]Ibid.

be without numbers and order?"[1] The practical principles of
knowing enable all to differentiate between that which is
honest and that which is dishonorable. As a consequence,
there is obedience to God, and these practical principles
are just as sure and certain as the knowledge of numbers.[2]

Melanchthon likens the practical principles, such
as the knowledge of the difference between good and evil,
and between honesty and dishonor, to sharing an image of
or likeness to the divine mind. Man was created in God's
image, then, what of his nature? What of this knowledge
impressed on the mind? What of the law of nature?
Melanchthon says that the "true definition of the law of
nature is that it is the knowledge of the divine law,
imparted to the nature of man."[3] The divine light in the
human mind is not extinguished, and through speculative and
practical principles, we are able to know the law of nature
which, in fact, is the divine law. Thus, the "understanding
of divine righteousness is implanted in men . . . ."[4]

Natural knowledge and obedience are united in the
divine law, for Melanchthon, because the knowledge of the

---

[1] Ibid.

[2] CR 21:711-712.

[3] CR 21:712.

[4] CR 21:714, also CR 21:713.

law of nature is actually knowledge of the divine law.
Melanchthon says that "the laws of nature are divine . . ."[1]

The duty, the office, or the function of the law
must be examined in order to understand its relation to
good works, as well as the moral imperative of those good
works. There is no doubt, says Melanchthon, that "the
divine law entreats [us to] interior and perfect obedience.
According to Deuteronomy 6:5: You shall love the Lord
God with all your heart."[2] Our corrupt and fallen nature,
however, is not able to muster this perfect obedience
because sin remains within us, and along with it doubt and
diffidence. Thus, we are not justified by obedience to the
law, because of our incapacity to fulfill its demands. If
works of the law do not merit the remission of sins, then of
what use is the law at all?[3]

The first function of the law Melanchthon calls
paedagogicus or politicus, "for God wishes to check the

---

[1]
CR 21:716. On this point see: Charles Leander Hill,
"An Exposition and Critical Estimate of the Philosophy of
Philip Melanchthon." Ph.D. dissertation, Ohio State University, 1938. Wilhelm Dilthey, Gesammelte Schriften. Band II.
Weltanschauung und analyse des Menschen seit Renaissance
und Reformation (Göttingen: Vandenhoeck und Ruprecht, 1957).
Ragnar Bring, Das Verhaltnis von Glauben und Werken in der
lutherischen Theologie (Munich: Kaiser Verlag, 1955). G. E.
M. Anscombe, "Modern Moral Philosophy." (Philosophy 33
January 1958), pp. 1-19.

[2]
Ibid.

[3]
Ibid.

disciplines of all men, even those who are not reborn,"
so that the crimes and faults of all are not united.[1]
This is why Paul says (1 Timothy 1:9) that the law is
not laid down for the just. Discipline is necessary
for all men, and Melanchthon provides four reasons why.
First, it is a command of God, and he ought to be obeyed.
Secondly, crimes are punished, either by the proper
magistrate or by God himself. Thirdly, God desires
public peace in order to establish a peaceful and
tranquil society for all. The fourth cause, reflecting
back to the first, Melanchthon calls paedagogia in Christum.[2]
This means living according to one's faith with a right
conscience in Christ. To act against Christ and the
Holy Spirit is to act against the conscience. It is
clearly indicated (1 Corinthians 6:9) that "fornicators,
idolaters, adulterers, etc. will not be able [to enter]
the Kingdom of God."[3] In the same sense John states
(1 Epistle 3:8) that "all who sin are from the Devil."[4]
One is not able to sin and at the same time follow
Christ and his Spirit as pedagogues. "It is necessary

---

[1] Ibid.

[2] CR 21:717.

[3] Ibid.

[4] Ibid.

to restrain sins and not resist the movement of the Holy
Spirit in the heart."[1]

The second use of the law Melanchthon terms
punishment or that which points out our sins. It "accuses,
frightens, and condemns all men in this corrupt nature."[2]
The law acts as the eternal judgment of God against sin, the
wrath of God which remains, and no one is able to be free of
the wrath of God simply by recognizing or acknowledging the
Son of God.[3] This knowledge of the law of God, impressed
upon the mind, is not to be taken lightly, nor is that
law to be considered mutable.[4] It is the judgment of God
against sin proclaimed throughout the ages. Melanchthon
says, as does Paul in Romans 1:18, that the wrath of God
is revealed from heaven against all man's iniquity.[5]

According to Melanchthon, Paul testifies to this
use of the law as a judgment or sentence. Paul says
(Romans 3:20) that it is through the law that we know sin.[6]
What Paul says is that "the law accuses and condemns sin,

---

[1] Ibid.
[2] CR 21:717-718.
[3] CR 21:718.
[4] Ibid.
[5] Ibid.
[6] Ibid.

[but] it does not destroy it."[1] Similarly, Paul states

(Romans 4:5) that "the law brings wrath."[2] He also

says (1 Corinthians 15:56) that the "sting of death is sin,

[and] the power of sin is the law."[3] Thus, for Melanchthon,

the law reveals sin present in us, and the fact that sin is

condemned by God, yet we are not free from it.

This use of the law reveals the sin, but it cannot

destroy or remove it. Melanchthon cites Paul's remarks in

Romans 7:9: "I was once alive apart from the law, that is,

I was secure not knowing the judgment of God. But afterward

[knowing the law] I became terrified when I realized my

weakness and my sins."[4] It was this use of the law that was

operative when the prophet reproved David for his adultery.[5]

After the recognition of sin comes contrition, and the voice

of the Gospel. The Lamb of God has destroyed sin and revealed

the loving mercy of God. God hates and condemns sin, "but

he desires to free believers [from sin] through the Son, who

was made the victim."[6] Paul, says Melanchthon, does exhort

---

[1] Ibid.
[2] Ibid.
[3] Ibid.
[4] CR 21:718-719.
[5] CR 21:719.
[6] Ibid.

us "to be terrified, not in that we are to die, but in order that we take refuge in the mediator."[1] Just as Paul states (Romans 11:32): "He has shut all under sin, so that he may have mercy upon all."[2]

The third use of the law, for Melanchthon, is applicable only to the reborn. The reborn and justified are, indeed, freed from the law. This means they are free from the curse or damnation of the law, or the wrath of God which is revealed through the law. Even though the reborn are freed from the curse of the law, it does show us that sin remains and that penitence is needed for the believer. For the reborn the law teaches "certain works, in which God desires us to exercise obedience."[3] It remains "an immutable divine order, that we obey God."[4] We are freed from the law, or damnation, because we are righteous by faith, because of the Son of God. Nevertheless, Melanchthon maintains that when it comes to obedience, "the law remains, evidently because the divine order remains. The justified are obedient to God, and have an inchoate obedience which,

---

[1] Ibid.
[2] Ibid.
[3] Ibid.
[4] Ibid.

in some way, is pleasing . . ."[1] The direction of works and the moral mandate elicited by the law remains, for the justified, as a means of being obedient to God. To obey God by pursuing certain works elucidated by the law is, for Melanchthon, the third use of the law.

In addition to the functions of the Mosaic prescriptions, says Melanchthon, the moral law is mandated by Christ in any number of scriptural quotations. Following the preaching of the Beatitudes in Matthew 5:21 are found such moral mandates. For an integral and perfect obedience to the law of God, a right order is required of all and must be enacted through interior and exterior actions.[2] Within this section, Christ condemns killing, says we should not be angry with our brothers, and condemns the act of adultery, as well as adultery in the heart. These sayings, remarks Melanchthon, are not just moral exaggerations of the Stoics, but are from Christ testifying that God is angry with human sins, and desires a specific moral law to be followed.[3]

As was noted earlier, the third use of the law, which prescribes works to be done, is properly applicable only to the justified. The moral mandate mentioned in the last paragraph, however, pertains to all. There is only "one

---

[1] Ibid.

[2] CR 21:720.

[3] Ibid.

and the same Gospel, by which all the saints from the
beginning of the world are saved for all times [those saints
include]: Adam, Noah, Abraham, Jacob, the prophets, and the
apostles."[1] This is not to imagine that the patriarchs
"are saved by the law of nature, the Jews by the law of
Moses, [and] we are saved by our own particular law."[2]
"Indeed, there is one moral law for all time, [for] all
people," but neither the patriarchs, nor the Jews, nor
Gentiles, nor ourselves are saved thereby, for no one is
able to satisfy the demands of the law.[3]

As was brought out in the previous section on
natural knowledge, Melanchthon maintained that the perception of this universal moral mandate is impressed on the
mind and is seen as part of God's order. Sin is not "the
order of God, but is a confusion and a terrible disturbance
of the divine order, which God always hates and curses."[4]
The moral law belongs to the one divine order. Considering
himself to be in agreement with Paul (notably in Romans 13)
Melanchthon states that order itself is "a series of persons
or things in agreement with (congruens) the rule of the
divine mind and it resides in us according to the law of
nature . . ."[5]

---

[1] CR 21:735.
[2] Ibid.
[3] Ibid.
[4] CR 21:992.
[5] Ibid.

Melanchthon draws his understanding of the immutability of this natural, moral law from his conception of
order within nature and of God's will. The "moral law is
not a mutable law, as that of a ceremony or of the
Twelve Tables, but the moral law is the eternal and immutable rule of the divine mind, proposing what is to be
done, and prohibiting and punishing what is not to be
done."[1] The fact that God elicits and approves obedience
through a natural or moral law is imparted to rational
creatures and is not liable to be lost from the mind. To
know God's desire for obedience and the eternal, immutable
moral law is like the knowledge of numbers; it is infused in
the mind and cannot be destroyed.[2] This rule, "the moral
law, always remains the order of the divine mind, in order
that the creature obeys."[3] For Melanchthon, the full obedience of the heart is revealed through works, and comes from
the eternal, immutable moral law which is impressed upon
the mind. The natural law (the moral law) calls us to the
testimony of faith in and through our works.

---

[1] CR 21:1042. The Twelve Tables were the earliest
code of Romans laws believed to have been composed by a
commission of decemviri legibus scribundis c. 450 B.C.
See H. F. Jolowicz, Historical Introduction to the Study of
Roman Law (2nd. ed., Cambridge: Cambridge University Press,
1952), The Oxford Classical Dictionary, Hammond and Scullard
(eds.) (Second Edition, Oxford: Oxford University Press,
1970), p. 1100.

[2] CR 21:1042.

[3] Ibid.

Syllogistic Arguments in the Loci of 1559

Aside from categories such as man's sinful condition,
the necessity of good works, the three specific causes for
doing good works, the rewards and merits granted to good
works, the meaning of faith and justification, the nature
of knowing, and the significance of the natural moral law,
the method Melanchthon employed most extensively in analyzing
the doctrine of good works is syllogistic argument. In no
other work does Melanchthon undertake so massive and strict-
ly rigoristic a treatment of the facets of the controversy
over good works. In this Loci, Melanchthon probes the
issues by proposing a major, minor, and conclusion
(followed by an analysis of one of the propositions) for a
total of eighteen times. Even though the topics or
questions raised overlap areas already examined within
other categories, the systematization and the analysis of
each syllogism is noteworthy and deserving of individual
treatment.

Righteousness means obedience according to all
precepts, begins Melanchthon. "Faith, of which we spoke,
is not actually a work of all precepts. Ergo we are not
justified by faith."[1] Melanchthon's response is that the
major is true, for "righteousness of the law is actually
obedience to all precepts."[2] Due to our corrupt nature we

---

[1]
CR 21:784.
[2]
Ibid.

are unable to satisfy the precepts of the law. Therefore, we are received or accepted, not by our obedience,
but on account of the Son of God. "Therefore, righteousness means one thing in the major, and another in the conclusion."[1] When Paul speaks of being justified by faith
(as in Galatians 2:16) he understands that by faith we
receive the remission of sins or acceptance because of
Christ the mediator, not because of our obedience. In
Romans 4:5 Paul states that "faith is imputed to him as
righteousness."[2] This differentiates, for Melanchthon,
that righteousness pertaining to the Gospel and faith,
from the righteousness of the law or obedience. Without
this distinction he feels the basic confusion between law
and Gospel will continue.

The second syllogism concerns the meaning of
faith. "It is impossible for knowledge alone to make one
righteous, faith is only knowledge (notitia), therefore it
is impossible for faith alone to make one righteous."[3]
Melanchthon responds to the minor. "Faith does not simply
mean knowledge, that is, the kind that is in the Devil, of
which James states (James 2:19): The demons believe and they

---

[1]
  Ibid.
[2]
  Ibid.
[3]
  CR 21:785.

tremble"[1] For Melanchthon, "faith means knowledge (notitia) in the intellect, assent to the promise of Christ, and trust in the will . . ."[2] It is therefore, not only that knowledge, though that is part of it, but also that trust which apprehends the promise. Faith receives the promise, therefore it is "necessary to understand it as the trust in the given mercy."[3]

Faith, Melanchthon understands as trust, but he does admit that present to trust is love.[4] Many other virtues ought to be present as well; but, when he says we are righteous by our trust, it should not be understood as on account of the worth of those virtues.[5] It is by God's mercy on account of the mediator that we are accepted, and it is fitting that this mercy be received or apprehended by faith. Our faith, then, is correlative to the mercy of God that is given because of his Son.[6]

The third syllogism is concerned with love. He who does not love remains in death, therefore, it is impossible to say that we are righteous by faith alone.[7]

1
 Ibid.
2
 Ibid.
3
 Ibid.
4
 Ibid.
5
 Ibid.
6
 Ibid.
7
CR 21:786.

Melanchthon admits that faith should not exist alone,
"but it does not follow that love is the cause of the
remission of sins. It is necessary for patience to
accompany faith, but it does not follow that our patience
is the cause of the remission."[1] The exclusive particles,
as sola fide, do not exclude virtues, but they do exclude
them from the cause of reconciliation, for Christ alone
was the cause of reconciliation.[2]

The fourth syllogism proceeds as follows: "We are
righteous by faith, faith is a work, therefore, we are
righteous on account of works."[3] "The major is understood
correlatively," says Melanchthon, "we are righteous by faith,
that is we are righteous by mercy because of Christ."[4]
We are not righteous "because faith is a virtue which merits
the remission by its worth."[5] Melanchthon does concede that
faith is a work, but he says it is a work like "love, patience,
or chastity."[6] These are feeble, weak, and languid, and
like faith, it is not due to the worth of the virtue that we

------

[1] Ibid.
[2] Ibid.
[3] Ibid.
[4] Ibid.
[5] Ibid.
[6] Ibid.

have the remission of sins.[1] It is fitting, he states,
for there to be some "instrument in us, by which we apprehend
the mediator interceding for us, [and] because of whom
the Father is propitious."[2]

In the fifth argument, Melanchthon turns to the
significance of God's grace. "We are righteous by grace,
grace is love infused in the heart, therefore, we are
righteous by infused love."[3] For Melanchthon, the minor
proposition errs. Grace actually means "the gratuitous
mercy or gratuitous acceptance because of Christ."[4]
To maintain that the remission of sins is due to our virtues
is to turn clearly from Paul's understanding of grace.[5]
We ought not to look to our qualities or virtues when we
anguish over the remission of sins, rather, we should take
refuge in the mediator. To reject the language of infusing
here, does not mean that Melanchthon rejects the gift of the
Holy Spirit. Melanchthon only wishes that grace be seen
primarily as an acceptance, or receiving, and not infusing.

The sixth syllogism begins by stating that it is
impossible to know the will of God towards us.[6] "To believe
that we are in grace is to affirm something of the will of

_____

1
 Ibid.
2
 Ibid.
3
 CR 21:787.
4
 Ibid.
5
 Ibid.
6
 Ibid.

God towards us."[1] Therefore, it is impossible to truthfully affirm the belief that "we are in grace."[2] Melanchthon says that the major is true, the will of God is not totally revealed by the Word of God. From the Gospel, however it is certain that Christ stands close to the heart of God the Father, so that we may "affirm that God is propitious towards us because of the mediator."[3] The condition of the human mind is such that the knowledge of God is obscured; consequently, the perception which enables us to affirm God's propitiousness towards us is obscured. The Gospel attests that the Son of God was freely sent and announces the promise, thus we believe and are confirmed in our belief.[4] To be sure, states Melanchthon, the condition of the law is added to this. "Even if penitence is necessary, nevertheless, the remission of [sins] does not depend on our worth, but is assured on account of Christ."[5] Because of Christ, then, we know (what would be otherwise impossible) that God is favorable and merciful towards us.

The seventh syllogism proceeds as follows: "No one is pleasing unless they have a new _habitus_ born from

---

[1]Ibid.

[2] Ibid

[3] Ibid.

[4] Ibid.

[5] Ibid.

the Holy Spirit. No one is able to affirm that they have
that _habitus_ because similar virtues can be born from
reason. As a result, no one is able to affirm that they are
pleasing."[1] Melanchthon denies the minor proposition. Even
if our reconciliation is not had because of our habits, "but
from the certain promise of God," nevertheless, new spiritual
movements occur when the heart is aroused by faith in
penitence.[2] These enable us to cry _Abba Pater,_ yet, "trust
looks to the mediator, not to our newness."[3] Melanchthon
adds a saying of John concerning the conscience (1 Epistle
of John 3:21): "If our heart does not condemn us, we have
trust in God, that whatever we ask for, we will receive from
him."[4] It is looking to the mediator and trusting in him
for our needs that our entreaties are assured. God's
favor is not due to the _habitus_, and our trust does not
look to ourselves, but Christ.

The eighth syllogism is concerned with the meaning
of faith. "The virtues of theology are distinct: faith
hope, [and] charity. If faith meant trust, it would be the

---

[1]
CR 21:788.
[2]
Ibid.
[3]
Ibid.
[4]
Ibid

same as hope, therefore, the distinction of the virtues would
not be retained."[1] Melanchthon states that he has always
held that these three be united, but that when it is said
men are justified by faith, it is to be correlatively
understood.[2] It is not on account of the worth of these
virtues that we are righteous, but due to the mediator.
Thus, "faith differs from the other virtues because it
apprehends, [and] the promise is applied to us."[3] It
accepts the present reconciliation, whereas, hope "expects
a future liberation."[4] As a rock is grasped, so is the
remission of sins, which is given to us because of the
mediator, and the faithful are assured.[5]

If faith is counted among the "theological virtues,"
says Melanchthon, "it is necessary not only to be understood
as knowledge, as the kind in the Devil, but that faith,
by which we approach God and invoke him. We do not
approach, however, in true fear, if we judge that we remain
in perpetual doubt."[6] It is that very doubt that produces

---

[1] Ibid.

[2] Ibid.

[3] Ibid.

[4] Ibid.

[5] CR 21:788-789.

[6] CR 21:789.

a flight from and a hatred of God. Faith does not operate
as one who hopes for a future liberation, but it accepts,
receives, grasps that which is graciously granted now.

"Evil works merit eternal penalties," begins the
ninth syllogism, "therefore, good works merit eternal life."[1]
The conclusion is seen to be valid, says Melanchthon, from
its contrary. It would "be valid if the contrary were
equally correct."[2] The evils we do are in contrast to the
law of God and the goods we do are never quite able to
satisfy the law of God. There remains in the saints a
certain helplessness and weakness, no matter how many good
works they perform or excellent virtues they possess. Many
interior evils remain, such as doubt, corrupt affections,
and diffidence. As Paul laments (Romans 7:24): "I am
a miserable man, who will free me from this body of death?"[3]
In their misery, says Melanchthon, "the pious acknowledge
their imbecility. They see that they do not satisfy the
law of God, and that they are not without sin. It is in
this humble state that they fly to take refuge in the
propitiator."[4] For Melanchthon, only the hypocrite dreams
of fulfilling the law through various external disciplines or

---

[1] Ibid.

[2] Ibid.

[3] Ibid.

[4] Ibid.

works. A certain freedom and joy is found in our corruptness and imbecility, according to Melanchthon, for it is in
this condition that we really seek the only one who can
free us. We must sink to the depths in order to understand
our inability to climb out and the need for the only one
who can really pull us out.

Sin is the hatred of, or enmity towards God,
continues the tenth syllogism: "therefore, righteousness is
the love of God."[1] Melanchthon is willing to concede this
position, except for the fact that love and hatred may not
be equally compared. Our love is lazy and is such that it
bears much that is foul and it even interferes with our
divine calling. Our love is incapable of fulfilling the law,
nor are we pleasing because of any personal perfection,
but we [and our love] are pleasing propter mediatorem.[2]

Following from the position that love is righteous,
is the statement that we are righteous by our love.[3] If
to be righteous, remarks Melanchthon, means to have virtues,
then this conclusion follows. However, it is not valid if
to be righteous means to be recipients of the remission
of sins. The first position means that righteousness is
not able to be understood as the thing which merits the

1
Ibid.
2
Ibid.
3
Ibid.

remission of sins, but only as virtue.[1] As if, says
Melanchthon, one were to say: "To pay a seller is just,
therefore, the one paying the seller is just."[2] One may
have the virtue of being just. Paying a debt is just, but
paying does not remit sin. Thus, love can be understood as
righteousness or justice, when considered a virtue, but we
are not justified by our love as virtue, for to be righteous
is to be a recipient.

"Righteousness is in the will," begins the eleventh
syllogism, "faith is not in the will, therefore, we are not
justified by faith."[3] The minor proposition is denied by
Melanchthon. Faith, for him, signifies the assent to the
promise of God, in the intellect, and it is united with
trust in the will. The promised reconciliation, through the
mediator, is desired and accepted.[4] If we do not desire and
accept the promised reconciliation fear and anxiety remain,
and peace is not able to exist for the conscience. Knowledge
of the Gospel does not suffice, for Paul says (Romans 5:1)
we are "justified by faith [and] we have peace."[5] He also
states (Romans 9:33): "He who believes in him will not be
confounded."[6]

---

[1]CR 21:789-790.

[2]CR 21:790.

[3]Ibid.

[4]Ibid.

[5]Ibid.

[6]Ibid.

Righteousness as well as faith is said to be in the will. To justify, says Melanchthon, means that the remission of sins and acceptance for eternal life comes from God.[1] "These come to us because of the mediator seated at the right [hand] of the eternal Father, nevertheless, it is fitting for them to be received by faith."[2] At the same time the Holy Spirit is given, along with a new light and new virtues, which we submit to God, and "eternal life is begun in us."[3] As Christ says (John 17:3): "This is eternal life, that they know you the only true God, and he whom you have sent Jesus who is Christ."[4] Faith and righteousness can be said to be in the will, but faith primarily looks to God. The remission of sins and eternal life is that something which comes from God, because of his Son.

In the twelfth syllogism, Melanchthon examines the meaning of faith, due to the question posed by the passage from James 2:24. "You see, therefore, that man is justified by works, not from faith alone."[5] Melanchthon states

---

[1]
 Ibid.
[2]
 Ibid.
[3]
 Ibid.
[4]
 Ibid.
[5]
 CR 21:791.

that the author, in this place, intends faith to be understood as a knowledge of history. This is the knowledge that
even the damned have, when it is said, "the demons believe
and they tremble." This kind of knowledge does not establish
man as righteous. When Paul speaks of faith, continues
Melanchthon, he means that trust in God's mercy is due to
Christ, and because of him do we receive reconciliation.[1]
James, then, does not disagree with Paul's meaning, but
James refutes the errors of those who held that they became
righteous because of a dogmatic profession. Melanchthon
maintained that this error was exemplified by the Jews who
held that they were righteous because of the profession of
their doctrines or ceremonies.[2]

Paul does not actually disagree with James' refutation. When James says that man is justified by works, he
is speaking of the "righteousness of works (iustitia
operum)," which Paul proclaims to be necessary.[3] James
does deny, however, that because of this righteousness
the remission of sins is granted. The verb "to justify"
should not be understood as "to reconcile," but it should
be seen as "to approve."[4] Man is justified by works, that

---

[1] Ibid.

[2] Ibid.

[3] Ibid.

[4] Ibid.

is, having the righteousness of works approved, [he is]
pleasing to God."[1] This is due to the fact that obedience
in the reconciled Melanchthon considers absolutely necessary.
If obedience is not manifested, "the person is not righteous,
nor pleasing, nor accepted, and transgressions against the
conscience remain."[2] It is fitting for men to have the
righteousness of works, if it is clear that works do not
procure the remission of sins and eternal life. They are
not pleasing because they satisfy the law, but because of
Christ (sed propter Christum).[3] Thus, the only real
difference between James and Paul (concerning the meaning
of faith) is one of emphasis. Melanchthon believes that the
righteousness of works through obedience is necessary, yet
it must not be seen as causally related to the remission
of sins.

Melanchthon begins his treatment of the thirteenth
syllogism by quoting 1 Corinthians 13:1: "If I have all
faith, [but] I do not have love, I am nothing."[4] Paul
admits that we need love, and that it is fitting for us
to express our love. Nevertheless, "it does not follow that

---

[1] Ibid.

[2] Ibid.

[3] Ibid.

[4] CR 21:792.

we receive reconciliation because of love, nor that we are pleasing because of love, that is, because it satisfies the law."[1] Love is not able "to exist unless preceded by faith, by which we receive remission and acknowledge [God's] mercy . . ."[2] It is due to another, namely Christ, that the person is able to stand assured of having reconciliation; he cannot look to personal qualities.[3] For Melanchthon, both are true: it is fitting for obedience to be present in the reconciled and yet, reconciliation is had on account of the Son of God.[4]

Matthew 19:17 indicates that if you wish to enter into life, begins the fourteenth syllogism, you will follow Christ's commands. Therefore, "we are able to satisfy the law and our obedience merits eternal life."[5] No, says Melanchthon, it is a great mistake to hold that men are able to satisfy the law and that the contumacy born within us is a thing not repugnant to or in opposition with the law of God. Furthermore, we cannot hold that our fulfillment of the law merits the reward of eternal life.[6]

---

[1]Ibid.

[2]Ibid.

[3]Ibid.

[4]Ibid.

[5]Ibid.

[6]Ibid.

Melanchthon considers these errors to arise from the failure properly to differentiate between the law and the Gospel. The law requires a complete obedience and it promises life. With the law there always remains the condition of that whole or complete obedience. Melanchthon's proposition, an disputed fact, is that no one is able to fulfill the demands of the law through obedience. The difference, then, between the law and the Gospel is found in John 6:40: "This is the will of him who sent me, that all who believe in the Son have eternal life."[1] Because of our infirm nature we cannot satisfy the law, but God wishes for us to receive eternal life because of his Son, and by faith. When we accept we begin that inchoate obedience that is necessary, but it does not satisfy the law of God.[2] When we are grafted to Christ by faith, then our obedience is pleasing because of the mediator.[3]

"Obedience is pleasing not because it satisfies the law, but on account of the mediator. Nevertheless, it is necessary for it to commence."[4] Melanchthon quotes Matthew 5:20 as attesting to the need for obedience. "Unless

---

[1] Ibid.

[2] CR 21:793.

[3] Ibid.

[4] Ibid.

your righteousness exceed that of the scribes and Pharisees, you will not enter into the kingdom of heaven."[1] The Pharisees taught external discipline, but the Gospel requires more.[2] The "righteousness of the pious overflows or excels in these six things," says Melanchthon, "penitence, faith, the newness from the Spirit, true invocation, following their calling, and the repression of the Devil."[3] That righteousness of the pious is a "new light or the beginning of eternal life (inchoatio vitae aeternae), which is and will be like the life, the wisdom, and the righteousness which the law proposes," namely, the clear knowledge and pure love of God.[4] Melanchthon does imply here that there is a development in justification. Nevertheless, he rules out justification that depends on the obedience to the law, even though that obedience is necessary. The righteousness of the pious person must be manifest through obedience, yet eternal life, (which the law proposes, but with its fulfillment as condition) is already here. It is revealed through that very obedience.

In the fifteenth syllogism, Melanchthon deals with the relationship between our forgiving others and God

---

[1] Ibid.
[2] Ibid.
[3] Ibid.
[4] Ibid.

forgiving us. "Forgive and you will be forgiven, therefore, our pardoning merits remission."[1] To forgive, says Melanchthon, is a precept, and to say you will be forgiven is a promise. To that promise is not, however, added the condition of pardoning. If such a condition were added, the promise would be made uncertain. As a result, on hearing of the promise we are to look to Christ and not to the state of our pardoning. Our obedience and pardoning are required, however, and are pleasing to God.[2] The moral precept which admonishes us to forgive is not causally related, for Melanchthon, to the promise of God that we will be forgiven.

"Great virtue especially justifies," begins the sixteenth syllogism, "love is a great virtue, therefore, love especially justifies."[3] The major is true, says Melanchthon, when applied to the righteousness of the law. If we satisfy the law, we are righteous on account of personal virtues. Due to the fact "that we do not satisfy the law, we are accepted on account of the mediator, and not because of any personal worth or because of our qualities."[4]

---

[1] Ibid.

[2] CR 21:794.

[3] CR 21:795.

[4] Ibid.

It does not follow from the major that great virtue greatly
reconciles, only the mediator reconciles. Even the reborn
recognize that weakness and infirmities remain and that
they are still incapable of fulfilling the law.

The greatest of all virtues, says Melanchthon, is
the love of God. Even the law (as revealed in Deuteronomy
6:5) tells us that we should love the Lord God with all our
hearts. The question posed by Melanchthon is "where is that
ardent flame of love?"[1] Only a small spark is found in the
saints and even that is difficult to retain. When we acknowledge this it becomes easier "to understand why it is
said that we are justified by faith."[2]

An important distinction can be brought out here
concerning faith and hope as virtues. Hope "is the personal
expectation of the future liberation promised by God."[3]
Faith differs in that it "receives the promise and applies
the benefits of the mediator to us."[4] Hope is not of this
kind, but it expects or looks to a future event. It is
understandable, then, why we do not say we are justified
by hope. This would not apply the mediator to us as is the

---

[1]
 CR 21:796.
[2]
 Ibid.
[3]
 Ibid.
[4]
 Ibid.

case, says Melanchthon, when we say we are justified by
faith. Another major difference is that faith "receives a
present benefit, a present reconciliation, without which
prayer is not possible."[1] Hope is that which looks to a
future event promised by God.

In this syllogism Melanchthon uses a psychological
argument to refute the position that we may fulfill the law.
Virtues, he says, even in the reborn are infirm and incapable
of fulfilling the law. That love that we muster for God seems
only to be a small spark and minimal at that. As a result,
our being justified is not through virtues, which are weak,
but by faith (not hope), which apprehends the promise of
God.

Many sins are forgiven, continues the seventeenth
syllogism, because Christ loved much, therefore remission
of sins is on account of love.[2] Melanchthon's response is
that absolution is twofold. First there is the private
absolution for the conscience. For this absolution, it must
be understood that faith receives the remission of sins
from without; it is not due to our virtues. This is the
reason, says Melanchthon, that Christ told the woman
(Matthew 9:22) that her faith had saved her.[3] Our faith

---

[1]
   Ibid.
[2]
   Ibid.
[3]
   CR 21:797.

does not depend on our love, but only on God's promised mercy. Second there is the public absolution before the Church, "which acts as a testimonial to personal conversion . . ."[1]

The sign of public confession and penitence indicates, for Melanchthon, that two churches exist. One is that which is made of hypocrites who do nothing but look to proper discipline and the law. The other preaches Christ and and true penitence and by true faith praise to God. This group acknowledges and testifies that Jesus Christ is the mediator. No matter how many handsome works the first group does, Christ still attributes praise to the works of those with faith in him. True worship of God is provided by: "penitence, faith, true prayer, love, kissing and cleansing the feet of Christ," and defending and honoring the services of the Church.[2] The Church of the hypocrites maintain that they are righteous by their disciplines without true penitence, faith, and fear of God. These people are without love, because the love of God and prayer is not able to exist unless the remission of sins, promised by the Gospel is known.

For Melanchthon, he who loves much does not receive the remission of sins except through faith. In fact, true love cannot exist without that remission. It is not love

---

[1] Ibid.

[2] Ibid.

through discipline that remits sins, but discipline or
works from love do attest to the remission of sins by
faith.

The eighteenth syllogism begins as follows: "Eternal
life is called reward, therefore, it is owed for works."[1]
Eternal life is a reward, says Melanchthon, because good
deeds are compensated, "even if given because of another,
namely, on account of Christ."[2] Melanchthon compares the
reward of eternal life to the inheritance of the Father
which is a reward to the son, because both depend on another
cause. Melanchthon considers his adversaries to provide a
far too strict, univocal meaning to works and rewards. It
is as though they hold the concepts of purchasing, winning
a prize, and receiving reward as one and the same.[3] Thus,
they establish a certain equality between obedience and
eternal life. "They call obedience meritum de condigno,
[and] they hold that men are able to satisfy the law of
God."[4] Moreover, they maintain that works amount to an
extra payment or can be even better than good (opera
supererogationis). For the adversaries, then, faith is
not spoken of as "receiving remission and the inheritance
of eternal life on account of Christ."[5] Even hope, then,

---

[1] CR 21:798.

[2] Ibid.

[3] Ibid.

[4] Ibid.

[5] Ibid.

becomes "the expectation of eternal life rising from our merits."[1] With so much debate over the meaning of merit, Melanchthon proposes a saying of St. Bernard: "Suffice it to be known of merit, that merit does not suffice."[2]

There must be penitence, faith, this inchoate obedience, or love in the reborn. Our works do not attain salvation, for it is freely offered and accepted by faith. Nevertheless, "God accepts our obedience, even if good works do not merit the remission of sins and the inheritance of eternal life. Obedience does merit other corporal and spiritual rewards in this life and in the future life."[3] Christ did say (Luke 6:23) that your reward will be great in heaven.

Life eternal, of course, is a reward, but it is not granted according to, or depending upon, works. Reward, for Melanchthon, is to be understood as compensation, "but not as granting reconciliation on account of our work. Furthermore, our inchoate obedience is not pleasing in and of itself, however, it is pleasing in the reconciled because of Christ."[4] Good works do not merit reconciliation, nor are they rewarded with eternal life. "In order for obedience to be pleasing, reconciliation necessarily must precede."[5]

---

[1]
Ibid.
[2]
Ibid.
[3]
CR 21:798-799.
[4]
CR 21:799.
[5]
Ibid.

Melanchthon summarizes this syllogism, and to an extent all of them, when he states that penitence in the believer is necessary.[1] The remission of sins is granted because of the Son of God, through grace, and "not on account of our worth."[2] Further, the "mind ought not to succumb to doubt, but conquer doubt by faith."[3] In addition, "it is necessary for there to be an inchoate obedience. It does not satisfy the law of God, but is pleasing in the reconciled because of the mediator. Sins do remain in the reborn, but there is a difference between sins against the conscience and those who remain in the saints."[4] Works in the reborn are necessary and are rewarded with corporal and spiritual rewards. Melanchthon distinguishes between those rewards and the reward of eternal life. What is rewarded is "earned," but only the mediator can "earn" eternal life. A causal connection between our works and salvation does not exist; it must come from another cause. In our case, we are rewarded eternal life as the gracious inheritance of a Father is given to the son, without the son directly earning it. Eternal life, then, is a reward propter aliam causam.[5]

---

[1] CR 21:799-800.

[2] CR 21:800.

[3] Ibid.

[4] Ibid.

[5] CR 21:798.

Conclusion

The effect of the Regensburg Colloquy, the Augsburg Interim, the Leipzig Interim, the attacks of Flacius, the Majoristic controversy, and the Osiander questions is a teaching concerning good works that is much more systematized, and to a certain degree more rigid, than that of the earlier Melanchthon.

The absolute necessity of the moral mandate or obedience in the reborn, Melanchthon holds to the very end; only the degree of emphasis varies. With a creeping antinomianism within the Evangelical party, Melanchthon insists, as he had done in the Loci of 1535, that works are necessary. Not being fearful of the ad salutem problem, he holds that Christians were created for good works, and that the Christian life itself is an outward confessing of the faith. Good works are necessary. This is more than just a moral suggestion; there exists a causal connection, namely, that an inchoate obedience will be present in the reborn. The reconciled person, acting out of a good conscience, will necessarily do good works. Melanchthon doesn't rule out the "ought" characteristic of works, or the "fittingness" of works, but of primary importance is that works "necessarily ought to follow."

Three primary causes for doing good works, which Melanchthon singles out, are: necessity, dignity, and reward. Works are necessary because God wishes them,

they retain faith, and they assist in helping to avoid
certain penalties for sins. The worth or dignity Melanchthon refers to is not that of the person, but of the
person's calling. A person does works according to his
calling. The final reason is reward merited by these
works. The rewards, of course, are spiritual and temporal,
but do not include the reward of everlasting life. Eternal
life is granted only through the mediator.

The promise of reconciliation that we have received
from the law bears the condition of the fulfillment of
that law. The condition of the law, however, is always
unfulfilled, according to Melanchthon. As a consequence,
the assurance of that promise cannot be guaranteed. Only
the Gospel and the grace given on account of Christ can
provide the benefits, which do not depend on the condition
of fulfillment of the law. If we had to fulfill the law,
the remission of sins would be hopeless. The gift of
salvation is granted freely on account of Christ, and not
due to any merits or personal worth.

For Melanchthon, another reason why we cannot merit,
is because God is furious over sin, thus we need a mediator.
God's wrath is so powerful, and immutable, that our works
cannot divert or deflect it. Our iniquities cannot withstand his wrath and our works cannot enable us to approach
his hallowed ground. As a result, we must hid, we must
take refuge in the only cover available, Jesus Christ the

mediator. It is only through Christ that our sins are
reputed to be righteous, we become heirs to eternal life,
and we are freed from the law and the condition of merit.
Although we are far from the perfection of the law and
righteousness, we are pronounced righteous by God.

A key reason for our inability to merit, according
to Melanchthon's writings, is the abiding sinful condition
of human nature. Central to his theology is the teaching
that sin remains, even after baptism, or that concupiscence
is sin. Its presence is ignored by all of us, he says,
but its oppression or burden is more than we can possibly
comprehend. These are not just venial sins or the privation of justice, but mortal sins. Human judgment, for
Melanchthon, tells us that our sinful state is a deprava-
tion or defect combating the law of God.

Due to this sinful condition, Melanchthon distinguishes between human righteousness and divine righteousness. One pertains to human discipline or earthly laws and
the other to that righteousness which destroys sin and
death. The human discipline, which cannot save us, is
much like a shadow. It is similar to the letter rather
than the spirit.

Even though we abide by a certain worldly right-
eousness, which cannot save, we must do our good works.
These works, even though imperfect, are pleasing to God.
Our contaminated obedience is received, not because of

our worth, but on account of the Son of God. As a result, prayer or invocation is pleasing according to the faith of the person. The invocation of the heathen or the Muslim, Melanchthon separates from the invocation of the Christian who has faith. The person, then, is not considered pleasing until received by God on account of the Son. Subsequently, works themselves are not pleasing unless the person is pleasing on account of acceptance by God. After the person is reconciled, through faith in Christ, works are received and they are pleasing to God; our sullied obedience is acceptable to God.

The works of the reborn are not only pleasing, according to Melanchthon, but they also merit, not salvation, but rewards. The works subsequent to reconciliation are pleasing and merit spiritual and corporal rewards in and after this life. Among the virtues granted rewards, Melanchthon includes: penitence, the fear of God, prayer, confession, patience, chastity, temperance, and diligence in one's calling.

To merit rewards, but not salvation, means that Melanchthon understands faith as correlative and justification as forensic. Justification is the imputation of righteousness or the acceptance for eternal life. Melanchthon does attest that God gives us the Holy Spirit. However, justification or reconciliation is above all being accepted, reputed, or pronounced righteous.

Melanchthon wishes to avoid speaking of righteousness as
something which arises from within, thus, it is imparted
to us from without. Likewise, faith is relative or correlative to the mediator. Due to God's mercy on account of
another are we reckoned as righteous. Thus, our faith is
correlative to that other, and this is why, for Melanchthon,
we can say that we are justified by faith. It is appropriate
to say "faith alone" in order to rule out the idea that
any personal dignity establishes us as righteous. Our faith
is a trust that we are reputed to be righteous because of
Christ. The use of the particles (sola fide, sola gratia)
is meant to transfer the cause of our justification to
Christ and away from us. Faith is not just knowledge, but
a trust in another and not in ourselves. As was indicated
earlier the natural moral law becomes increasingly
important for Melanchthon as a reason for doing good works.
Perception of that law is not limited to the reborn, but
all men can perceive God's signs in themselves and in
nature (the effects in the world). The natural knowing
process enables us to perceive not only the contingency
of the world, and the mind itself, but the necessity for
order and the difference between honesty and falsehood. Just
as the ability to judge morally is impressed on the mind,
so is the eternal and immutable rule of law of the divine
mind. This natural moral law, which directs us to obedience
of the heart toward God, becomes the primary reason

for doing good works.

Melanchthon's division of the principles of speculative
nature and practical nature establishes the "scientific"
existence of the moral imperative. Its integralness with
God is shown through the definition of the law of nature
as the knowledge of the divine law, imparted to the nature
of man. Thus, natural law and obedience to it become one
with the divine law and obedience to it. The divine law
calls us to obedience, even if we are unable to perfectly
fulfill it. Thus, good works are "naturally" necessary.

The law functions in three distinct ways, for
Melanchthon. It acts as pedagogue or in a political
sense when it functions as the guide for the universal
discipline of all humankind. It also acts as the eternal
judgment of God against sins by revealing sin, then condemning its presence. The final function is to elucidate,
for the reborn, the means (or works) of being obedient to
God. Even though the reborn are freed from the law as a
means of achieving salvation, still they must obey God
by pursuing certain works proposed by the law. The law
calls us to the testimony of faith in and through our
works. God elicits and approves obedience through his
eternal and immutable law.

The eighteen syllogisms of the Loci of 1559 may
be characterized by five predominant categories: 1) the
distinction between human and divine righteousness, 2) a

proper understanding of faith, 3) the meaning of love, 4) God's grace and reward, and 5) sin.

The first category, Melanchthon establishes as a starting point or presupposition for his entire theology. If there is no real difference between law and Gospel, all is vain. This categorical differentiation means there cannot exist one righteousness between man and God. For Melanchthon, they are distinct because of sin. Human and divine righteousness are distinct or else law would be Gospel, which for him, clearly is not the case. Due to Melanchthon's understanding of the distinct character of the two righteousnesses, he repeatedly emphasized the forensic nature of justification, that which must come from without.

The second major category is faith. Faith is not simply an historical knowledge, but it is trust. It is not, as hope, that which looks to a future expectation. Faith, for Melanchthon, is that which trusts, accepts, and receives. Likewise, it is relative to that which gives or bestows. It is a virtue in the sense that it is virtuous, but it is not an infused virtue by means of which reconciliation is had. It is a work insofar as it is an instrument which apprehends. As well, Melanchthon says, faith is in the will to the extent that it desires the reconciliation that it receives in trust.

Love, the third category, is described in the syllogisms as something that must exist, but which cannot be

ascribed as the cause for the remission of sins. Just as
patience should exist in the reconciled, yet patience does
not reconcile, likewise, love does not reconcile. In
loving we are able to forgive, as well, but forgiving does
not make us forgiven. Finally, Melanchthon is convinced
that true love, patience, or forgiving are unable to exist
without faith having already been present. Faith must
precede love.

Melanchthon writes of grace, the fourth category
here, as something which accepts, receives, takes in or
admits. It is not something that is infused, even though
Melanchthon speaks of the Holy Spirit being given. At the
same time, grace is not something which resides, or
inheres, nor is it a habitus. It is not that which slowly
grows or develops from within, as inhering, but that which
is granted now, from without. It is God's favor, his disposition toward a merciful promise as his own way of relating
to fallen mankind. Finally, God grants, by grace, eternal
life as a reward not earned by us, but propter aliam.

The fifth category Melanchthon deals with in the
syllogisms is sin, or the sinful state of all men. The
abiding presence of sin, even after reconciliation, prevents
us from fulfilling the demands of the law. Our inability
to reach perfection by discipline, according to Melanchthon,
is due to our sinful state which causes us to need another,
namely, a mediator. The need for Christ the mediator

would be altogether obviated if sin did not abide in us, and we were able to fulfill the law. Thus, our abiding sinful condition is an extremely important ingredient in Melanchthon's entire theology.

CONCLUSION

The overwhelming number of writings treating
Melanchthon actually turn out to be treatments of Luther
and Melanchthon, with great emphasis on Luther (Greschat,
Bring, Schäfer), or they are examinations of Melanchthon and
Lutheran confessional literature (Bente, Quere, Green, Klug,
Stahlke), which attempt to show how Melanchthon is in union
with or wavers from the orthodoxy of these documents. Other
writings which have contributed much to Melanchthonstudien
have dealt with his philosophy (Hill, Herrlinger, Wiedenhofer, Maurer), his ethics (Bauer, Dittrich, Mayer, Schäfer,
Thieme), and his understanding of the Lord's Supper (Neuser,
Quere). To date, however, no one has attempted to treat
in a systematic and historically developed manner Melanchthon's doctrine of good works. Treatises have been written
touching on his doctrine of justification as he presented it
in various periods of his life (Maurer, Greschat, Green, Bring,
Eichhorn, Engelland, Mayer), but no one has examined, in
detail how he understood the role of good works. How did
he define them? Were works important to him? Did he maintain that works are necessary? How did he relate works to
faith? What ancillary categories did Melanchthon use in order
to establish a specific teaching regarding good works?

In this study I have attempted to reveal, in historical
context, the function of works for Melanchthon, the reasons
for them, the language used to describe them, and the
categories he brought to his teaching on this topic. I have
attempted to answer, by textual examination of the most
pertinent writings of Melanchthon, the questions; are works
needed, and if so, why?

As a response to the Catholic <u>Confutatio</u>, the
Apology stood as Melanchthon's first systematic treatise
dealing especially with the doctrine of good works. He
says in it that works are fitting, (<u>oportet</u>), that they
ought (<u>debeat</u>) to be performed, and that they are necessary
(<u>necesse esse</u>) for a moral Christian life. Works follow
upon the remission of sins; they are not the cause of that
remission. God commands us to do good works, we are granted rewards for our works, but they do not win salvation or
the remission of sins.

Melanchthon also states, in the Apology, that the
doctrine of merit must be repudiated for it detracts from
the glory of Christ. Works are not pure in themselves and
do not win salvation. Rather, there is only one cause for
the remission of sins, and that is Christ. It is through
Christ that we are reputed to be righteous; external works
cannot make us righteous. Melanchthon distinguishes between
the Gospel and all that philosophy, which advocates like

the Jews and Muslims, works as a means of meriting salvation.
The terrified conscience is aware that our stained works cannot appease God's wrath, but that remission of sins is a
reward for the deeds of another. Our own deeds are contemptuous, have no value in and of themselves, and cannot
possibly merit anything.

Also in the Apology, Melanchthon further defined
faith as that which receives or accepts the promise of God.
For him it is not simply the knowledge or recognition of
Christian mysteries. Faith, as "the substance of things
hoped for," (Hebrews 11:1) is reckoned as justice by God.
It does not possess or earn salvation, but looks to another,
Christ.

From 1531 to 1534 Melanchthon was not directly concerned with the Confutatio, but, as his letters to Brenz
indicate, with an over-emphasized teaching on our own
"newness" due to the presence of the Holy Spirit within
the soul. He maintained that this novitas was not sufficient in itself, but that faith is required which accepts
righteousness extra nos. In addition, Melanchthon was of
the opinion, from reading astrological signs, that an
impending catastrophe obviated excessive theological debate
on these issues, even though he continued to develop
syllogistic arguments as an important method for doing just
that. From watching the stars, Melanchthon was quite certain

that some cosmic disaster was about to occur. As a result,
he felt that theological debate concerning justification
was pedantry and that the message from the stars was much
more important.

Especially in the Commentary on Romans of 1532 a
shift is indicated from the ethical mandate (we should do
good works) to the position that one who is justified will
(causally) do good works. Within this same work, Melanchthon is concerned with the emphasis on inner renewal in
the writings of Osiander. As a result, he emphatically
emphasizes the doctrine of the imputation of God's righteousness. He underscores this doctrine by stating that
faith is correlative to that which grants righteousness.
By these means he wished to keep righteousness outside of
us, and prevent any notion of merit.

The Loci of 1533 agrees with the Apology in
emphasizing the need, even the necessity, of good works.
Melanchthon does begin, however, to speak of works "meriting" rewards--but not salvation. Salvation is merited only
on account of Christ. Righteousness itself is even more
strongly presented as something extra nos. In this version
of the Loci, Melanchthon begins to differentiate between
persons and works. This leads him to argue that works are
incapable of making a person pleasing to God. The function

of the law as a guide is mentioned but not nearly as much as
in the later writings. For Melanchthon, the notion that we
have a terrified conscience that needs to be pacified becomes
a major category. In addition, Melanchthon begins to grant
that works are pleasing to God once a person has been
reconciled by faith in Christ. Faith imputatively fulfills
the law since we are reputed righteous by God just as if we
had fulfilled the law.

Before the appearance in 1535 of the second _Loci_, we
find that Melanchthon's concepts of works has developed only
in a limited fashion. The impact of the controversy which
saw works as a _causa sine qua non_ certainly led him to
change his tune. Melanchthon describes how he had emphasized
the doctrine of the imputation of grace, when infused grace
was discussed. At the same time, he felt the need for a
reinforced emphasis on good works, lest they be neglected
by those who, thinking they could do no good anyway, would
abandon them.

It is also during this period that Melanchthon
stresses the necessity of good works for salvation. This
does not mean that he wished works to share as a cause of
the remission of sins. Christ remains the only cause, but
one who is justified _will_ do good works. The state of
being justified _necessarily_ brings about works, or otherwise
that state would not exist.

In considering the _Loci_ of 1535, I have characterized
the teachings of Melanchthon on works by using the following
categories: the necessity of works, the worth of works,
causes for doing good works, the natural law as cause, the
necessity of the moral law, corrupt works as pleasing, the
meaning of faith, the significance of rewards, and
syllogistic arguments.

Over against the previous texts of Melanchthon, the
Loci of 1535 is markedly more philosophical and reveals an
increased interest, on the part of Melanchthon, in natural
law. Melanchthon defends the role of natural reason in
perceiving practical moral principles, whereby the law of
nature is known. Moreover, Melanchthon identified that law
as the Decalogue, and he maintained that by obedience to the
natural moral law we obey the law of God.

Melanchthon denies the possibility of merit, and
yet he attests to the need for works, in the case of the
justified. It is as a result of his interest in natural
knowledge and natural law, as well as through his background
in classical thinkers, that Melanchthon arrives at a
theology of good works. Concurrently, he arrives at the
need for works from the doctrine of imputation, which
necessitates a moral mandate, lest works be seen as worth-
less. During this period we find that the establishment of
natural reason, natural judgment and natural law, becomes

an important category along with Melanchthon's increased emphasis on imputative justice and the moral mandate.

During this period 1535-1541 Melanchthon unequivocally defines justification as the imputation of righteousness, and the non-imputation of sins. Surprisingly, along with this definition, Melanchthon does not distinguish between person and work to the extent that he had in the earlier Loci. Within this period, the causes for doing good works are more pronounced than in previous years.

The pacification of the terrified conscience is not emphasized by Melanchthon during these years. Rather, he exhorts his readers to do good works, because they are pleasing to God. In addition, he renews the earlier emphasis on reward.

Throughout the colloquia, the Interims, battles with Eck, and arguments with Agricola, Flacius, and Osiander, Melanchthon attempted (during the years 1543 to 1560) to conciliate an agreement with the Catholics and appease those of his own party, who felt that he was compromising Evangelical doctrine. The Leipzig Interim had held that works are necessary for salvation, yet it denied that salvation is merited through works. The Regensburg Book had accomplished little more than to alienate Melanchthon from some of the Evangelical party. During the years 1550 to 1552 we find Melanchthon defending himself on three fronts. These include: attacks by Flacius, the controversy caused by Melanchthon's

participation in the Interims, the Osiandrian controversy
and the problem over the phrase "good works are necessary
for salvation." About 1553, Melanchthon, by his own repeated
emphasis on imputative righteousness countered Osiander's
renewed emphasis on novitatem.

Throughout these later years, in documents other
than the Loci of 1559, Melanchthon did not deny that works
are necessary for salvation. By reason of formal cause,
without interpreting it as merit, he was of the opinion
that one could hold the position that "works are necessary
for salvation." As a result, I agree with F. Bente. Even
thought Bente wished to show how unorthodox Melanchthon was,
he was correct in this matter. Melanchthon qualified his
phrasing of "necessary for salvation" by simply saying it
is misunderstood and therefore should be avoided. The
evidence I have presented from writings following the Loci
of 1535 indicates that Melanchthon would have used the
phrase again had he felt that it would not have been con-
troversial. Melanchthon did not deny the meaning of the
phrase, as I explained earlier, but only acted out of
prudence in regard to its use.

Like the Loci of 1535, the Loci of 1559 contains
categories such as the necessity of works, causes for doing
good works (necessity, dignity, and reward), the function
of the natural law, the meaning of faith, and works as
pleasing. The one major category given a larger consideration

in the Loci of 1559 is the human condition abiding in sin.
Melanchthon counters what he considers to be a developing
antinomianism, as well as those who attack his insistence
on works, with a renewed emphasis on our sinful condition
and the necessity of doing good works.

Melanchthon's theology of good works developed
from the early period of his life. Initially he repudiated
both philosophy and the "natural." His later writings,
however, attest to an appreciation for the interaction of
the natural and the divine. We saw how he actually considered works of little value, until the Confutatio brought
to bear some of Melanchthon's own presuppositions regarding
an ethical "ought." Within the Apology, we see Melanchthon
struggling to systematize the Evangelical position. The
Commentary of 1532 and the Loci of 1533 are evidence of
Melanchthon's attempt to clarify a doctrine of good works
which excluded both merit and antinomianism. He even
incorporated syllogistic arguments to "build" or "establish"
a position. Throught the 1540s and 1550s we see how he
consciously is moderating his own position in an attempt to
reconcile the right-wing followers of Luther's who feel he
has gone too far in compromising with the Catholics. In the
last period of his life, we see how his concern over antinomianism again led him to emphasize the "necessity" of
works in the reborn. Consequently, works for Melanchthon
are no longer simply an ethical mandate.

The questions arise: Did Melanchthon have one
doctrine of good works? Did he come up with an answer
acceptable to the Catholics and the Evangelicals? The
answer to both questions is no; I have shown the various
categories Melanchthon used when treating works, and how
they varied during given periods, depending on the circum-
stances. There was no single doctrine proposed by Melanchthon, nor one completely acceptable to either the Catholics
or the Evangelicals. Melanchthon tried desperately to walk
between what he considered to be the two extremes, merit
and antinomianism. At first, his denial was of merit, but
he soon realized (probably his humanistic presuppositions
simply brought to bear) the fact that works "ought" to be
done. It became obvious to him, that an ethical mandate
was not enough to enforce works, so Melanchthon had to
conclude to the fact that the reborn will (causally) do
good works. Was he naive on this point? Or did he feel
that this was the only possible alternative? Depending
on one's point of view, he was both. As a result of this
study, I conclude that it was the only viable alternative
that occurred to him. He continued to say one "ought" to
do good works, but he reinforced this by saying that they
are causally connected, you will do good works, if you are
reborn.

Subsequent to Melanchthon's day, Lutheranism has
been rife with debates concerning Luther, Melanchthon, and
Lutheranism. Many consider the teaching of each of these

to be one and the same; others hold them as distinct
entities and traditions. Melanchthon considered the
dynamics that Luther dealt with more as logical principles
and themes. Luther's concern for concepts and principles
did not include any system of logical consistency and
unity. He regarded a pastoral theology of his own understanding of the Word of God more important than a classroom
theology which was logical and coherent. Melanchthon,
however, perceived reality with the background of a
classicist; he was concerned with value and ultimate unity.
Luther actually attacked a system of value and ultimate
unity, the late Medieval Catholic Church. Building the
post-Medieval Church was not Luther's concern. Melanchthon,
on the other hand, saw as a consequence of Luther's attack,
positive dynamics arising from the crumbling unity.
Unconsciously, yet out of psychological necessity, Melanchthon
attempted to envision that new system of value and unity.

ARG   Archiv für Reformationsgeschichte. Gütersloh, 1903-

CH   Church History. Publication of the American Society of Church History. 1923-

CR   Corpus Reformatorum. Philippi Melanthonis Opera quae supersunt omnia. Ed. C.G. Bretschneider. 28 vols. Halle, 1834-60.

DTC   Dictionnaire de Theologie Catholique. Ed. A. Vacant, E. Mangenot, and A. Amann. Paris, 1930-50.

EKL   Evangelisches Kirchenlexikon. Ed. H. Brunotte and Otto Weber. 2nd ed. 4 vols. Göttingen, 1956-61.

ELC   The Encyclopedia of the Lutheran Church. Ed. Julius Bodensieck. 3 vols. Minneapolis, 1965.

LThK   Lexikon für Theologie und Kirche. Ed. J. Hofer and K. Rahner. 2nd ed. 10 vols. Freiburg, 1957-66.

MBW   Melanchthons Briefwechsel. Ed. Heinz Scheible. Stuttgart-Bad Cannstatt, 1977-

NCE   New Catholic Encyclopedia, 16 vols. New York, 1967.

Lexicon   Mediae Latinitatis Lexicon Minus. J. F. Niermeyer. Leiden, 1976.

ODCC   The Oxford Dictionary of the Christian Church. Ed. F. L. Cross and E. A. Livingstone. 2nd ed. London, 1974.

RGG   Die Religion in Geschichte und Gegenwart. 3rd ed. 6 vols. plus index. Tübingen, 1957-65.

RPTK   Realencyklopädie für protestantische Theologie und Kirche. Ed. Herzog. 24 vols. Leipzig, 1805-82.

StA   Melanchthons Werke in Auswahl (Studienausgabe). Ed. Robert Stupperich. 7 vols. Gütersloh, 1951-75.

WA   D. Martin Luthers Werke. Kritische
Gesamtausgabe. Weimar, 1833-

WAB   D. Martin Luthers Werke. Kritische
Gesamtausgabe: Briefwechsel. Weimar, 1930-

ZKG   Zeitschrift für Kirchengeschichte. Stuttgart,
1877-

ZTK   Zeitschrift für Theologie und Kirche.
Tübingen and Leipzig, 1950-

BIBLIOGRAPHY

Primary Sources

Die Bekenntnisschriften der evangelisch-lutherischen Kirche.
    5th edition. Göttingen: Vandenhoeck and Ruprecht,
    1963.

Bindseil, Henricus Ernestus. Philipp Melanchthon. Epistolae,
    iudicia, consilia, testimonia aliorumque ad eum
    epistolae quae in Corpore Reformatorum desiderantur.
    Hildesheim/New York: Georg Olms Verlag, 1975.

_____. Epistolae, iudicia, consilia, testimonia
    aliorumque ad eum epistolae quae in Corpore
    Reformatorum desiderantur. Halle: 1874.

Bretschneider, C. G. and Bindseil, H. E., eds. Philippi
    Melanthonis Opera quae supersunt. Corpus Reformatorum,
    28 vols. Halle/Braunschweig: C. A. Schwetsche and
    Son, 1834-60.

Camerarius, Joachim. De Philippi Melanchthonis ortv, totivs
    vitae cvrricvlo et morte, implicata rervm memorabilivm
    temporis illivs hominvmque mentione atque iudicio,
    cum expositionis serie cohaerentium: narratio
    diligens et accvrata Ioachimi Camerarii . . . Leipzig:
    Ernestus Voegelin Constantiensis, 1566.

Chytraeus, David. Summa doctrinae de vera Dei agnitione:
    seu Descriptio Dei vsitata, in locis theologicis
    Philippi: explicata praelectionibus Dauidis Chytraei,
    editis per Johannem Frederum. Wittenberg: Z.
    Lehmanum, 1584.

Cochlaeus, Johannes. De Sola Fide: Philippica Tertia . . .
    in Apologiam Philippi Melanchthonis, De quarto,
    quinto et sexto articulis Lutheranae Confessionis,
    ubi disceptatur de sola fide, quam Lutherus asserit,
    'Philippicae Quator Iohannes Cochlei, in Apologiam
    Philippi Melanchthonis Ad Carolum V. Imperatorem
    Romanorum . . .'Leipzig: [Nicolaus Faber], 1534.

Hartfelder, Karl. Melanchthoniana Paedagogica. Eine
    Ergänzung zu den Werken Melanchthons im Corpus
    Reformatorum. Leipzig: B. G. Teubner, 1892.

300

Luther, Martin. D. Martin Luthers Werke. Kritische
Gesamtausgabe. Weimar: Herman Böhlaus Nachfolger,
1881ff.

_____. Luther's Works. Edited by Jaroslav Pelikan,
et al. St. Louis: Concordia Publishing House,
1958ff.

Major, John. Iohannis Maioris Ioachimi Exequiae reverendo,
& clarissimo viro Philippo Melanthoni, in Academia
Vitebergensi factae. De rebus item diuinis eiusdem
poëmata. Wittenberg: 1561.

Melanchthon, Philip. Loci praecipvi theologici. Nvnc denvo
cvra et diligentia summa recogniti, multisque in
locis copiose illustrati, per Philippvm Melanthonem.
Cum appendice disputationis de coniugio. His
accesservnt definitiones theologicae, quarum in
Ecclesia usus est, eodem autore . . . Wittenberg:
I. Crato, 1559.

_____. De Oratione Ciceronis. Leipzig: Jacobus
Berwaldus, 1543.

_____. Discrimen Legis et Evangelii. Tübingen:
Hulderichum Morhardum, 1523.

_____. In Evangelivm Ioannis, annotationes Philippi
Melanchthonis. Tübingen: Hulderichum Morhardum,
1523.

_____. Epistolae selectiores aliqvot. Philippi
Melanthonis. Editae a Casparo Pevcero . . .
Wittenberg: I. Crato, 1565.

_____. Ethicae doctrinae elementa et enarratio libri
qvinti Ethicorvm. Edita et recognita Vitebergae
anno 1553. Avtore Philippo Melanthone. Wittenberg:
[H. Krafft], 1554.

_____. Loci commvnes theologici, iam postremo cura ac
diligentia summa recogniti, & locis aliquot aucti.
per Philippum Melanchthonem. Accessit locorum tam
communium, quam scripturae, obiter declaratorum, rerum
quoq, trigeminus index. Basil: Ioannem Oporinum,
1550.

_____. Liber continens continva serie Epistolas Philippi
Melanchthonis scriptas annis XXXVIII. ad Ioach.
Camerar. Pabep. nvnc primvm pio stvdio et accvrata
consideratione hvivs editvs, cvrante evm exprimendvm
Ernesto Voegelino. Leipzig: 1569.

_____. Die Loci communes . . . in ihrer Urgestalt
nach G. L. Plitt. In 3. Auflage von neuem
herausgegeben und erläutert von. D. Th. Kolde.
Leipzig: A. Deichert, 1900.

Scheible, Heinz., ed. Melanchthons Briefwechsel. Heidelberger
Akademie der Wissenschaften. vols. 1 and 2. Stuttgart/
Bad Canstatt: Fromman-Holzboog, 1977-78.

Stupperich, R., ed. Melanchthons Werke in Auswahl.
Studienausgabe. Gütersloh: 1951-75.

Supplementa Melanchthoniana. Werke Philipp Melanchthons Die
im Corpus Reformatorum Vermisst Werden. 5 vols.
Leipzig: Verein fur Reformationsgeschichte, 1910-29.
Reprint Minerva G. M. B. H. Frankfurt, 1968.

Secondary Sources

Agnoletto, Attilio. La Filosofia di Melantone. Milan:
Marzorati, 1959.

Aland, Kurt. Die theologische Fakultät Wittenberg und ihre
Stellung im Gesamtzusammenhang der Leucorea während
des 16. Jahrhunderts. 450 Jahre Martin-Luther-
Universität. Halle/Wittenberg: 1952.

Althaus, Paul. The Theology of Martin Luther. trans.
Robert C. Schultz. Philadelphia: Fortress Press, 1966.

Anscome, G. E. M. "Modern Moral Philosophy." Philosophy 33
(January 1958):1-19.

Avis, P. D. L. "Moses and the Magistrate: A Study in the
Rise of Protestant Legalism " Journal of Ecclesiastica
History 26 (April 1975):149-172.

Bauer, Clemens. "Die Naturrechtsvorstellungen des jungen
Melanchthon." In Festschrift für Gerhard Ritter.
Tübingen: J. C. B. Mohr, 1950.

Bauer, C. "Melanchthons Naturrechtslehre." Archiv für
Reformationsgeschichte 42 (1951):64-98.

Bauer, Karl. Die Wittenberger Universitätstheologie und
die Anfänge der Deutschen Reformation. Tübingen:
J. C. B. Mohr, 1928.

Beck, Nestor. "Faith and Works: A Study of Articles IV-VI
and XX of the Augsburg Confession (1530)." Ph.D.
dissertation, Concordia Seminary, St. Louis, 1973.

Bente, F.   "Historical Introductions to the Symbolical Books
     of the Evangelical Lutheran Church." In Concordia
     Triglotta. St. Louis: Concordia Publishing House,
     1921.

Bindseil, Heinrich Ernst. Bibliotheca Melanthoniana . . .
     Halle: Typis Hendeliis, 1868.

Bizer, Ernst. Theologie der Verheissung. Studien zur
     theologischen Entwicklung des jungen Melanchthon
     (1519-1524). Neukirchen/Vluyn: Verlag des
     Erziehungsvereins, 1964.

Blatter, August. Die Thätigkeit Melanchthons bei den
     Unionversuchen 1539-1541. Bern: Genossenschafts-
     buchdruckerei, 1899.

Blumenberg, Hans. Die kopernikanische Wende. Frankfurt/
     Main: Suhrkamp Verlag, 1965.

Boisset, Jean. Mélanchthon. Éducateur de l'allemagne.
     Paris: Éditions Seghers. Collection dirigée par
     André Robinet, 1967.

Bornkamm, Heinrich. Das Jahrhundert der Reformation;
     Gestalten und Kräfte. Göttingen: Vandenhoeck and
     Ruprecht, 1961.

_____. Philipp Melanchthon. Göttingen; Vandenhoeck
     and Ruprecht, 1960.

_____. "Melanchthons Menschenbild." In Philipp
     Melanchthon: Forschungsbeiträge zur vierhundertsten
     Wiederkehr seines Todestages dargeboten in Wittenberg
     1960, edited by Walter Ellinger. Göttingen:
     Vandenhoeck and Ruprecht, 1961.

_____ et al. Philipp Melanchthon. 1560-1960.
     Gravenzande/Niederlande: Europäische Bücherei, 1961.

Bouman, Herbert J. A. "Retrospect and Prospect; Some
     Unscientific Reflections of the Four Hundredth
     Anniversary of the Formula of Concord." The
     Sixteenth Century Journal 8 (1977):85-104.

Bray, John S. "The Value of Works in the Theology of Calvin
     and Beza." The Sixteenth Century Journal 4 (1973):
     77-86.

Brecht, Martin. "Iustitia Christi: Die Entdeckung Martin Luthers." Zeitschrift für Theologie und Kirche 74 (1977):179-223.

Breen, Quirinus. "The Subordination of Philosophy to Rhetoric in Melanchthon. A Study of his Reply to G. Pico della Mirandola." Archiv für Reformationsgeschichte 43 (1952): 13-28.

_____. "The Two-Fold Truth in Melanchthon." Review of Religion 9 (January 1945): 115-136.

_____. "The Terms 'Loci Communes' and 'Loci' in Melanchthon." Church History 16 (1947): 197-209.

Bring, Ragnar. "Glaube und Werke." Zeitschrift für systematische Theologie 12 (1935):498-551.

_____. Das Verhältnis von Glauben und Werken in der lutherischen Theologie. Munich: Kaiser Verlag, 1955.

Bromiley, Geoffrey W. Historical Theology: An Introduction. Grand Rapids: Eerdmans, 1978.

Brüls, Alfons. Die Entwicklung der Gotteslehre beim jungen Melanchthon, 1518-1535. Bielefeld: Luther-Verlag, 1975.

Brunner, Emil. Man in Revolt. trans. Olive Wyon. Philadelphia: Westminster Press, 1947.

Brunstäd, Friedrich. Theologie der lutherischen Bekenntnisschriften. Gütersloh: C. Bertelsmann Verlag, 1951.

Bullemer, Karl. "Quellenkritische Untersuchungen zum I. Buche der Rhetorik Melanchthons." Ph.D. dissertation, Würzburg, 1902.

Büttner, Manfred. Die Geographia Generalis Vor Varenius. Geographisches Weltbild und Providentialehre. Wiesbaden: Franz Steiner Verlag, 1973.

Buttler, Gottfried. "Neues Interesse an Melanchthon. Ein Literaturbericht." Monatschrift für Pastoraltheologie 53 (March 1964):109-120.

Caserta, Nello. Filippo Melantone (dall'umanesimo alla Riforma). Rome: Edizioni Ita, 1960.

Clemen, Otto. Studien zur Melanchthons Reden und Gedichten.
        Leipzig: M. Heinsius, 1913.

Cochrane, Arthur. "The Act of Confession-Confessing."
        The Sixteenth Century Journal 8 (1977):61-83.

Cohrs, Ferdinand. Philipp Melanchthon, Deutschlands
        Lehrer. Ein Beitrag zur Feier des 16. Februar 1897.
        Halle: Verein für Reformationsgeschichte, 1897.

Colungo, Alberto and Turrado, Laurentio. Biblia Sacra Iuxta
        Vulgatam Clementinam. Nova Editio. Madrid:
        Biblioteca De Autores Cristianos, 1977.

Cox, F. A. The Life of Philipp Melanchthon, Comprising an
        Account of the Most Important Transactions of the
        Reformation. Boston: Gould, Kendall, and Lincoln,
        1835.

Crofts, George Daniel. "Philip Melanchthon's Views on Church
        Councils." Ph.D. dissertation, University of
        Colorado at Boulder, 1971.

Debus, Allen G. The Chemical Philosophy. Paracelsian
        Science and Medicine and the Sixteenth and Seventeenth
        Centuries. New York: Science History Publications,
        1977.

Denys, Edward Paul. "Philip Melanchthon's Unique Contribution
        to Education." Ph.D. dissertation, Loyola University
        of Chicago, 1973.

Dilthey, Wilhelm. Gesammelte Schriften. II Band.
        Weltanschauung und Analyse des Menschen seit
        Renaissance und Reformation. Göttingen: Vandenhoeck
        and Ruprecht, 1957.

Dittrich, Ottmar. Geschichte der Ethik. Die Systeme der
        Moral vom Altertum bis zur Gegenwart. 4th vol.
        Von der Kirchenreformation bis zum Ausgang des
        Mittelalters. I. Die Reformatoren und der
        lutherisch-kirchliche Protestantismus. Leipzig:
        Felix Meiner, 1932.

Dobrzycki, Jerzy., ed. The Reception of Copernicus'
        Heliocentric Theory. Holland: D. Reidel Publishing
        Co., 1972.

Drickamer, John M. "Did Melanchthon Become A Synergist?"
        The Springfielder 40 (Spring 1976):95-101.

Dueck, Abe. "An Unpublished Letter Pertaining to Developments Prior to the Colloquy between Bucer and Melanchthon." Archiv für Reformationsgeschichte 66 (1975):141-151.

Ebeling, Gerhard. Luther: An Introduction to His Thought. trans. R. A. Wilson. Philadelphia: Fortress Press, 1970.

Eichhorn, A. "Die Rechtfertigungslehre der Apologie." Theologische Studien und Kritiken 60 (1887): 415-491.

Elert, Werner. Die Augustana und der Gedanke der christlichen Solarität. Rede bei der Augustana-Feier der Theologischen Fakultät Erlangen. Erlangen: Palm and Enke, 1931.

_____. The Structure of Lutheranism. Translated by W. A. Hansen. St. Louis: Concordia Publishing House, 1962.

Ellinger, Georg. Philipp Melanchthon. Ein Lebensbild. Berlin: R. Gärtner, 1902.

Encyclopedia of the Lutheran Church, 1965 ed. S.v. "Interims of Augsburg and Leipzig," by Philip J. Schroeder.

Engelland, Hans. Melanchthon: Glauben und Handeln. Munich: C. Kaiser, 1931.

_____. Die Frage der Gotteserkenntnis bei Melanchthon. Munich: C. Kaiser, 1930.

_____. Allein aus Gnaden! Die Lehre von der Rechtfertigung. Munich: C. Kaiser, 1936.

_____. "Der Ansatz Der Theologie Melanchthons." In Philipp Melanchthon. Forschungsbeiträge zur Vierhundertsten Wiederkehr seines Todestages dargeboten in Wittenberg 1960, edited by Walter Elliger. Göttingen: Vandenhoeck and Ruprecht, 1961.

Eschenhagen, Edith. "Beiträge zur Sozial- und Wirtschafts-geschichte der Stadt Wittenberg in der Reformationszeit." Ph.D. dissertation, Halle-Wittenberg, 1927.

Fagerberg, Holsten. Die Theologie der lutherischen Bekenntnisschriften von 1529 bis 1537. Göttingen: Vandenhoeck and Ruprecht, 1965.

_____. A New Look at the Lutheran Confessions (1529-1537). Translated by Gene J. Lund. St. Louis: Concordia Publishing House, 1972.

Ficker, Johannes. Die Konfutation des Augsburgischen Bekenntnisses. Ihre erste Gestalt und ihre Geschichte. Leipzig: Verlag von Johann Ambrosius Barth, 1891.

Fischer O.S.B., Bonifatius. Novae Concordantiae Bibliorum Sacrorum Iuxta Vulgatam Versionem Critice Editam. 5 vols. Stuttgart-Bad Cannstatt: Friedrich Frommann Verlag Gunther Holzboog GmbH and Co., 1977.

Forell, George Wolfgang. "The Formula of Concord and the Teaching Ministry." The Sixteenth Century Journal 8 (1977): 39-47.

Fortman, S.J., Edmund J. The Theology of Man and Grace: Commentary. Milwaukee: Bruce Publishing Co., 1966.

Fraenkel, Peter. Zwanzig Jahre Melanchthonstudium. Sechs Literaturberichte (1945-1965). Geneva: Droz, 1967.

_____. Testimonia Patrum. The Function of the Patristic Argument in the Theology of Philip Melanchthon. Geneva: Droz, 1961.

Friedensburg, Walter. Geschichte der Universität Wittenberg. Halle: M. Niemeyer, 1917.

Friesen, A. "Philip Melanchthon (1497-1560), Wilhelm Zimmerman (1807-1878) and the dilemma of Muntzer historiography." Church History 43 (June 1974): 164-182.

Galle, Friedrich. Versuch einer Charakteristik Melanchthons als Theologen und einer Entwicklung seines Lehrbegriffs. Halle: Johann Friedrich Lippert, 1840.

Geiger, Ludwig. Johann Reuchlin. Sein Leben und seine Werke. Leipzig: Duncker and Humboldt, 1871.

Gerrish, B. A. Grace and Reason: A Study in the Theology of Luther. Oxford: Clarendon Press, 1962.

Geyer, Hans-Georg. Von der Geburt des wahren Menschen. Probleme aus den Anfängen der Theologie Melanchthons. Neukirchen/Vluyn: Verlag des Erziehungsvereins, 1965.

Gilbert, Felix. History: Choice and Commitment. Cambridge: Harvard University Press, 1977.

Graesse, J. G. Th. Orbis latinus oder Verzeichnis der wichtigsten lateinischen Orts- und Ländernamen. Ein Supplement zu jedem lateinischen und geographischen Wörterbuch. Berlin: Richard Carl Schmidt and Co., 1909.

Green, Lowell C. "Melanchthon, Philipp." In The Encyclopedia of the Lutheran Church, edited by Julius Bodensieck for the Lutheran World Federation, vol. 2. Minneapolis: Augsburg Publishing House, 1965.

_____. "Formgeschichtliche und inhaltliche Probleme in den Werken des jungen Melanchthon. Ein neuer Zugang zu seinen Bibelarbeiten und Disputationsthesen." Zeitschrift für Kirchengeschichte 84 (1973):30-48.

_____. "Faith, Righteousness, and Justification: New Light on Their Development Under Luther and Melanchthon." The Sixteenth Century Journal 4 (April 1973):65-86.

_____. "Influence of Erasmus upon Melanchthon, Luther and the Formula of Concord in the Doctrine of Justification." Church History 43 (June 1974): 183-200.

_____. "Erasmus, Luther, and Melanchthon on the Magnus Consensus: The Problem of the Old and the New in the Reformation and Today." Lutheran Quarterly 27 (November 1975):364-381.

_____. "Luther Research in English-Speaking Countries Since 1971." In Lutherjahrbuch. Gottingen: Vandenhoeck and Ruprecht, 1977.

Greschat, Martin. Melanchthon neben Luther. Studien zur Gestalt der Rechtfertigungslehre zwischen 1528 und 1537. Witten: Luther Verlag, 1965.

Gritsch, Eric W. and Jenson, Robert W. Lutheranism: The Theological Movement and Its Confessional Writings. Philadelphia: Fortress Press, 1976.

Grotefend, Otto. "Beiträge zum Briefwechsel Melanchthons." Zeitschrift für Kirchengeschichte 28 (April 1907): 58-70.

Haendler, Klaus. "Offenbarung- Geschichte- Glaube. Bemerkungen zum Glaubensbegriff Melanchthons." In Reformatio und Confessio. Festschrift für D. Wilhelm Maurer zum 65. Geburtstag am 7. Mai 1965, edited by Friedrich Wilhelm Kantzenbach and Gerhard Müller. Berlin/Hamburg: Lutherisches Verlagshaus, 1965.

_____. Wort und Glaube bei Melanchthon. Eine untersuchung über die Voraussetzungen und Grundlagen des melanchthonischen Kirchenbegriffes. Gütersloh: Verlagshaus Gerd Mohn, 1968.

Haikola, Lauri. "A Comparison of Melanchthon's and Luther's Doctrine of Justification." Dialog. A Journal of Theology. 2 (Winter 1963): 32-39.

Hammer, Wilhelm. Die Melanchthonforschung im Wandel der Jahrhunderte. Ein beschreibendes Verzeichnis. 2 vols. Gütersloh: Gerd Mohn, 1967, 1968.

_____. "Melanchthon, inspirer of the study of astronomy; with a translation of his oration in praise of astronomy (De Orione, 1553). Popular Astronomy 59 (June 1951): 308-319.

Harnack, Adolf von. "Philipp Melanchthon." Die Antike 7 (1931): 181-185.

Harrison, Jr., Richard L. "Melanchthon's Role in the Reformation of the University of Tübingen." Church History 47 (September 1978): 270-278.

Hartfelder, Karl. Philipp Melanchthon als Praeceptor Germaniae. Berlin: A. Hofmann and Co., 1889; reprint ed., Nieuwkoop: B. DeGraaf, 1964.

Heninger, Jr., S. K. The Cosmographical Glass. Renaissance Diagrams of the Universe. San Marino, California: The Huntington Library, 1977.

Heineck, Hermann. Die älteste Fassung von Melanchthons Ethik. Berlin: R. Salinger, 1893.

Herrlinger, Albert. Die Theologie Melanchthons in ihrer geschichtlichen Entwicklung und im Zusammenhange mit der Lehrgeschichte und Culturbewegung der Reformation. Gotha: Friedrich Andreas Perthes, 1879.

Herte, Adolf. Die Lutherbiographie des Johannes Cochläus. Eine quellenkritische Untersuchung. Münster in Westfalen: Aschendorff, 1915.

_____. Die Lutherkommentare des Johannes Cochläus,
kritische Studie zur Geschicht-Schreibung im Zeitalter
der Glaubensspaltung. Münster in Westfalen:
Aschendorff, 1935.

_____. Das katholische Lutherbild im Bann der
Lutherkommentare des Cochläus. Münster in Westfalen:
Aschendorff, 1943.

Heyer, Friedrich. "Les solutions proposeés par les
différentes confessions chrétiennes au probleme de
la foi et des ouvres." Translated by Jacques-Noël
Peres. Positions Lutheriennes 24 (1976):2-13.

Hildebrandt, Franz. Melanchthon: Alien or Ally? Cambridge:
Cambridge University Press, 1946.

Hill, Charles Leander. "An Exposition and Critical Estimate
of the Philosophy of Philip Melanchthon." Ph.D.
dissertation, Ohio State University, 1938.

_____. The Loci communes of Philip Melanchthon.
With a Critical Introduction by the Translator.
Boston: Meador Publishing Co., 1944.

_____. Melanchthon. Selected Writings translated
by Charles Leander Hill, edited by Elmer Ellsworth
Flack and Lowell J. Satre. Minneapolis: Augsburg
Publishing House, 1962.

Hillerbrand, Hans J. Landgrave Philipp of Hesse, 1504-1567,
Religion and Politics in the Reformation. Reformation
Essays and Studies, no. 1. St. Louis: Foundation
for Reformation Research, 1967.

Hirsch, Emanuel. "Melanchthon und das Interim." Archiv für
Reformationsgeschichte 17 (1920):62-66.

Holl, Karl. "Die Rechtfertigungslehre im Licht der Geschichte
des Protestantismus." In Gesammelte Aufsätze zur
Kirchengeschichte. III Der Westen, by Karl Holl.
Tübingen: J. C. B. Mohr, 1928.

Huschke, Rolf Bernhard. Melanchthons Lehre vom Ordo
politicus; ein Beitrag zum Verhältnis von Glauben
und politischem Handeln bei Melanchthon. Gütersloh:
Gerd Mohn, 1968.

Jedin, Hubert. Des Johannes Cochläus Streitschrift De libero
arbitrio hominis (1525), ein Beitrag zur Geschichte
der vortridentinischen katholischen Theologie.
Breslau: Müller and Seiffert, 1927.

Kantzenbach, Friedrich Wilhelm. Evangelium und Dogma. Die
    Bewältigung des theologischen Problems der
    Dogmengeschichte im Protestantismus. Stuttgart:
    Evangelisches Verlagswerk, 1959.

Kawerau, Gustav. Die Versuche. Melanchthon zur katholischen
    Kirche zurückzufuhren. Halle: Verein fur
    Reformationsgeschichte, 1902.

Klug, Eugene F. and Stahlke, Otto F. Getting Into the Formula
    of Concord. A History and Digest of the Formula.
    St. Louis: Concordia Publishing House, 1977.

Költzsch, Franz Heinrich. Melanchthons philosophische Ethik.
    Freiberg: Graz and Gerlach, 1889.

Kolb, Robert. "Georg Major as Controversialist: Polemics in
    the Late Reformation." Church History 45 (December
    1976): 455-468.

_____. "Nikolaus von Amsdorf on Vessels of Wrath
    and Vessels of Mercy: A Lutheran's Doctrine of
    Double Predestination." Harvard Theological Review
    69 (July-October 1976): 325-343.

Kolde, Theodor. Historische Einleitung in die Symbolischen
    Bücher der Evangelisch-Lutherischen Kirche. Gütersloh:
    C. Bertelsmann, 1913.

Lewis, Charlton T., Short, Charles. A Latin Dictionary;
    Founded on Andrews' Edition of Freund's Latin
    Dictionary. Revised, Enlarged, and in Great Part
    Rewritten. Oxford: Oxford University Press, 1879.

Lieberg, Hellmut. Amt und Ordination bei Luther und
    Melanchthon. Göttingen: Vandenhoeck and Ruprecht,
    1962.

Little, David. "Calvin and the Prospects for a Christian
    Theory of Natural Law." In Norm and Context in
    Christian Ethics, edited by Outka and Ramsey. New
    York: Charles Scribner's Sons, 1968.

Macquarrie, John. Three Issues in Ethics. New York: Harper
    and Row, 1970.

Maier, Heinrich. An der Grenze der Philosophie. Tübingen:
    J. C. B. Mohr, 1909.

Manschreck, Clyde L. Melanchthon on Christian Doctrine.
Loci Communes 1555. Translated and edited by Clyde
Manschreck. Introduction by Hans Engelland. New
York: Oxford University Press, 1965.

_____. Melanchthon: The Quiet Reformer. New York/
Nashville: Abingdon Press, 1958.

Matheson, Peter. Cardinal Contarini at Regensburg. Oxford:
Clarendon Press, 1972.

Matthes, Karl. Philipp Melanchthon. Sein Leben und Wirken,
aus den Quellen dargestellt. Altenburg: Julius
Helbig, 1841.

Maurer, Wilhelm. "Zur Komposition der Loci Melanchthons
von 1521. Ein Beitrag zur Frage Melanchthon und
Luther." Luther-Jahrbuch 25 (1958):146-180.

_____. "Der Einfluss Augustins auf Melanchthons
theologische Entwicklung." Kerygma und Dogma 5
(1959):165-199.

_____. Melanchthon-Studien. Gütersloh: G. Mohn,
1964.

_____. "Melanchthons Loci communes von 1521 als
wissenschaftliche Programmschrift. Ein Beitrag zur
Hermeneutik der Reformationszeit." Luther-Jahrbuch
27 (1960):1-50.

_____. Der Junge Melanchthon. Zwischen Humanismus
und Reformation. vol. 2. Der Theologe. Göttingen:
Vandenhoeck and Ruprecht, 1969.

_____. "Studien uber Melanchthons Anteil an der
Entstehung der Confessio Augustana." Archiv für
Reformationsgeschichte 51 (1960):158-206.

_____. "Melanchthon als Humanist." In Philipp
Melanchthon: Forschungsbeitrage zur vierhundertsten
Wiederkehr seines Todestages dargeboten in Wittenberg
1960, edited by Walter Elliger. Göttingen:
Vandenhoeck and Ruprecht, 1961.

Mayer, Cornelius. "Rechtfertigung durch Werke?" Theologische
Quartelschrift 154 (1974): 118-136.

Mehl, Roger. "Les implications anthropologiques, éthiques et
ecclésiologiques de la doctrine de la justification
par la foi." Positions Lutheriennes 24 (1976): 15-24.

Meinhold, Peter. Philipp Melanchthon: der Lehrer der Kirche. Berlin: Lutherisches Verlagshaus, 1960.

Meissinger, Karl August. Der katholische Luther. Munich: Leo Lehnen Verlag, 1952.

Muehlenberg, Ekkehard. "Synergia and Justification by Faith." In Discord, Dialogue, and Concord. Studies in the Lutheran Reformation's Formula of Concord, edited by L. W. Spitz and W. Lohff. Philadelphia: Fortress Press, 1977.

Müller, Konrad. :Philipp Melanchthon und das kopernikanische Weltsystem." Centaurus. International Magazine of the History of Mathematics, Science and Technology. 9 (1963): 16-28.

Müller, Gerhard. "Alliance and Confession: The Theological-Historical Development and Ecclesiastical- Political Significance of Reformation Confessions." Translated by Herbert J. A. Bouman. The Sixteenth Century Journal 8 (1977): 123-140.

McNeill, John Thomas. "Natural Law in the Teaching of the Reformers." Journal of Religion 26 (July 1946): 168-182.

McSorley, Harry J. Luther: Right or Wrong? An Ecumenical-Theological Study of Luther's Major Work, The Bondage of the Will. Minneapolis: Augsburg Publishing House, 1969.

Neuser, Wilhelm. Der Ansatz der Theologie Philipp Melanchthons. Neukirchen: Kr. Moers, 1957.

_____. "Melanchthons Abendmahlslehre und ihre Auswirkung im unteren Donauraum." Zeitschrift für Kirchengeschichte 84 (1973): 49-59.

Niermeyer, J. F. Mediae Latinitatis Lexicon Minus. Leiden: E. J. Brill, 1976.

_____. Mediae Latinitatis Lexicon Minus. Abbreviationes Et Index Fontium. Leiden: E. J. Brill, 1976.

Oberman, Heiko A. Werden und Wertung der Reformation: vom Wegestreit zum Glaubenskampf. Tübingen: J. C. B. Mohr (Paul Siebeck), 1977.

Oyer, John Stanley. Lutheran Reformers Against Anabaptists:
Luther, Melanchthon and Menius and the Anabaptists
of Central Germany. The Hague: Martinus Nijhoff, 1964.

_____. "The Writings of Melanchthon Against the
Anabaptists." Mennonite Quarterly Review 26 (1952):
259-279.

Patterson, W. Brown. "The Anglican Reaction. Response to
the Formula of Concord." In Discord, Dialogue, and
Concord. Studies in the Lutheran Reformation's
Formula of Concord, edited by L. W. Spitz and W.
Lohff. Philadelphia: Fortress Press, 1977.

Pauck, Wilhelm. Melanchthon and Bucer. Philadelphia:
Westminster Press, 1969.

Pelikan, Jaroslav. From Luther to Kierkegaard. A Study in
the History of Theology. 2nd ed. St. Louis:
Concordia Publishing House, 1963.

Pöhlmann, Horst George., trans. and ed. of Apologia
Confessionis Augustanae by Philip Melanchthon.
Gütersloh: Gütersloher Verlagshaus Gerd Mohn, 1967.

Preus, Robert D. The Theology of Post-Reformation Lutheranism:
A Study of Theological Prolegomena. St. Louis:
Concordia Publishing House, 1970.

Quanbeck, Warren A. "The Formula of Concord and Authority
in the Church." The Sixteenth Century Journal 8
(1977): 49-60.

Quere, Ralph. Melanchthon's Christum Cognoscere: Christ's
Efficacious Presence in the Eucharistic Theology of
Melanchthon. Bibliotheca Humanistica & Reformatorica,
XXII. Nieuwkoop: B. DeGraaf, 1977.

_____. "Melanchthon on Sign, Presence, and Benefit:
The Genesis of Melanchthon's Doctrine of Christ's
Efficacious Presence." Ph.D. dissertation, Princeton
Theological Seminary, 1970.

_____. "Christ's Efficacious Presence in the Lord's
Supper: Directions in the Development of Melanchthon's
Theology After Augsburg." Lutheran Quarterly 29
(February 1977): 21-41.

_____. "Melanchthonian Motifs in the Formula's
Eucharistic Christology." In Discord, Dialogue, and
Concord. Studies in the Lutheran Reformation's Formula
of Concord, edited by L. W. Spitz and W. Lohff.
Philadelphia: Fortress Press, 1977.

Ranke, Leopold von. Deutsche Geschichte im Zeitalter der
    Reformation. Ungekürtzte textausgabe. Wien: Im
    Phaidonverlag, 1934.

Realencyklopädie für Protestantische Theologie und Kirche.
    1905 ed. S.v. "Rechtfertigung."

Richard, James William. Philip Melanchthon, the Protestant
    Preceptor of Germany, 1497-1560. New York: Putnam,
    1898; reprint ed., New York: Lenox Hill, 1974.

Riemann, Otto. Philippi Melanchthonis, Studia Philosophica.
    Quam rationem Et Quid Momenti Ad Ejus Theologiam
    Habuerint, Quaeritur. Halle: Universitate
    Fridericiana Halensi, 1885.

Ritschl, Albert. Die christliche Lehre von der Rechtfertigung
    und Versöhnung. vol. 1. Die Geschichte der Lehre.
    4th ed. Bonn: A. Marcus and E. Webers Verlag, 1903.

Ritschl, Otto. Dogmengeschichte des Protestantismus.
    Grundlagen und Grundzüge der theologischen Gedanken-
    und Lehrbildung in den protestantischen Kirchen.
    vol. 3. Die reformierte Theologie des 16. und 17.
    Jahrhunderts in ihrer Entstehung und Entwicklung.
    Göttingen: Vandenhoeck and Ruprecht, 1926.

_____. "Der doppelte Rechtfertigungsbegriff in der
    Apologie der Augsburgischen Konfession." Zeitschrift
    für Theologie und Kirche (1910): 292-338.

Rogness, Michael. Philip Melanchthon, Reformer Without Honor.
    Minneapolis: Augsburg Publishing House, 1969.

Roos, Keith L. The Devil in 16th Century German Literature:
    The Teufelbücher. Bern: Herbert Lang; Frankfurt/
    M.: Peter Lang, 1972.

Rump, Johann. Melanchthons Psychologie, (seine Schrift De
    Anima) in ihrer Abhangigkeit von Aristoteles und
    Galenos . . . Kiel: E. Marquardsen, 1897.

Schäfer, Rolf. Christologie und Sittlichkeit in Melanchthons
    Frühen Loci. Tübingen: J. C. B. Mohr, 1961.

_____. "Melanchthons Hermeneutik im Römerbrief-Kommentar
    von 1532," Zeitschrift für Theologie und Kirche 60
    (October 1963): 216-235.

Schäfer, Rudolf. Philipp Melanchthons Leben, aus den Quellen
    dargestellt. Gütersloh: C. Bertelsmann, 1894.

Scheible, Heinz., ed. Die Anfänge der reformatorischen Geschichtsschreibung. Melanchthon, Sleiden, Flacius und die Magdeburger Zenturien. Gütersloh: Gütersloher Verlagshaus Gerd Mohn, 1966.

Schlink, Edmund. Theology of the Lutheran Confessions. Translated by P. F. Koehneke and H. J. A. Bouman. Philadelphia: Fortress Press, 1961.

_____. Theologie der Lutherischen Bekenntnischriften. Munich: Chr. Kaiser Verlag, 1948.

Schmidt, Carl. Philipp Melanchthon. Leben und ausgewählte Schriften. Elberfeld: Verlag von R. L. Friderichs, 1861.

Schott, Erdmann. "Melanchthon als evangelischer Theologe." In Philipp Melanchthon: Forschungsbeiträge zur vierhundertsten Wiederkehr seines Todestages dargeboten in Wittenberg 1960, edited by Walter Elliger. Göttingen: Vandenhoeck and Ruprecht, 1961.

Schwarzenau, Paul. Der Wandel im theologischen Ansatz bei Melanchthon von 1525-1535. Gütersloh: Carl Bertelsmann Verlag, 1956.

Seebach, Julius. "Melanchthon's Doctrine of the Will." Lutheran Quarterly 30 (April 1900): 190-210.

Seeberg, Reinhold. Lehrbuch der Dogmengeschichte. vol. 2. Die Dogmengeschichte des Mittelalters und der Neuzeit. Erlangen/Leipzig: A. Deichert, 1898.

Seigel, Jerrold E. Rhetoric and Philosophy in Renaissance Humanism: The Union of Eloquence and Wisdom, Petrarch to Valla. New Jersey: Princeton University Press, 1968.

Sick, Hansjörg. Melanchthon als Ausleger des Alten Testaments. Tübingen: J. C. B. Mohr, 1959.

Søe, N. H. "The Three Uses of the Law." In Norm and Context in Christian Ethics, edited by Outka and Ramsey. New York: Charles Scribner's Sons, 1968.

Spahn, Martin. Johannes Cochläus. Ein Lebensbild aus der Zeit der Kirchenspaltung. Berlin: Felix L. Dames, 1898.

Sperl, Adolf. Melanchthon zwischen Humanismus und Reformation. Forschungen zur Geschichte und Lehre des Protestantismus. vol. 15. Munich: Chr. Kaiser Verlag, 1959.

Spitz, Lewis W. The Reformation, Basic Interpretations.
        Lexington, Mass.: D. C. Heath and Co., 1972.

_____. "The Formula of Concord, Then and Now." The
        Sixteenth Century Journal 8 (1977):9-21.

Steinmetz, David C. Reformers in the Wings. Philadelphia:
        Dortress Press, 1971.

Stern, Leo. Philipp Melanchthon: Humanist, Reformer,
        Praeceptor Germaniae. Festgabe des Melanchthon-
        Komitees der Deutschen Demokratischen Republic.
        Halle: 1960.

Stoeckhardt, George. "General Justification." Corcordia
        Theological Quarterly 42 (April 1978):139-144.

Stroebel, Georg Theodor. Versuch einer litterär Geschichte
        con Philipp Melanchthons Locis theologicis als dem
        ersten evangelischen Lehrbuche. Altdorf: L.
        Schüpfel, 1776.

_____. Miscellaneen Literarischen Inhalts, gröstentheils
        aus ungedruckten Quellen. Nuremberg: Martin Jacob,
        1782.

Strommen, Merton P.; Brekke, M. L.: Underwager, R.C.; and
        Johnson, A. L. A Study of Generations: Report of a
        Two-Year Study of 5,000 Lutherans Between the Ages
        of 15-65; Their Beliefs, Values, Attitudes, Behavior.
        Minneapolis: Augsburg Publishing House, 1972.

Stupperich, Robert. "Die Rechtfertigungslehre bei Luther
        und Melanchthon 1530-1536." In Luther und Melanchthon.
        Referate des Zweiten Internationalen Lutherforscher-
        kongresses, edited by Vilmos Vajta. Göttinger:
        Vandenhoeck and Ruprecht, 1961.

_____. "Die Reformatoren und das Tridentinun." Archiv
        für Reformationsgeschichte 47 (1954): 20-63.

_____. "Melanchthoniana und andere unbekannte
        Reformatoria. A. Widmungen." Archiv für
        Reformationsgeschichte 45 (1954):253-260.

_____. Der Unbekannte Melanchthon. Wirken und
        Denken des Praeceptor Germaniae in neuer Sicht.
        Stuttgart: W. Kohlhammer Verlag, 1961.

Tappert, Theodore G., trans. and ed. The Book of Concord.
        The Confessions of the Evangelical Lutheran Church.
        Philadlephia: Fortress Press, 1959.

318

_____. "Melanchthon in America." In Luther und Melanchthon. Referate und Berichte des Zweiten Internationalen Kongresses für Lutherforschung, edited by Vilmos Vajta. Göttingen: Vandenhoeck and Ruprecht, 1961.

Temkin, Owsei. Galenism. Rise and Decline of a Medical Philosophy. Ithaca/London: Cornell University Press, 1973.

Thieme, Karl. Der Geist der lutherischen Ethik in Melanchthons Apologie (1531-1931). Giessen: Alfred Töpelmann, 1931.

Thorndike, Lynn. A History of Magic and Experimental Science. New York: Columbia University Press, 1941.

Thulin, Oskar. Bilder der Reformation. Aus den Sammlungen der Lutherhalle in Wittenberg. Berlin: Evangelische Verlagsanstalt, 1953.

Troeltsch, Ernst. The Social Teaching of the Christian Churches. Translated by Olive Wyon. New York: Harper and Row, 1960.

Vajta, Vilmos., ed. Luther und Melanchthon. Referate und Berichte des zweiten Internationalen Kongresses für Lutherforschung. Göttingen: Vandenhoeck and Ruprecht, 1961.

_____, and Weissgerber, Hans., eds. The Church and the Confessions. Philadelphia: Fortress Press, 1963.

Verkamp, Bernard J. "The Limits upon Adiaphoristic Freedom: Luther and Melanchthon." Theological Studies (1975): 52-76.

Volz, Hans. "Melanchthons Anteil an der Lutherbibel." Archiv für Reformationsgeschichte 45 (1954): 196-233.

Wallmann, Johannes. Der Theologiebegriff bei Johann Gerhard und Georg Calixt. Tübingen: J. C. B. Mohr, 1961.

Walter, Johannes von. Luther und Melanchthon während des Augsburger Reichstags. Gütersloh: C. Bertelsmann, 1931.

Weissgerber, Hans. "The Valid Confessional Symbols." In The Church and the Confessions, edited by Vilmos and Weissgerber. Philadelphia: Fortress Press, 1963.

Whitley, W. T., ed. The Doctrine of Grace. New York: The Macmillan Company, 1931.

Wiedenhofer, Siegfried. Formalstrukturen humanistischer und reformatorischer Theologie bei Philipp Melanchthon. Frankfurt/M. and Munich: Peter Lang, 1976.

Williams, George H. The Radical Reformation. Philadelphia: Westminster Press, 1962.

Wolf, Ernst. Philipp Melanchthon: evangelischer Humanismus. Göttingen: Vandenhoeck and Ruprecht, 1961.

Zeeden, Ernst Walter. Martin Luther und die Reformation im Urteil des Luthertums. Studien zum Selbsverständnis des lutherischen Protestantismus von Luthers Tode bis zum Beginn der Goethezeit. vol. 1. Freiburg: Verlag Herder, 1950.

Zeller, Eduard. Geschichte der Deutschen Philosophie seit Leibniz. Munich: Druck und Verlag von R. Oldenbourg, 1875.

INDEX

TOPICAL AND ANALYTICAL INDEX

A

Abba, Pater, 260
Abraham, 78, 80, 153
accedere, 103
accepta, 74
acceptatio, 151
accipit, 55, 164
Achilles, 216
ad alterum, 62
addendum est, 86
ad salutem, 191, 278
ad vitam aeternam, 151
affectus, 168
Agricola John, 11, 118,
        170, 186, 192, 293
ἀκριβολογίαν και
        λεπτολογιαν, 186
alia iustitia, 108
Ambrose, 125
ambulare, 20
Amsdorf, Nicholas von, 186
Anabaptist, 2, 170
Anscombe, Gertrude E.M.
        129, 246
Anselm, 84
Anti-Christ, 42, 43
Apology, 11, 21, 23, 28,
        30, 31, 35, 36, 40,
        42, 44, 47, 55, 58,
        64, 65, 66, 67, 68,
        71, 74, 75, 83, 87,
        101, 111, 113, 120,
        154, 174, 288, 289,
        290, 295
apprehendunt, 148
apprehendere, 85
apprehenditur, 165
Aristotle, 41, 72, 84, 125,
        173, 192
        Ethics, 84
Assembly at Celle (1548),
        176
assentiri promissioni Dei,
        56
Athanasius, 125

Augsburg Confession, 13, 17,
        21, 22, 64
Augsburg Interim (1548), 176,
        278
Augustine, 84, 102, 125, 150,
        192

B

Barnes, Robert, 125
Basel, 185
Basil, 125, 192
Bauer, Clemens, 10, 287
beneficium Christi, 157
Bente, Friedrich, 6, 9, 22, 23,
        287, 294
Bernard, 192, 276
Bizer, Ernst, 84
Blumenberg, Hans, 112
Bona opera
        bekehrung nöthig sei, 184
        bona opera ita necessaria
                sunt ad vitam aeternam,
                128
        causa sine qua non, 119, 171,
                291
        da ist keine Gnade, 184
        de condigno, 47, 48, 90, 146
        debeat, 28, 65, 288
        debere, 201
        debiti, 202
        dignitas, 91, 104, 133
                dignitatem, 201
                dignitas nostra, 92
                dignitas propria, 132
        est necessaria, 75
        fide iustificamur, 77, 113,
                152
        fide sit medium inter fidem
                et opera, 70
        formaliter, 106
        hoch vonnöthen, 184

Bona Opera cont.
  impletio, 102
  inchoatio, 99, 100
  inchoatio novitatis, 199
  inchoatio vitae aeternae,
     270
  indigna, 97, 113
  iustitia carnis, 89, 90,
     147, 160
  iustitia humanae rationis,
     223
  iustitia operum, 266
  necessaria ad salutem, 121
  necessaria sequi debet nova
     obedientia, 201
  necessaria sequi debet re-
     conciliationem, 127,
     197
  necesse sit retinere legem
     moralem, 141
  non propter nostram digni-
     tatem, 149
  opera supererogationis, 275
  oportet, 28, 65, 85, 86, 91,
     92, 123, 129, 189, 288
    oportere, 201
    oportuit, 149
    ornavi, 120
  per accidens, 145
  perfecta obedientia, 165
  quae sequi fidem debet, 107
  quia sequi reconciliationem
     necessario debent, 128
  Retinendae fidei, 202
  sancta, 33
  sequens, 94
  sequi debet, 127
  sequi debet obedientia
     nostra, 129
  sola opera, 18
  zur seligkeit, 191
  zur seligkeit nöthig seyn,
     185
Bonfio, Secretary to Campeggio,
    14
Bonaventure, 84, 125, 192
Brekke, Milo L., 3
Brenz, John, 23, 67, 68, 69, 70,
    71, 111, 112
Bretschneider, Carolus, 84, 125,
    192
Brieger, Theodor, 177
Bring, Ragnar, 6, 7, 9, 143, 287

Bucer, Martin, 122, 177
Bugenhagen, John, 183

C

Calvin, John, 187
Camerarius, John, 14, 15, 18,
    21, 72, 111
Campeggio, Cardinal, 13
Carlowitz, Christopher von,
    182
Carlstadt, Andreas, 111
Casterato, Nello, 4
Catholic Confutatio, 13, 14,
    15, 16, 17, 18, 20, 22,
    58, 288, 289, 295
Celle Interim, 183
Celsus, 125
chamo et freno, 135
Cherinthus, 84
Chrysostom, John, 193
Cicero, 84, 125, 139, 172,
    193, 222
Cochlaeus, Johannes, 14, 18,
    111
compensatio, 123
concurrere, 36
confidamus, 157
congruo mereri, 45
consistere, 103
consummatio legis, 144, 217
contra legem Dei, 224
Cordatus, Conrad, 118, 119,
    120, 121, 122
Corvinus, Antonius, 74
credamus, 157
credo remissionem peccatorum,
    233
Cruciger, Casper, 8, 118, 119,
    121
cultus, 42
Cyprian, 84, 125

D

dat vitam aeternam, 205
de iustificatione hominis, 178
De natura deorum, 139
debita, 47

deberetur, 63
Decalogue, the, 37
Diet of Augsburg, 14, 181,
     182
Diet of Worms, (1541), 176
Dietrich, Veit, 14, 121
dignitas vocationis non
     personae, 205
dilectio, 105
Dilthey, Wilhelm, 138
disciplina, 85
Dittrich, Ottmar, 10, 287
Double justice, 177-179

                E

Ebion, 84
ecclesiam et gentes pugnantes
     cum Evangelio, 223
Eck, Johannes, 11, 13, 14, 16,
     18, 177, 178, 180, 192,
     193, 293
efficimur consortes divinae
     naturae et filii Dei,
     178
Eichhorn, Albert, 287
Elert, Werner, 64
Ellinger, George, 4
Engelland, Hans, 10, 287
Epiphanius, 193
erben, 184
ethnicos, 81
Euripides, 125
Eusebius, 193
exclusive particula, 131
ex opere operato, 28, 80
extra nos, 74, 83, 93, 105,
     112, 114, 289, 290

                F

Fabio, 159
facilis est responsio, 87
Ficker, Johannes, 13, 16
fide, 97, 113, 166, 237
     medium, 70, 71
     quia fide iusti sumus, 106
fiducia, 63, 76, 83, 85, 99,
     117, 152, 155, 157, 166,
     233, 234, 237

fiducia ad alterum, 240
fiducia Christi, 90, 148
fiducia in Christum, 90, 148
fiducia misericordiae, 92
fiducia vana, 49
Flacius, Illyricus, 11, 185,
     186, 187, 191, 192, 278,
     293
flagitia, 89
Formula of Concord, 3, 5
Fourth Assembly of the Lutheran
     World Federation at
     Helsinki, 3

                G

Gallas, Nicholas, 186
George, Duke of Saxony, 115
George of Anhalt, 186
German Evangelical Party, 2
Gerson, 125, 193
Graf, Dom Ernest, 177
Granvella, Nicholas, 177
gratis, 131, 210
Green, Lowell C., 6, 287
Gregory Nazianzen, 126, 193
Gregory Neocaesariensis, 193
Gregory the Great, 125
Greschat, Martin, 3, 6, 8, 190,
     287
Gropper, John, 177
Grynaeus, Simon, 72

                H

habitus, 48, 61, 83, 259, 260,
     285
Hansen, Walter A., 64
Hartfelder, Karl, 4, 169, 170
Helding, Michael, 181
Henninger, Josef, 178
Henry VIII, 125
Herrlinger, Albert, 10, 287
Herte, Adolf, 18
Hesiod, 84, 125, 172, 193
Hill, Charles Leander, 10, 112,
     246, 287
Hirsch, Emanuel, 84

Homer, 125, 193
honorem mediatoris, 38
hostia, 149
Hugo, 193
humilitas, 179

I

inhabitationem, 190
impii, 146
imputare, 112
    imputatio, 83, 113
    imputationem iustitiae,
        178
    imputatum est, 153
    imputatur nobis, 98
    imputetur, 102
Interims, the, 11
intra nos, 74, 83
intuens, 83, 113
irae nemo resistere potest,
        213
Irenaeus, 84, 125, 193
Isaiah, 84
Isocrates, 125
iudicium, 88
ius naturae, 140
iustificare, 231
iustitia, 61, 101, 108, 143,
        156, 165, 166

J

Jedin, Hubert, 177, 178
Jeremiah, 84, 222
Jerome, 84, 125, 193
Joachim, Elector of Branden-
        burg, 183
John, 84, 125, 193
Johnson, Arthur L., 13
Jolowicz, Herbert F., 253
Jonas, Justus, 119, 120, 121
Jung, Eva-Maria, 177

K

Klug, Eugene, 6, 8, 287
κοιναὶ ἔννοιας, 138, 244
Kolb, Robert, 8, 188, 190

L

legem Dei, 118
Leipzig Interim (1548), 176,
        183, 186, 278, 293
levia mala, 219
Lewis, Charlton T., 42
lex naturae, 89, 138, 172
Lipgens, Walter, 177
Luke, 125, 193
Luther, Martin, 1, 5, 14, 17,
        22, 30, 64, 69, 119, 17
        287, 295, 297

M

Magdeburg, 186
Mainz, Elector of, 115
Major, George, 187
Majoristic Controversy, 278
Manschreck, Clyde, 4
Marcion, 193
Mark, 193
Mathesius, John, 187, 192
Matheson, Peter, 177
Matthew, 84, 125, 193
Maurer, Wilhelm, 10, 112, 129
        287
Maurice, Duke and Elector of
        Saxony, 183
Maxcey, Carl. E., 179
Mayer, Cornelius, 287
mediatorem Christum, 213
Meinhold, Peter, 4, 84
Melanchthon, Philip
    Commentary on Romans, 11,
        74, 82, 83, 103, 113
        124, 174, 290, 295
    Loci of 1521, 131, 173
    Loci of 1533, 11, 67, 84,
        92, 93, 96, 98, 99,
        101, 103, 113, 154,
        174, 290, 291, 292,
        295
    Loci of 1535, 11, 115, 118
        121, 124, 125, 126,
        127, 130, 131, 133,
        134, 136, 141, 146,
        151, 154, 158, 164,
        169, 171, 201, 237,
        278, 294

Loci of 1559, 10, 11, 176,
190, 192, 194, 195,
202, 208, 215, 221,
224, 228, 231, 240,
243, 254, 283, 294,
295
Loci Communes Theologici,
118, 124
Schwartzerd, Phillip, 4
mendacia, 186
manifesta mendacia, 187
mercedes
post hanc vitam in coelis,
180
merces, 47
mercedem, 180
mercedes, 47
merentur, 134
merentur praemia spiritualia
et corporalia, in hac
vitam, 206
meritum
meritum condigni, 45
meritum congrui, 45
meritum de condigno, 45, 275
meritum de congruo, 45, 90,
146
metalepsin, 219
Meyer, Cornelius, 10
modum justificationis, 29, 61
Möller, Wilhelm, 83
monachatus, 52
motus, 27, 32, 87
motus in voluntate, 234
Müller, Nikolaus, 4
mundiciem, 37, 101

N

necesse est, 28, 29, 92, 104,
127
necessario, 29
necessario sequi debet, 96
necesse esse, 32, 65, 288
Nero, 159
Neuser, Wilhelm H., 10, 287
Niermeyer, Jan F., 42, 43, 47,
52, 101, 149, 161
noticia, 76
noticia historiae, 56, 76
noticiam, 57
novitas, 68, 83, 111, 112,
113, 130, 153, 211,
289

notitia, 155, 255, 256
novitas
nova, 82
nova obedientia sit, 121,
123
novitatem, 189, 190, 199,
294

O

obedientia ac poenitentia, 87
officia, 163
Otto, 186
ordinatio, 203
Origen, 84, 126, 193
Osiander, Andreas, 11, 71, 78,
83, 278, 290, 294

P

paedagogia, 88, 90, 146
legem paedagogiam, 136
paedagogia in Christum, 247
paedegogicus, 246
paedagogus, 88, 159
papatus, 43
Paul, 84, 126, 152, 153, 154,
155, 156, 159, 165, 184,
189, 193, 199, 203, 204,
210, 219, 220, 223, 224,
226, 228, 231, 233, 238,
242, 247, 248, 248, 249,
252, 255, 258, 264, 266,
267
Paul of Samosata, 84, 126
πελαγιανιζειν, 45
Peter Lombard, 125, 193
Pflug, Julius von, 177, 181
Phidias, 126
ψιλονεικια, 182
Photiorus, 194
Pistorius, John, 177
Plato, 84, 126, 194
plenitudo legis, 107
Plutarch, 194
poenitentia, 85, 208
politicus, 246
Pomponius Atticus, 84, 159,
223

post hanc vitam in coelis, 180
post hanc vitam praemia aeterna dabunter, 231
practica principia, 244
praemia, 205
principia speculabilia, 244
προλημψεις, 138, 244
pronunciari, 98
   pronunciator iusti, 99
propter aliam, 285
propter Christum, 94, 95, 117, 123, 129, 148, 150, 151, 157, 165, 170, 199, 205
   propter Christum fide, 215
   propter Filium Dei, 224
   propter filium Dei gratis, 206
   propter mediatorem, 206, 207
   propter mediatorem Christum, 217
   sed propter Christum, 267
Pygius, 194

Q

qualitas, 93, 164
Quere, Ralph, 6, 11, 287
quia sumus in Christo, 150

R

Rahner, Karl, 178
Recess of Celle, 183
Regensburg Book of 1541, 293
Regensburg Colloquy of 1541, 278
Regensburg Diet of 1541, 176, 177
Reich Gottes, 184
remitto
   remittitur, 102
   remittuntur, 78
renovatio, 75, 78, 82, 83, 113, 127, 147
   renovata, 32
reputare, 73
Richards, James W., 4, 13, 22, 23

Rosenberg, Manfred, 177
ruunt in delicta, 200

S

Samosatenus, 194
saniores, 117
Schaefer, Rudolf, 4
Schäfer, Rolf, 6, 287
Schenk, James, 170
Schenk, Wilhelm, 177
Schmalkaldic League, 177, 181, 182
Schnepf, Erhard, 186
Schwenckfeld, Kasper, 111
Scipio, 151, 159, 231
Scotus, 126
Seebass, Gottfried, 84
sentire, 89
Servetus, 84, 126, 194
Short, Charles, 42
sola fide, 17, 75, 115, 187, 236, 237, 239, 257, 282
   sola, 187
   sola gratia, 239, 282
   sola fide iustificamur, 180, 186
Sophocles, 194
Spalatin, George, 22
speciem distributivae iusticia, 62
Sperl, Adolf, 10
Spitz, Lewis W., 11
Stahlke, Otto F., 6, 8, 287
Stapleton, Thomas, 1
Stern, Leo, 4
στοργας, 216
Strommen, Merton, 3
Stupperich, Robert, 4, 10, 177
sycophanta, 122

T

Tertullian, 84, 126, 194
Themistocles, 84, 154
Theodosius, 194
Thieme, Karl, 10, 287
Thomas Aquinas, 126
Tschackert, P., 84
Tubingen, 185

U

Underwager, Ralph C., 3

V

Vajta, Vilmos, 10
Valentinians, 84
Valentinus, 126
Valla, Laurentius, 194
vestigia, 138, 240
velle et accidere, 166
vestigium Dei, 137
veterem hominem, 118
victima, 149
Virgil, 126
vivificare, 97
    vivificant, 90

W

Wiedenhofer, Siegfried, 10,
    170, 287
William of Ockham, 193
Williams, Judith L., 13, 14
Wimpina, Konrad, 14
Wycliff, John, 126

X

Xenophon, 84, 126, 139, 159,
    172, 194

Z

Zeno, 126